Maharashtra
MAXIMUS

Maharashtra
MAXIMUS
The State, Its People & Politics

SUJATA ANANDAN

RUPA

Published by
Rupa Publications India Pvt. Ltd 2018
7/16, Ansari Road, Daryaganj
New Delhi 110002

Sales Centres:
Allahabad Bengaluru Chennai
Hyderabad Jaipur Kathmandu
Kolkata Mumbai

ISBN: 978-81-291-4999-2

First impression 2018

10 9 8 7 6 5 4 3 2 1

The moral right of the author has been asserted.

Printed in India by Repro Knowledgecast Limited, Thane

For my sisters
Aparna (Chitra)
who mended my broken wings
and
Sushama (Gopa)
who helped me fly again.

You can lead and motivate people without a certificate or title,
what you need to do is to tell people
a compelling secret that was only known to you.

—Michael Bassey Johnson

Contents

Foreword

I was born in Bombay (as it was called then) into a Maharashtrian family, but I often wonder if I am truly a Maharashtrian. I do not say this out of any sense of disloyalty or disenchantment or alienation; it's just that, again and again, you come up with this vexing question: *Who* is a Maharashtrian?

Although born in India's financial capital, it was not then a part of Maharashtra. Then at one time, when the Shiv Sena was in one of its extreme agitational moods, Bal Thackeray had proclaimed that only someone who had lived for the last fifteen years in Maharashtra could call himself a Maharashtrian. I hadn't.

The reason for that was my father worked in the railways, and every few years he went on a new posting to a different part of the country. We went West, we went East, we went North (but for some reason, never South), so as children we heard many languages, and were immersed in many cultures. Outside the house, we spoke English; at home Marathi. My mother, Vasumati, was a really well-known writer, so I listened to her read her latest short story, but all my own reading was from English literature. Now I speak Marathi at home, but think and write in English. So am I a Maharashtrian?

My parents celebrated all the Maharashtrian religious festivals, particularly Ganeshotsav. This was at once a joy and trial when we were in Gorakhpur in UP. Who made Ganapatis there? No one. So we had to send for one from Bombay. Once installed, for ten days our house reverberated to the sound of the aarti and the aroma of delicious prasad, as friends and colleagues—not a Maharashtrian among them, alas—came in different batches every day for darshan and pooja. Now that I have been back in Mumbai for over four decades after my studies in England, I 'celebrate' Ganeshotav with my ears plugged. So, though fully qualified under the Thackeray definition, am I a Maharashtrian?

This question arose in my mind while reading Sujata Anandan's *Maharashtra Maximus*. That's because the more I read, the more I realized that the complexities of Maharashtra are labyrinthine, way beyond my understanding. I like her initial formulation about the Power of Three: that things have always gone in threes for Maharashtra—three regions of pre-Independent India (Marathwada, Vidharbha and Bombay State), were merged to make the state we now call Maharashtra. The state has three major crops (sugarcane, cotton and onions) which have a great impact on its politics. Pre-Independence, the geographical region we now inhabit had three distinct ruling dynasties...

Three, however, is a simple number. Nothing in Maharashtra is simple. Name three of the greatest reformers of modern India. Indisputably, their numbers will include Jyotiba Phule, Lokmanya Tilak and B R Ambedkar (three again). Phule was a social reformer who worked tirelessly in the nineteenth century for the eradication of untouchability and the caste system, and with his wife Savitribai Phule pioneered women's education in India. In fact, they opened the very first school for girls in India in 1848.

Bal Gangadhar Tilak is considered the first leader of India's Independence movement. (In fact the British called him the 'Father of Indian unrest'.) His famous battle cry reverberated all over India: 'Swarajya is my birthright and I shall have it'. Tilak is also remembered for starting the Marathi weekly *Kesari* which acted as a conscience-keeper of the Independence movement, but most of all, for transforming the worship of Ganesh from a family pooja into the very public Sarvajanik Ganeshotsav, a deliberate move to instill pride in our traditional values, and thus start strong nationalistic feelings against British rule.

B R Ambedkar's contribution to the country hardly needs reiteration. From chairing the committee that drafted the Indian constitution, to being the country's first law minister, to starting the Dalit Buddhist movement, his influence on the country is felt even today.

There are some connections we can draw here. Ambedkar spent crucial years in Baroda and was financially supported by Baroda state's Maratha ruler Sayajirao Gaekwad. This enabled Ambedkar to study overseas, and find employment on his return. Sayajirao's long reign was characterised by significant social and educational reforms, especially when it came to the caste system and untouchability, as well as the education and status of women. In the history of India's maharajas, Sayajirao will probably rank as the most enlightened and reformist of them all.

Tilak's swarajya was a call for independence in the beginning of the last century. But Shivaji Bhonsle, better known as Chhatrapati Shivaji Maharaj, formulated the concept of swaraj well in advance of the concept of India as a nation state. For him it was a term signifying independence from foreign rule. He is, indisputably, the greatest figure in Maharashtra's history, and one of our country's greatest historical figures.

How did a people who produced so many of India's greatest thinkers, rulers and reformers produce in more recent times, entities like the RSS and the Shiv Sena? Sujata's book has much information and insights about them; most of us also know a bit about their basic philosophy which is the opposite of what the great names mentioned above stood for. Both RSS and the Sena stand for exclusion and hostility for the 'other'. The RSS ideology is a harking back to the past, and not a looking forward to the future; while the Sena, even when it ruled the state, did not build any institutions of lasting value. It could do that, even today, but does it have the will to do so?

These are the contradictions that bedevil the state. 'Maharashtra Dharma' is now a long-forgotten phrase, perhaps more aptly described as Maharashtra Dharna. The state is immersed in caste-driven politics, the pull of powerful lobbies dominated by sugar barons, farmers' co-operatives which don't help the farmer but the politicians who head them...

As a Maharashtrian, I ask myself why is it that someone like Sharad Pawar couldn't become prime minister when he had two clear chances of being selected? Other questions, at a more basic level follow. Why are Maharashtrians so reluctant to go outside the state (or the country) in search of opportunities? Why is it that the state's major business and industries have not been started or promoted by Maharashtrians?

You also wonder why after so many years is there a continuous agrarian crisis, and why cries of utter despair are not heard and end in farmer suicides? Why are irrigation schemes, so obviously needed urgently, only been riddled with rampant corruption?

I have been a follower of Sujata Anandan's weekly *Hindustan Times* column for quite some time now. What has always struck me is that her easy access to the state's leading politicians has neither impaired her objectivity nor her willingness to call a spade a spade. These same virtues are strongly evident in this book which looks at Maharashtra's political history with a clear and objective eye.

I wish the picture she painted was brighter. I wish her observations led her to more optimistic predictions. But, then, she is dealing with reality, and she tells it as it is.

Anil Dharker

Introduction

One problem anyone writing about Maharashtra faces is the obvious one: what is the historical Maharashtra, and who are the original Maharashtrians?

These days, nearly everything in Maharashtra is defined in terms of Shivaji from giant statues to militant organizations. And certainly, there was much to admire in Shivaji's life and, especially, his legacy. In 1647, when he was only 17, Shivaji had begun to create an independent Maratha zone around today's Pune. By the time he died in 1680 he had created a vast if far-flung (its regions were not necessarily contiguous) empire.

Shivaji's successors were less glorious (and eventually, the Peshwas or prime ministers, seized control of the empire) but his influence endured. In 1730, fifty years after Shivaji death, the Marathas controlled much of central and modern India: the Scindias and the Holkars in what we call Madhya Pradesh today, the Gaekwads in Baroda, the Peshwas on the West Coast and the Bhonsles in Berar from where they conducted regular raids into Bengal and Orissa. All this was a consequence of Shivaji's original quest to extend the influence of his people.

Looking back, we like to think of this as the Maratha Empire though, in strict caste terms, the kings were not all Marathas. The Peshwas were Brahmins and the Holkars of Indore were Dhangars, members of a pastoral community.

This era forms the core of the modern idea of Maharashtra. Today's powerful leaders from Western Maharashtra (men like

Sharad Pawar) look back to their Maratha heritage, as did their predecessors; Vasantdada Patil, YB Chavan and so many others.

Even later politicians with no connection to the Marathas, acted as though they were directly descended from Shivaji. Bal Thackeray, a gifted cartoonist at Bombay's *Free Press Journal*, was not a Maratha; his caste, the CKP's, is approximate to North India's Kayasthas. But when he founded the Shiv Sena, not only did he appropriate Shivaji's name, he also adopted a martial tradition not normally associated with cartoonists, calling himself the Senapati and encouraging his sainiks to commit acts of violence.

Because of this aggressive Maratha-glorification and Shivaji-worship, the Brahmins, who were an important part of the independence movement in the early twentieth Century (Lokmanya Tilak, Gopal Krishna Gokhale and many others), were sidelined, especially within the ruling Congress establishment: during 1999-2014, the Congress-NCP government in Maharashtra did not appoint a single Brahmin cabinet minister for 15 years.

And yet, the Brahmins had their revenge, becoming founders of the RSS in the 1920s and creating a whole strain of nationalist thought which eventually challenged the secular-Congress narrative at a national level. In Maharashtra today, the Chief Minister Devendra Fadnavis is a Brahmin, so is his great rival within the BJP, Nitin Gadkari.

And the national agenda in India these days is often set by the Marathi-speaking Brahmins of the RSS. The power of the elderly thinkers of Nagpur probably exceeds anything the Peshwas ever managed.

So you could conceivably argue that though we tend too often to talk of the heritage of Maharashtra in terms of Marathas and would-be senapatis, the real contribution to Indian politics has come from a group that was, till recently, ignored in state politics.

Which still leaves us with the problem of place. Today's Maharashtra is an artificial, political construct. It was created only in

1960 after a local movement complained about being part of the old Bombay State (which included parts of today's Gujarat) and being ruled by Gujaratis. (Morarji Desai, a Gujarati, was chief minister).

Even now, Maharashtra includes districts and towns that have historically been associated with other regions (Aurangabad was part of Hyderabad) and some of its areas continue to demand autonomy; for instances Vidarbha, parts of which may be more logically placed in Madhya Pradesh. On the other hand, many Marathi-speaking areas in Goa (where Manohar Parrikar, a Marathi-speaking Brahmin, from the BJP, was chief minister till recently) seem like extensions of Maharashtra.

And then, there is the problem of Mumbai/Bombay. Figures differ and are controversial but everyone broadly agrees that something like 60 per cent of the population of Mumbai comprises non-Maharashtrians. The state's politicians say that this is a consequence of migration to the city from elsewhere in India and perhaps it is. But equally, other figures show that 70 per cent of migrants to Mumbai come from other parts of Maharashtra.

So how Maharashtrian is Mumbai, really? Well, originally at least, not very. The city was created by the British who reclaimed much of it from the sea, and then developed by Parsis, Gujaratis, Muslims and other communities. The Maharashtrians always had a large role to play—the textile mills which first contributed to the city's prosperity, ran on the basis of their hard work. But there is no evidence to suggest that their role was significantly greater than that of many other communities.

And you could argue that were it not for a political decision—the naming of Bombay as the capital of the new state of Maharashtra in 1960—they would have no special claim to it. In fact, there are few historical connections: the great Maratha Kingdoms never included Bombay and even the RSS chose Nagpur as its headquarters.

For all Maharashtrian politicians, Mumbai/Bombay has remained a source of glamour, envy and outrage. When Bal

Thackeray's Shiv Sena first hit the headlines in 1966, it was because the Senapati campaigned against Gujaratis and 'Madrasis' (he meant Malayalis, I suspect but was not really sure of the difference) who, he claimed, were taking away the city's prosperity. Then, in the 1980s, he switched to an anti-Muslim platform, distorting Shivaji's legacy (the Maratha army always depended on Muslim generals), before settling down to a policy of beating up taxi drivers from UP (or 'bhaiyyas' as he called them).

You can sense the hunger to dominate Bombay in the aggravation over its name. Many cities have had their names changed: Madras is Chennai, Bangalore is Bengaluru, Calcutta is Kolkata and so on.

But only in Bombay / Mumbai does the new name matter so much. Cinema halls will be attacked if a character dares refer to Bombay rather than Mumbai. Shopkeepers will be threatened if their signboards do not give their address as 'Mumbai'.

So why should it matter so much? Nobody will beat you up in Bengaluru if you still use the old name. Why is Mumbai so different?

I guess it is because of the central conflict between the city and the state: Maharashtrians run Mumbai now and want us all to acknowledge that.

So where is Maharashtra headed now?

Sujata Anandan, whose knowledge and understanding of Maharashtra politics is unrivalled, takes the line that the state is going through a bad patch. The Marathas, for instance, are now rudderless and directionless. The glory days of Shivaji are long forgotten. And perhaps, going forward, Maharashtra politics will not be so dependent on the Marathas and their leadership. Hence the current discontent, the agitations and the political demands.

But it is not as though the non-Maratha elements in state politics have done much better. Maharashtra, we are always told, is India's richest state. But I'm not sure it is the most advanced state any longer. A new climate of nasty, petty, vindictive parochialism has taken hold with bans on everything from beef to stand-up comedy.

A state that has yet to find its centre both geographically and ethnically, is now in the process of losing its humanity and its heart.

Perhaps, this is just a phase.

But I don't think anyone can predict where Maharashtra is headed without understanding the background. Sujata's book is so invaluable because it looks beyond today's headlines and shows us the origins of today's Maharashtra and its concerns.

Nobody who cares about Indian politics can afford not to understand Maharashtra and, therefore, can afford not to read this book.

Vir Sanghvi

1

Maharashtra Dharma

Marathas gave to India the concepts of
Swaraj and federalism, and kept it largely Hindu.

Three is a significant number for Maharashtra, with three regions of pre-independent India—Marathwada, Vidarbha and Bombay State—merging to make the modern state; three crops—sugarcane, cotton and onions—influencing modern-day politics; and three distinctive political rules before independence—Shiv Shahi, Peshwai and the British. In ancient times, Maharashtra was ruled by three dynasties—the Satvahanas, Vakatakas (who gave Maharashtra the Ajanta and Ellora caves in Aurangabad) and the Rashtrakutas (250 BCE to 972 CE). Later, it was ruled by the Western Chalukyas, the Cholas and the Yadavs, until Islamic powers seized India in the medieval era.

These Islamic rulers, starting with the Bahmanis, set up the Qutubshahi, the Adilshahi and the Nizamshahi kingdoms (nizams were at one time viceroys to the Mughals), which overlapped the territories of modern-day Maharashtra. The territory of what constitutes Maharashtra today was constantly under siege by Mughal rulers struggling to subjugate other Muslim kingdoms of the Deccan, and bring all of India under a single Islamic dynasty (the Chugtais).

The British seized much of the present-day territory after three Anglo-Maratha wars, the last of which was in 1818. During (and even before the intensification of) the freedom struggle, three reformists—Jyotiba Phule, Lokmanya Tilak and B.R. Ambedkar (among others)—left an indelible mark on Indian polity. Among the several nineteenth century stalwarts, three stood out. They were Justice M.G. Ranade (fighting for social upliftment among the masses before political liberation), Vishnushashtri Pandit (pioneer in widow remarriages) and Lokhitavadi Gopal Hari Deshmukh, who was the founder president of the Arya Samaj in the state.

In modern times, three chief ministers stand out for greatly influencing the course of the state and leaving a permanent stamp on its society. These chief ministers are Yashwantrao Chavan, Vasantrao Naik and Sharad Pawar, all of who kept up the tripartite spirit of the Phule-Shahu-Ambedkar philosophy that was the underpinning of their governance at all times. Then, again, three castes—Mahar, Maratha and Brahmin—have had an immense impact on Maharashtra's politics. Not surprisingly, the state's logo is the 'Trimurti' (derived from the Ajanta caves), and there are three theories about why the state is called Maharashtra, meaning the greatest of all nations.

It is largely believed that the state began to be known as Maharashtra from the time of the Rashtrakuta dynasty, but the basic derivation seems to come from the Maharashtri language (later known as Marathi), which was an offshoot of ancient Prakrit. The Marathas claim that it was their rule over the territories of modern Maharashtra (indeed much of it is Maratha country) that gave the state its name. But this claim is bitterly contested by the Mahars, one of the three dominant castes of the state, who believe the state is named after them—'Mahar-rashtra', hence 'Maharashtra'.

Modern-day Maharashtra has seen three phases in its neo-socio-political formation since India's independence from British rule in 1947. It was under three separate governments soon after independence—Bombay State, Central Provinces and Berar, and Hyderabad State—all of which saw major struggles to integrate with each other and emerge as one Marathi-speaking state. But the beginning, for the purpose of this book, was the dawn of Maratha rule starting with Chhatrapati Shivaji, son of Shahaji, who was a mansabdar in the army of Mughal Emperor Shah Jahan and later an officer in the Bijapur army. Shivaji established the Maratha empire and the concept of Swaraj or independence. At that time, though, this independence was from Islamic rule and the idea of Swaraj was confined to a Maratha state.

The Maratha rule of Shivaji and his descendants is credited with keeping much of India 'Hindu', even though Shivaji was a secular ruler who had many Muslims as generals in his army. These Muslim generals hated the Mughals and the various Islamic sultanates across India, and were only too willing to collaborate with Shivaji to defeat these powers. In fact, Aurangzeb's elder son Akbar conspired with Shivaji's son Sambhaji to defeat his father. When Aurangzeb finally captured Sambhaji, the Maratha King was brutally tortured to get him to reveal the names of the other Mughal collaborators in his army. But Sambhaji steadfastly refused and was dismembered by Aurangzeb before being put to death.

However, much of the Maratha expansionism and empire-building took place under later kings, particularly Shivaji's grandson Shahu, who, however, never took to the battlefield. His wars were fought for him by his prime ministers, the Peshwas, who were not Kshatriyas but Chitpavan Brahmins. One of these Peshwas was Bajirao I, who along with his son Nanasaheb, often collaborated with the declining Mughals to keep out other Islamists, particularly the Afghans, from the north. The Peshwas were also the first dynasty of prime ministers in India. In the kingdoms of the ancient times, including Shivaji's, the post of prime minister was not hereditary. This changed when a grateful Shahu promised Bajirao's father, Vishwanath Ballal, that his son could inherit the job for the services the father had rendered to him not just for expanding the Maratha dominions but also securing the release of Shahu's mother from Mughal imprisonment. Five generations of Vishwanath's progeny continued in that post until the British defeated them in 1818.

The fight for Swaraj and independence from the British was taken up by other stalwarts in later centuries. Maratha rule in India is very significant because Shivaji's descendants captured and established many principalities across North, West and South India and also seized large portions of the east (there is a Mahratta Ditch Lane in Kolkata, after a ditch built by the British East India Company to keep Maratha raiders away from their factories).

In fact, at its peak, the Maratha territory stretched from Tanjore in the south to Peshawar and Khyber Pakhtunkhwa, which is in modern-day Pakistan, in the north. They also laid claim to Kabul and Kandahar in Afghanistan and, in between, they had their sardars in Gujarat and Madhya Pradesh as well—Gaekwads in Baroda, Scindias in Gwalior and Holkars in Indore. The Bhonsales in Nagpur had charge of territories in the east, including Bengal and Orissa. Other confederates included the Puars (Pawars) in Dewas, a branch of the Bhonsales in Tanjore, Patwardhans in Miraj, Ghorpades in Mudhol (Karnataka) and Vinchurkars in Pune, their capital, which, at one time, between the Islamic and British conquests, had become the de facto capital of India.

Thus the Peshwas had formed a confederacy of Maratha states through large territories of modern-day India, which, in a way, was the precursor to federalism in the later Indian Republic. They had registered a presence even in Delhi but had not quite conquered the capital, a feat that eludes even the modern-day leaders of Maharashtra. They lost much of their territory in wars with the Afghan Durrani empire, particularly the Third Battle of Panipat in 1761. To a large extent, Tipu Sultan halted the march of later Maratha rulers in the south, after which it took them several years to recover. But even so they held sway over large swathes of

India, including Attock (now in Pakistan), leading Charles Metcalfe, then the acting governor general of Bombay Province, to say in 1806, 'India contains no more than two great powers, British and Mahratta, and every other state acknowledges the influence of one or the other. Every inch that we recede will be occupied by them.'

He was right, for from Shivaji's jagirs of Pune and Supa in the seventeenth century, the Maratha dominions had expanded by the late eighteenth century from Pune to the southern banks of the Yamuna River in the north and to the northern banks of the Tungabhadra River in the south, barring the nizam's territory across the eastern half of the Deccan plateau (the western half was all Maratha territory). In the west, their dominions stretched to Kutch and Kathiawar and the eastern parts of Rajputana. Central India, too, was in their possession from Bundelkhand to the Central Provinces and Berar, and Malwa. The Mahanadi delta in the east from Balasore to Cuttack in modern-day Orissa belonged to them as well. Lahore and other parts of Punjab were lost to them forever after the battle of Panipat in 1761, but they stretched their dominions to Rohilkhand, Oudh and Bihar in the east. But, like Punjab after Panipat, they lost Mysore to Haider Ali and his son Tipu Sultan, and Tanjore was seized by the British in 1799.

The British had to fight three wars with the Marathas to vanquish them: the First Anglo-Maratha War took place in 1775 when the East India Company intervened in a succession struggle within the family of the Peshwa rulers based in Pune. But it was the Second Anglo-Maratha War in 1805 that really diminished the Maratha power. In the Third Anglo-Maratha War in 1817–1818, the Marathas were completely routed by the East India Company. During this war, the British seized all the territories belonging to the Peshwa rulers (who had been ruling in the name of Shivaji's descendants since the late eighteenth century) and appropriated them to British India.

The ceding of these territories gave the British control over most of present-day India and Pakistan, particularly as the Peshwas had already captured much of the coastal western regions from the Portuguese with the help of the formidable naval fleets set up by Kanhoji Angre—Shivaji was among the first kings in India to establish a navy of his own. Land fortifications were a major feature of the Maratha military and had been built from Shivaji's times.

In fact, Bajirao Peshwa was an exceptional military ruler who did not lose a single battle. Even if the Peshwas under his son Nanasaheb and Nanasaheb's cousin Sadashivrao Bhau became too ambitious in later years and lost the Third Battle of Panipat in 1761 (which pushed Maratha expansionism and their empire back by nearly a quarter century), there are many historians who believe that the battle was an essential one for India. For even that resounding defeat meant that India saved much of its territory in the north during Partition. Had the Marathas not fought the Third Battle of Panipat, much of North India would have been ceded to Pakistan at the time of Partition. But fortunately for India, even the victorious Afghan King Ahmed Khan Abdali recognized their might and pleaded with the vanquished Marathas to take charge of Delhi and give up their claims to Attock, leaving Punjab by and large to him. By comparison, even Bengal, which was another reformist state during the nineteenth century, did not come anywhere close to achieving this feat. The rulers of Bengal, essentially Mughal subedars, were content with their territories and entertained no thoughts of expansionism. In the case of the Marathas, however, there was an underlying philosophy that sustained Maratha empire-building, which was lacking in the other kingdoms of medieval and pre-modern India.

The ascendancy of Shivaji and of the inheritors of his legacy would not have been possible without this philosophy—what historian V.K. Rajwade describes as 'Maharashtra Dharma', a phrase first appearing in the lexicon of Sant Ramdas, Chhatrapati Shivaji Maharaj's resident saint and political adviser. Maharashtra had many saints in medieval times, but they were mostly confined to what is known as the Bhakti movement and the Varkari tradition, wherein they attempted to equalize society and militated in their own way against caste discrimination.

But, as one historian has said, despite the presence of these saints, religion, particularly the Hindu religion in Maharashtra, 'did not bend to the extreme of other-worldliness' as many social scientists have also testified. Thus, among these saints rose Sant Ramdas who first evolved the concept of Swaraj and linked it to Maharashtra Dharma, while Shivaji attempted to integrate people of all classes and castes in his kingdom under the banner of Maharashtra Dharma.

Maharashtra Dharma, simplified for those unfamiliar with the term, meant not just Hindu dharma but also nationalism. It manifested in seventeenth century India in various ways such as the protection of the cow, protection of Brahmins, a fight for independence from Muslim kings (Swaraj) and an attempt to restore morality in Indian/Hindu society, which many felt had been destroyed by the Islamic rulers.

When in the early twentieth century, Bal Gangadhar Tilak, one of India's greatest freedom fighters, roared against the British, 'Swarajya is my birthright and I shall have it!' it was not just the fanciful stringing of words to produce a slogan that would resonate at the time and, perhaps, even beyond the times. Tilak's 'birthright' had a historical context and it was not without reason that he had begun public celebrations of the Ganpati and Shivaji festivals a few years earlier. The 10-day Ganeshotav in 1893 was, of course, an attempt to thwart the British ban against Indian gatherings, but the Shivaji festival was clearly the revival of the legend of a brave and significant warrior king—who is credited with saving India from a complete Islamic takeover—so he was not lost in the mists of time as a forgotten hero.

The Marathas, particularly, are justifiably proud of maintaining the native character of their land through the ages. It was a feat that was also attempted by the Sikhs and the Bundelas (the Rajput and Jat kings from time to time collaborated with the Islamic kings to defeat various rivals, including the Marathas). But, as Rajwade states, neither community had the unity, determination and leadership required to accomplish this goal. Even Bengal, which influenced and led Maharashtra in the reformist movements of the nineteenth century, could not protect its territory from conquests, eventually leading to the partition of Bengal in the early twentieth century and the secession of East Bengal at the time of Partition.

It is this spirit of Maharashtra Dharma, unique to the Marathas, that helped them keep the flag of Swaraj flying for nearly two centuries after Shivaji's death, sometimes under Maratha rulers and at other times under the Peshwas, both fully believing in the superiority of Maharashtra Dharma. It must, however, be mentioned that while Sant Ramdas, who formulated Maharashtra Dharma, might have had the intention of protecting the Hindu religion, the later Marathas and the Peshwas were secular by nature. They fought against the Jat and Rajput kings and raided the largely Hindu Bengal (though ruled by a Mughal governor); sometimes they patronized the nizam, while at other times they fought against him.

At the core of their expansionism was less religion and more extortion of revenues, such as chauth, a fourth of the amounts due to the local kings. Also implicit in their philosophy of expansion was the concept of sardeshmukhi, a recognition of their supremacy; and Swaraj, freedom to govern their core territory, the Deccan, by themselves without interference from the Islamic conquerors. One tends to forget that between the two hundred years of various Islamic rulers and the 150 years of British rule, India was largely governed for nearly 200 years by the Marathas under the shadow of a receding Mughal dynasty. They may have demanded a price for their protection of various other Indian kingdoms and dynasties, but Maratha rule left an indelible stamp on the way the nation would shape itself after independence.

It was only in the early twentieth century, with the advent of Mohandas Karamchand Gandhi, that Maharashtra Dharma ceased to be the domain of Maratha territory, and nationalism acquired a more pan-Indian character under the Congress-led struggle for freedom. But the advent of Gandhi and his attempts to secularize the nationalist movement by including Muslim leaders in the freedom struggle also gave rise to militant Hinduism in Maharashtra that saw the birth of both the Hindu Mahasabha, the Rashtriya Swayamsevak Sangh (RSS) and the Veer Savarkar brand of militant, often violent, nationalism. However, N.C. Kelkar, who was a fierce Tilak supporter and initially hostile to Mahatma Gandhi, did not believe the two forms of nationalism were irreconcilable, and Acharya S.D. Javadekar alleviated the hostility between the muscular Tilakites and the pacifist Gandhi by establishing a link between the two.

Writing in various Marathi newspapers at the time, Javadekar said Tilak and Gandhi both stood between the moderates (Ranade) and those with more extreme views (Savarkar). While Tilak's nationalism was of the extreme kind, he believed in a non-violent struggle, which was Gandhi's conviction too. Gandhi believed that religion was the opium of the masses, and Tilak had a similar view. In fact, Tilak mixed religion with politics by starting the Ganpati and Shivaji festivals, one to defy the British and the other to raise the nationalist spirit in the hearts and minds of the citizens. So while Mahatma Gandhi would later be declared the father of the nation, Tilak was most certainly the father of Indian nationalism in the eyes of Kelkar, Javadekar and most other Maharashtrian leaders of the early twentieth century who struggled to find their place under Gandhi's growing influence, not just in Maharashtra but in the whole of India as well.

If Maharashtra was the torchbearer of Indian nationalism, it also led, along with Bengal, the social reforms in the nineteenth century. These reforms gave a distinct shape to the socio-political atmosphere in Maharashtra and the rest of India. Many of these reformists have been forgotten today, reduced to just names of streets. One of these reformists was Justice M.G. Ranade who achieved a fine balance between his loyalty to his employers and the desire to see society pulled out of its mire to become a more equal sphere for all sections. Justice Ranade fought against caste discrimination (influencing Dr B.R. Ambedkar's thoughts and actions in later years) and child marriage. However, he could not practise what he preached and, and at the age of forty, after the death of his wife, he gave in to family pressure and married an eleven-year-old girl. But that is another story.

It must be stressed that Maharashtra Dharma did not limit itself to political expansionism and empire-building in the seventeenth and eighteenth centuries. In the nineteenth century, Maharashtra Dharma underwent various transformations and evolved as a liberal nationalist movement focused on social reform, ahead of political independence from the British. According to Rajendra Vora, this Maharashtra Dharma was interpreted by leading reformists like Ranade, Lokhitvadi, G.G. Agarkar and Balkrishna Gokhale at various times in the mid to late nineteenth century as a movement based on the principle of individual liberty. Along with political independence, there had to be social reform and economic liberation, a philosophy that struck at the very core of entrenched caste prejudices that denied such liberties to large masses of the Indian population, across the country.

These reformists were moderates, and their philosophy was bitterly opposed by militant nationalists like Tilak and Kelkar who wanted political independence ahead of reform in the Hindu social system. Notably, this clash of the titans of the nineteenth century reformist movement in Maharashtra was largely among Brahmins who held different views on Indian and Hindu society.

But Maharashtra also gave rise to reformists like Jyotiba Phule, B.R. Ambedkar and Shahu Maharaj, the ruler of Kolhapur, all of whom also interpreted Maharashtra Dharma to mean the integration of all castes and communities. They bitterly opposed its Brahminical interpretation, which excluded them from basic freedoms and liberties. In fact, Phule claimed Shivaji for a Shudra king because of his stress on integration of all sections of society with the king/leadership, a position that was mostly held by Kshatriyas and Brahmins. The presumption was that Shivaji would not have stressed on integration if he were upper-caste.

However, Shahu Maharaj of Kolhapur (not his grandson, but a later twentieth-century descendant of Shivaji's), stressed his Kshatriya origins while setting up a radical party to oppose Brahmin domination of the political movement. But while he was influenced by Phule, Shahu Maharaj preferred to put an Arya Samajik interpretation on Maharashtra Dharma. His affirmative action during his early twentieth century rule—he would employ Dalits and backward classes specifically in his administration—influenced Dr Ambedkar to include reservations for the deprived sections of society, including Scheduled Castes and Scheduled Tribes, in the Constitution of independent India several decades later. Like Phule and Ranade, Ambedkar also believed that British rule was an essential element of social reform in the country.

It is worth noting that those leaders who wished for the equalization of society were opposed to the early exit of the British, because they believed it was only under the neutral and liberal British that society could be reformed and the debilitating caste system be put to an end. Meanwhile, organizations like the RSS opposed the exit of the British for quite the opposite reason—they feared power would go to the hands of the non-upper castes in an Independent India, and British neutrality was preferable to domination. The reformist leaders were not wrong for it was British support that led to the ending of sati, made widow remarriage possible by the enactment of stringent laws against the witch-hunting of social reformists, and gradually began to put an end to child marriage as well.

A bitter debate on social reforms and political independence raged from the mid-nineteenth century to the early twentieth century until it led to a confluence of the views of Tilak and Gandhi in the early twentieth century (though Tilak was no more by the time Gandhi landed on Indian shores). Unlike Savarkar, who believed in 'terrorist nationalism', Tilak was militant but non-violent and Mahatma Gandhi was non-violent but aggressively determined that the British must quit India. From the early twentieth century onwards, Gandhism began to rapidly take over even Maharashtra Dharma, for it combined elements of the integration of society first propagated by Chhatrapati Shivaji Maharaj, with the absolute determination that the British must quit India, which was integral to the philosophy of the Tilakites. In between, it took in the reforms sought by leaders like Phule (in the past century) and Ambedkar.

Gandhism was 'an idea whose time had come', to quote Victor Hugo, and very soon, leading stalwarts of the freedom movement in Maharashtra, such as Yashwantrao Chavan, saw the writing on the wall and quickly made their choice. But Gandhi's stress on integrating Muslims with the rest of the population went against the idea of Maharashtra Dharma, which was essentially a philosophy evolved for independence from Islamist rule. Thus, one can say that Gandhism led directly to the establishment of militant Hindu groups like the Hindu Mahasabha and the RSS. But even if these extremist groups do not follow the essential principles of Shivaji's Maharashtra Dharma today, they define the political present and future of India.

COMMUNITIES

Properly speaking, global thinking is not possible... Look at one of those photographs of half the earth taken from outer space, and see if you recognize your neighbourhood. The right local questions and answers will be the right global ones. The question, 'What will this do to our community?' tends toward the right answer for the world.

—Wendell Berry

We cannot seek achievement for ourselves and forget about progress and prosperity for (others)... Our ambitions must be broad enough to include the aspirations and needs of others, for their sakes and for our own.

—Cesar Chavez

2

'Now Scrub Our Utensils!'

The bad blood between Maharashtrians and Gujaratis is centuries old.

The city of Mumbai, where the Gateway of India is located, has always been the centre of conflict between the various communities in the country. This is the city that makes Maharashtra the leading state in the country, acting like the gateway to the rest of India for Maharashtrians from different regions of the state. But it is a city built not just by Maharashtrians alone. Large sections of people from across India have contributed to what it is today. Though some political parties may wish to lay exclusive claim to Mumbai today, their xenophobic campaigns, aimed at ridding the metropolis of all its non-Maharashtrian residents, are clearly not just short-sighted but also historically incorrect. That is because the city has had a chequered past in terms of ownership and its resident communities, and no singular ethnic group can claim exclusive rights over its land and its people.

The seven islands that were joined together by the British to create the city of Bombay—as the city was known then—were actually ruled by Muslim kings until the advent of the Western colonialists. As a result, the biggest landlords of Mumbai are still Muslim and Christian trusts and these communities continue to control large swathes of land within the domain of the seven islands. The original ruler of these seven islands was Sultan Mohammad Shah who 'sold' two islands to the Portuguese in the sixteenth century in return for their protection against the Mughals.

Emperor Aurangzeb had been camping in the Deccan for years in order to enforce the rule of his dynasty throughout India. The most troublesome of these Deccan powers were the Qutubshahi and Adilshahi kingdoms. Although Aurangzeb had not yet cast his eye upon what then seemed like a ragtag group of islands, Sultan Mohammad Shah feared it could be just a matter of time before he was overpowered and subjugated by the Mughals. Eventually, however, the Portuguese took over all the islands from the local rulers but seemed to have no idea what to make of the disparate pieces of land mostly occupied by indigenous fishing communities, such as the Kolis, who even today dominate the fishing industry and are considered the original inhabitants of Mumbai.

However, when Prince Charles II married Catherine of Braganza in 1662, the islands passed as her dowry into the possession of the British, who believed they had been cheated out of substantial sums and handed a dud by the Portuguese. It was not until the mid-nineteenth century that the British recognized the strategic value of these islands and began the process of reclaiming land from the waters surrounding the disparate islands to join them into a single mass of land.

The British laid roads and railways and soon Bombay developed into a strategic naval defence installation as well as a viable commercial seaport, displacing Surat in Gujarat from its pre-eminent position in this regard. The Gateway of India is a monument that was meant to showcase the British Empire and was built to mark the visit of King George V and Queen Mary ahead of the Delhi Durbar in 1911. However, the Gateway could not be completed by 1911 and was finished much later.

Once the British began to give primacy to Bombay over

Surat, much of Surat's trading activities shifted to Bombay as did many of its resident entrepreneurs—Gujaratis, Bohra, Khoja Muslims and Parsis, who soon gave Bombay an uncharacteristically Gujarati flavour. Perhaps the migration of these communities from neighbouring Gujarat was essential because Maharashtra did not have its own traditional class/caste of traders. The Deshashtha Brahmins of the Konkan region came closest to the traditional trader class, but they were essentially moneylenders and did not perform the duties that the banias and other groups from Gujarat had done for centuries.

Bombay was under British administration long before the Third Anglo-Maratha War ceded other territories in Maharashtra, notably around Pune and western Maharashtra, to the colonial powers. Thus Bombay had a liberal and anglicized character, which influenced even native Maharashtrians who either frequently visited the island city or made it their home. The Bombay Presidency under the British later morphed into Bombay Province and then into a bilingual (Gujarati and Marathi) state after independence. It became the capital of Maharashtra after a bitter contest between Maharashtrians and Gujaratis, prior to the states' reorganization in 1960.

However, the events that occurred in the years after the Portuguese gifted the territories they held to the British, until Bombay's emergence as Maharashtra's capital, had a huge bearing on the fortunes of the rest of the state. The fact that Bombay is still India's financial and commercial capital, that it continues to be cosmopolitan in nature and is more liberal and westernized than other districts or other leading cities of Maharashtra, and that there is no single monolithic culture that defines the Bombay or Mumbai of the twenty-first century, is all due to the British influence in the period stretching from the nineteenth century to the early twentieth century. That British influence is visible in the politics of the city even today.

Soon after the British had developed Bombay—a name they inherited from the Portuguese who thought it was a good (bom) port (bahia) and hence named it Bombay—as a major seaport in the mid-nineteenth century, they faced a huge industrial crisis back home. This crisis was caused by a major failure of the cotton crop in the United States of America, which was the chief source of raw cotton for the textile mills of Manchester. Britain used this raw cotton to produce rich fabrics, which were exported to foreign markets, including markets in Europe, Far East and India. Looking to augment their supply of raw cotton, the British began to encourage cotton farming in western India. As it turned out, most of their raw cotton came from the Central Provinces and Berar region, which is part of present-day Vidarbha. This region was also a major supplier of oilseeds and jowar.

The transport of raw cotton from the interiors to the ports of Bombay and onwards to Britain did not come without some risks. Much of the raw material tended to be destroyed by seepage and the vagaries of nature. Hence the British encouraged, in a limited fashion, the setting up of textile mills within the reclaimed city, which soon became a mini-Manchester of the east. Even today, vast tracts of land in the modern metropolis are mill lands established in those times. These mills, set up by the British and enterprising individuals from neighbouring Gujarat, have greatly contributed to the demographic composition of Mumbai, and continue to influence its politics today. For while the mill owners were almost all rich Gujaratis, their workers were local Maharashtrians, and since the city's native settlers were largely fishermen, much of the workforce came from the hinterland of Maharashtra.

With the collapse of the Peshwai in the early nineteenth century and the gradual end to the balutedar system in the villages, these sections of society were in need of employment (balutedars were village servants, but not mere servitors. They performed functions essential to the survival of the village, such as carpentry, pottery, weaving, scavenging etc., in return for which they were looked after well by the village council and provided with food, housing and other essentials). Thus, as the village councils collapsed, the balutedars migrated to the attractive British-ruled port town of Bombay where industries, including those catering to the production of oilseeds and infrastructure building, were coming up rapidly.

But the British did not need only blue-collar workers. They had headquartered a huge province in Bombay and were greatly in need of white-collar workers for the middle and lower levels of their administration. To cater to this need, the British set up schools and colleges in Bombay, and the traditional classes, notably Brahmins who were privileged in terms of education, began to send their children to these institutions. Soon, educated young Indian men and women began populating the British administration as clerks, accountants, and even supervisors and managers, under an overall British management.

The educational institutions set up by the British meant that castes and communities that were traditionally barred from learning and acquiring superior knowledge did not need to remain in the dark ages any longer. Thus, people from all castes and communities, including the backward Dalits and the untouchables, began migrating to Bombay for better prospects. An English education became synonymous with liberalism, and Bombay contributed enormously to the reformist movement in Maharashtra.

Many of the state's nineteenth century reformists had some association with the city, and the British administration supported them in ending practices like child marriage and sati, and encouraged widow remarriage by the enactment of laws. The fact that Bombay was governed by rulers who did not encourage discrimination or untouchability in their administration, and did not interfere in the people's cultural peculiarities, contributed enormously to the liberal outlook of the whole of Maharashtra and the development of its socialist character by the mid-twentieth century. This liberalism influenced other parts of Maharashtra after independence, making it one of the most progressive states of modern-day India with a distinctive socialist ethos that marks the state as one of the most forward-looking of the times.

This cosmopolitan nature of Bombay also helped to pioneer many progressive movements in the state. However, once the British left India and Bombay in the hands of the local citizenry, the skewed nature of the city's socio-politics became apparent. The colonial rulers had set up the Bombay Municipal Corporation (BMC) to govern the fast-growing metropolis, but the only people who were allowed to vote, until 1947, were those who paid income tax. The fact that these income taxpayers were mostly Gujarati, Muslim Bohras, Parsis and Sindhis underlined not just their economic status but their privileged positions of influence as compared to the local people who, even during independence, constituted 50 to 60 per cent of the city's population. Therefore, local residents grumbled that Bombay was a city of the rich who needed the poor to service their needs.

Most of the corporators and mayors of Bombay hailed from the Gujarati, Muslim Bohra, Parsi and Sindhi communities. Later, South Indians also migrated to Bombay to take over the administration of the state. All these communities dominated the higher echelons of the bureaucracy and the middle level and clerical opportunities in the city. Local Maharashtrians found that they were mostly confined to the chawls and textile workforces of Bombay. Even Marathi politicians who had joined Gandhi and the Congress Party felt the discrimination between themselves and the Gujarati leaders of the erstwhile Bombay State.

Maharashtra Dharma, of course, had undergone a transformation under Mahatma Gandhi to include all sections of society, including the Muslim minorities. But now the bigger divide was between the Gujarati entrepreneurs who had made Bombay what it was over a century-and-a-half of their enterprise, and local Maharashtrians who wanted exclusive charge of their own state capital. This led to the dawn of the Samyukta Maharashtra Movement (SMM, formally launched in 1956), which brought together all streams of political thought and philosophy. It unnerved India's first Prime Minister, Jawaharlal Nehru, who was compelled to concede Bombay to Maharashtrians rather than to the Gujaratis who wanted the city for their own state capital in the event of a reorganization of the states. This bitterness between the Maharashtrian and Gujarati communities is evident in the state's politics even today.

Morarji Desai was the chief minister of Bombay State in the years when the SMM took root and his superior attitude towards Maharashtrians may have helped to cede Bombay to Maharashtra. The turning point in the agitation came when he ordered the police to fire on a protesting mob at Flora Fountain, which resulted in the martyring of 106 protestors, a fact that has not yet been forgotten by the local populace. Flora Fountain was subsequently renamed Hutatma Chowk and the Martyrs' Memorial there stands as a permanent reminder of the sacrifice of human lives for a unified Maharashtra. Perhaps if Desai had refrained from firing at the protestors, Bombay may have continued as a bilingual state or even ended up as the capital of Gujarat, as the influencers were stronger on the Gujarati side than among the Maharashtrian leaders.

Maharashtrian leaders who were stalwarts of the SMM had coined the slogan: *'Mumbai aahe aamchi, nahi konache baapachi'* (Mumbai is ours and belongs to nobody else's father). The slogan sounds rude, but the political language of Maharashtra has always had an element of rusticity; the leaders did not mean to offend, it was simply an assertion of their ownership of the city. But the slogan enraged Desai and he responded, *'Mumbai tumchi, ataa bhaandi ghasaa aamchi'* (Mumbai may be yours, but get back to scrubbing our utensils), thereby implying that Maharashtrians were inferior to Gujaratis. Desai's response propagated old myths and underlined the fact that Gujaratis were the richer community while Maharashtrians were merely servants in their homes, fit only to scrub their utensils.

The bad blood between Gujaratis and Maharashtrians is centuries old. Closer to modern times, keeping up that bitterness, Maharashtra's minor potentates did not permit the British to build dams that would help to irrigate Gujarat, as these would submerge many villages in Maharashtra. After independence, although B.G. Kher, a Maharashtrian, was made the first chief minister of a bilingual Bombay State, his cabinet and subsequently the cabinet under Morarji Desai, was over-represented by Gujaratis, making Maharashtrian leaders uncomfortable. There was a growing feeling among Maharashtrian leaders—who had less influence with the Centre owing to Desai and before him Sardar Vallabhbhai Patel— that most funds being allocated to Bombay State were being used for projects in Gujarat rather than in Maharashtra. Additionally, they were convinced that the hinterland would never get justice in a bilingual state dominated by Gujaratis.

The Congress Party, during the freedom movement, had promised to reorganize the states on the basis of language, but after independence, party leaders changed their minds for fear that linguistic states would lead to a balkanization of India. However, pressure on the Congress was building from all sides, including from the Madras and Calcutta provinces. After the death of a Telangana activist who was fasting to demand a separate state for the Telugu-speaking areas from Madras State, Pandit Nehru gave in and set up a states' reorganization committee in 1953.

Now the battle for Bombay started in right earnest as the Gujaratis, led by the Mahagujarat Andolan and encouraged by Desai, were determined that, in the event of bifurcation, Bombay must go to Gujarat as the state capital. Maharashtrian leaders were equally determined that Bombay belonged to them. Socialist parties and communist leaders intensified the agitation for a unified

Maharashtra while debate raged on the future of Bombay, with serious consideration being given to turning it into a city-state or union territory.

This conflict between Gujaratis and Maharashtrians in Bombay was identical to of the trouble between Maharashtrians and Hindi-speaking people in the Central Provinces and Berar, and the Maha-Kaushal areas of Central India. Maharashtrians began to feel the pinch of the discrimination against them in terms of financial allocations and development of their areas, and wanted to separate from the Hindi-speaking majority of their state, that is, the Central Provinces and Berar. Hyderabad State had similar problems. The nizam, traditionally, had paid scant attention to the people living in his territories in Marathwada, who continued to remain backward even after the nizam's territories were ceded to India after the police action of September 1948. The agitation was greatly intensified in all three regions by the Marathi-speaking people, and Yashwantrao Chavan, one of the tallest leaders of the time, who was being projected as a reincarnation of Chhatrapati Shivaji Maharaj, ultimately prevailed upon Nehru to cede Bombay to Maharashtra.

Much water has flowed under the bridge since then, but the bitterness between the Gujaratis and Maharashtrians in Mumbai has not quite gone away. In fact, it might have intensified and the fault lines have become more apparent after the ascension of Narendra Modi to power at the Centre. Once upon a time this bitterness was limited to the Gujaratis and Maharashtrians in the Congress leadership. Today it manifests itself in the everyday existence of these communities, not the least because the Congress Party no longer exclusively represents them. Both these communities are clearly divided between the Bharatiya Janata Party (BJP), seen as the Gujaratis' party, and the Shiv Sena, which projects itself as the only representative of everything Marathi and Maharashtrian, as was manifest in the elections to the Brihanmumbai Municipal

Corporation in February 2017 where the two parties ran neck and neck reflecting the narrow gap between Marathi and Gujarati residents of the city.

Some political commentators believe this could be a deliberate ploy by the two parties to carve up the votes of the two communities between themselves. For without this extreme polarization, the Gujaratis and the Maharashtrians might have joined other parties, such as the Maharashtra Navnirman Sena of Raj Thackeray, which could have mopped up a large chunk of the Marathi vote.

The lack of a traditional trading/business community among Maharashtrians meant that even after the states' reorganization, the Gujaratis and other communities, including the Marwaris, Punjabis and Sindhis, continued to dominate the business of Maharashtra. Even today, Maharashtrian entrepreneurs can be counted on the fingers of just one hand. This has led to a unique situation with barely any shift in the centuries' old tradition of the Gujarati and Marwari business communities—at one time encouraged by Chhatrapati Shivaji to settle in his territory—dominating the lives of the Maharashtrian people in the villages and cities of Maharashtra.

Soon after the states' reorganization, Maharashtra's Congress Party leaders discovered they still did not have a voice in New Delhi, and Bombay continued to be dominated by Gujaratis (in business), South Indians (in bureaucracy) and Communists (in politics). These Congress leaders subtly and covertly encouraged the establishment of a regional force that would take on these three groups and rid Bombay of their combined influence. Thus, Bal Thackeray and his Shiv Sena emerged from nowhere and burst upon the scene with a lasting vengeance.

Supported by the Congress, the Shiv Sena made short shrift of these three groups in less than a decade of its existence. While the South Indians and Communists were by and large vanquished, overpowering the Gujarati sense of entrepreneurship proved tougher than expected, though the Gujaratis wisely stayed out of the line of Bal Thackeray's fire as far as possible. Over the course of time, the Shiv Sena went out of fashion, and it was the BJP that helped revive this sleeping tiger.

The BJP emerged from the ashes of the Jan Sangh in the late 1970s after a major controversy over its dual membership in the Janata Party government of Morarji Desai. (Desai became the prime minister after the Congress Party's defeat in 1977.) For a long time, the BJP experimented with Gandhian socialism but got nowhere. Then, its late-leader Pramod Mahajan forged an alliance with Bal Thackeray in the mid-1980s, enabling the two parties to improve their electoral performance which, until then, had been dismal given that both had a similar voter base (just 13 per cent at the time) and won barely a seat or two in the State Assembly and Lok Sabha when they contested independent of each other. These were also the years when the BJP took up the Babri Masjid campaign in Ayodhya. After the demolition of the mosque in 1992 and the subsequent riots in Mumbai in December 1992 and January 1993, the Shiv Sena and the BJP together stormed to power in Maharashtra in 1995, albeit with a shortfall in numbers that was made up by 45 Congress rebels in a house of 288 legislators.

Mahajan had clearly recognized the distrust of Maharashtrians for Gujaratis and blunted Thackeray's antipathy towards the community by leading the alliance in Maharashtra. The alliance trundled along happily until Mahajan's death in 2006 and the emergence of Narendra Modi as the Hindu Hriday Samrat, a title that Thackeray, at one time even more extremist than the BJP, had appropriated for himself. But it was not just the fight for supremacy among Hindus that caused the Shiv Sena, even in Thackeray's lifetime, to begin backtracking on the alliance. It would not support the Vishwa Hindu Parishad's bandh calls, it refused to endorse many of the BJP's programmes, it dug in its heels over shares of the electoral pie in Maharashtra, it even supported two Congress candidates, Pratibha Patil and Pranab Mukherjee, for president.

The emergence of Modi among the tallest leaders of the BJP infuriated Bal Thackeray—he had not forgotten Morarji Desai's insults to Maharashtrians, going so far as to refuse to erect a memorial to India's former prime minister who passed away when the Shiv Sena was ruling Maharashtra. Thackeray did not want another Gujarati to dominate Maharashtra and Maharashtrians. That distrust was carried forward by Thackeray's son and heir Uddhav Thackeray. Modi's complete disregard of the Shiv Sena in the run-up to the Lok Sabha elections in May 2014 strengthened Uddhav Thackeray's resolve not to concede another inch to the BJP during the assembly elections that followed in October 2014. This led to the break-up of the precarious alliance between the two parties, which had lasted for a quarter of a century despite some very turbulent circumstances.

Its shortfall in numbers in the assembly elections compelled the BJP to ally with the Shiv Sena in government, but that has not helped in smoothing the ruffled feathers of the Shiv Sena leadership. This led the two parties to fight against each other in the BMC polls and Uddhav to declare that never again will his party ally with the BJP in any election—a promise and a threat that has held true by and large, though they continue together in government as a withdrawal by the Sena would lead to a toppling of the government.

Apart from the political fault lines—the Shiv Sena is emerging as a bigger opposition to the BJP than either the Congress or the Nationalist Congress Party (NCP)—the divide between the two parties is apparent within the socio-economic fabric of Mumbai as well. In June 2015, Gujaratis and Maharashtrians living in a housing society in Kandivli in North Mumbai nearly came to blows over something as basic as food—a Maharashtrian family, not caring about a Brahma puja being offered by the Gujaratis in the building, turned down their appeals and went ahead with their decision to cook fish for lunch. Tempers flared and the police had to intervene. This incident caused Shiv Sainiks to reassert their protectionism of local Maharashtrians who, unlike Gujarati Hindus and Jains, are non-vegetarians—even sections of Maharashtrian Brahmins are meat and fish eaters, though they might eschew beef. The promotion and, in some cases, the imposition of vegetarianism by the BJP, now run by Gujaratis, does not sit well with the Shiv Sena. An uneasy calm prevails between the two communities at all levels of society in Mumbai.

The distrust is not limited to Gujaratis and Maharashtrians or vegetarians and non-vegetarians, but runs deep among the emergent communities of Mumbai, which continues to be a city of a poor majority that is dominated by the rich minority. But today, the poor are not Maharashtrians alone—they include North Indians from several states of India, Muslims as well as Hindus settled in slums and ghettos, who are all part of the vote banks for the BJP and the Shiv Sena as well as the Congress and the NCP.

The BJP believed that it would be able to contain and perhaps destroy the Shiv Sena by breaking their alliance and striking out on its own in 2014 and again in 2017. But it might have been too early to write the epitaph of Bal Thackeray's party, which continues to dominate the city of its birth, even after a hard-fought civic poll when the BJP pulled out all the stops, and even after its original inhabitants—the Maharashtrians—have dwindled to 40 per cent or less of the total population. The Shiv Sena keeps the Maharashtrian spirit and ethos in the city alive and ensures that the community is not marginalized in its own city and state capital. With a mix of terror and defiance of opposing forces, it has made sure that no one dares to ask a Maharashtrian to scrub utensils again.

3

Sugar and Its Spice...

Marathas have always kept all other
communities on a tight leash.

In the first week of January 2016, the RSS organized a show of strength at Marunji village on the outskirts of Pune. The event was billed as a Shiv Shakti Sangram and was aimed at underlining the growing influence of the RSS cadres in Maharashtra. This was the RSS's interpretation of Chhatrapati Shivaji's Maharashtra Dharma, which they had failed to popularize among the masses despite trying for nearly a century, both before and after independence. However, even after the installation of an ideologically compatible government both in New Delhi and Mumbai, the RSS was struggling for recognition and acceptance among the masses.

The RSS had chosen Pune for this latest show of strength not without good reason. The Shiv Shahi and the Peshwai rule of the seventeenth and eighteenth centuries had ensured that Pune was the de facto capital of India with a token allegiance to the Maratha seat of power in Satara and Kolhapur, in western and southern Maharashtra respectively. In many ways, Pune has remained the de facto capital of Maharashtra to this day, not the least because of the absence of a traditional trading community in the state, among Maharashtrians.

Despite the xenophobic campaigns of the Shiv Sena, Mumbai has remained a cosmopolitan metropolis with most job-givers belonging to the communities that had settled in Bombay Province before independence. Mumbai's demographic composition has undergone a subtle shift over the years with more middle and lower level settlers and migrants hailing from North India grabbing jobs in more than 160 service sectors in the city, without which it would not be able to exist.

However, while Bombay, after the bitter struggle of the Samyukta Maharashtra Movement, was installed as the capital of Maharashtra, Pune continued to exercise an overwhelming influence on the state's fortunes, not the least because it was the heart of the cooperative movement in the state. The rural elite that governed Maharashtra uninterrupted for nearly five decades after independence hailed mostly from western Maharashtra, and were by and large Marathas. Sugar played a major role in the state's politics at the time, and continues to do so today. To some people, that sugar has tasted bitter, to others it has been the spice of their existence.

Post-independence, Maharashtra was politically influenced by three caste groups—Brahmins, Marathas and Dalits—with the Marathas holding the other two on a tight leash, sometimes co-opting them to power and at other times marginalizing them so that the influence of both Brahmins and Dalits was restricted to the fringes of polity. While Dalit leaders might have been patronized and made part of the power structure from time to time, Brahmins were kept strictly at bay from actual power structures.

Nevertheless, Maratha leaders co-opted Brahmins to many institutional bodies to keep the hegemony of the upper castes intact. But there was always a good deal of distrust between the two upper-caste communities in Maharashtra—the Marathas saw the Brahmins as usurpers of power from Shivaji's descendants, and the intellectual battles between Shahu Maharaj of Kolhapur and Lokmanya Tilak in the early twentieth century reinforced this prejudice. The Marathas had felt marginalized for at least a century before the defeat of the Peshwas in the nineteenth century.

Yashwantrao Chavan, the first chief minister of unified Maharashtra, saw the wisdom of keeping all sections of the population happy, and included a fair number of Brahmins not just in his government and Cabinet, but also in the subsidiary power structures of the state. He set up many literary, cultural and educational institutions in which he installed members of the Brahmin community, thus keeping them engaged and otherwise happy so that they continued to influence society and government in the state.

This exercise defeated the RSS's attempts to drive a wedge between the Brahmins and Marathas, and limited the organization's expansionist plans over the next few decades. Thus, the RSS was confined to Nagpur and limited to an ideological manifestation of a particular stream of thought instead of being considered the representative of the general Hindu population or even the upper-caste/Brahmin segment. Meanwhile, Maratha politicians mostly affiliated to the Congress set about capturing the hearts and votes of the people of western Maharashtra, using sugar as a major tool in that exercise of ensuring the restoration of the Maratha domination of the state.

The doyen of the cooperative movement in Maharashtra was Vithalrao Vikhe Patil who organized the region's sugarcane farmers into Asia's first cooperative. This cooperative worked extremely well, benefitting both the farmers and the rural elite. The Maharashtra government then sanctioned the setting up of several cooperative banks to finance these sugar factories, with the apex cooperative bank always being strictly under the control of the doyens of the ruling party. Being part of a cooperative meant the farmer was assured of a minimum price for the procurement of his sugarcane and had a guaranteed market at the time of sowing.

Thus, he could borrow with ease and the banks were also assured of repayments in good time.

But the Maharashtra government cleverly limited the farmers to 'zones', which meant that no farmer from within the specified radius of a particular sugar cooperative could offer his cane for crushing at any other sugar factory. The elected chairpersons of these sugar cooperatives were always either the local Member of Legislative Assembly (MLA) or a Member of Parliament (MP), and voting against either of them meant voting against their own interests. Were the Congress candidate to lose his assembly election or the Lok Sabha election, he held the farmers in his zone responsible, and as a result delayed the cane crushing (crushing season usually begins in November and could stretch up to April each year). The later the cane is crushed, the less is its sugar yielded, causing the farmer to suffer a loss in compensation and procurement. Consequently, the farmer voted for his cooperative factory chairman even if he was not ideologically inclined to do so.

This has been the closest to cadre-building that the Congress has managed in the century or more of its existence, and it worked well for the party over the decades—economics influenced voter choices, and politics was determined by the business interests of the main players. Bombay was ruled by a succession of Marathas from western Maharashtra and the Congress Party's major stake since the state's reorganization was always in western Maharashtra.

It is, therefore, not without reason that when Sharad Pawar, a three-term Congress chief minister of Maharashtra, split the party to strike out on his own, his NCP was weighed down by sugar barons from western Maharashtra. Even the Congress then could not overcome the hegemony of the Maratha rulers of the state. The Marathas, riding piggyback on the Congress, held the reins of power after independence strictly in their own hands, except when Vasantrao Naik, who hailed from Vidarbha and belonged to a non-ruling community, reigned as the longest serving chief minister of the state from 1963 to 1974.

It was a necessary corollary of power in those days that you could not hold office without Maratha endorsement; even the Peshwas kept up a token subservience to Shivaji's descendants in Kolhapur and Satara. Thus, Naik's development programmes were mostly focused on western Maharashtra, which grew by leaps and bounds. That resulted in the people of his native Vidarbha region accusing Naik of according them stepmotherly treatment—and many of them continue to argue for a separate state in order to secure justice and development but, more importantly, freedom from Maratha domination.

So strong was the grip of the Marathas on the cooperatives and the Congress, that the party in Maharashtra was hardly impacted after the Congress split in 1969, and once again in 1978. Even Pawar's first rebellion in 1978—which was a split among the Marathas rather than the Congress as Pawar acted in his own interests and against those of Chavan and then Chief Minister Vasantdada Patil—did not make much of a dent in the Congress's overall hegemony over Maharashtra, except for replacing one Maratha leader with another as the head of Congress affairs.

However, according to Suhas Palshikar, former professor of political science at the Savitribai Phule University in Pune and now director of the think tank Lokniti, then Prime Minister Indira Gandhi hated to be beholden to Maratha leaders and so tried to cut them down to size by placing a trusted aide, Abdul Rehman Antulay, at the helm of affairs in the state. The Congress won the assembly elections in 1980, and despite the major role played by Vasantdada Patil in that victory, Indira Gandhi sent A.R. Antulay to Maharashtra as the state's chief minister, not realizing that this decision would damage the Maratha ethos, and thus Congress hegemony in the process.

Marathas, from the dawn of their kingdom in the seventeenth century, had always fought against the Muslim domination of their territory. Modern-day Maratha leaders, although having imbibed the secularism and co-existential philosophies of Shivaji, nevertheless felt they were betraying the Chhatrapati's cause of self-rule in their state. These modern-day Maratha leaders then, including Pawar, saw Antulay as a throwback to the Islamic rulers against whom their ancestors had fought for Swaraj and were soon on the lookout for an opportunity to destabilize Antulay.

When Antulay slipped up in the allocation of cement quotas to builders against donations to fund government schemes (though, admittedly, all the donations were accounted for by cash receipts and cheque payments), they saw their opportunity to displace him, this time with a Maratha as the chief minister (they wanted Patil but had to settle for Babasaheb Bhosale instead). The success of anyone but a Maratha was not acceptable, even though Antulay had only been extending to the urban milieu—the game the sugar barons were playing in the rural areas.

However, the Maratha hegemony had been damaged due to the distrust that existed between the succeeding Prime Minister, Rajiv Gandhi, and Patil, who soon displaced Bhosale as chief minister. Patil was not beyond playing the ancient Maratha game of cutting Delhi down to size—during the run-up to the Bombay municipal elections in 1985, he once again brought up the Centre's alleged desire to turn Bombay into a union territory or a city state. Unknowingly, Patil sounded the death knell of Maratha hegemony in the state with that statement because it roused the sleeping tiger Bal Thackeray and changed the political equation in the state forever. Suddenly, even people outside Bombay began to see the Shiv Sena—a self-proclaimed guardian of Shivaji's legacy—as a credible alternative to Marathas and the Congress. They trusted the Shiv Sena more with the fortunes and well-being of their state.

The Shiv Sena won that election resoundingly, achieving a majority of its own for the first time. Its earlier victories were achieved either when it was in a coalition with mainstream parties or with the support of fringe groups like the Muslim League to make up the shortfall in its numbers in the election of a mayor. This victory was the first of many and the Shiv Sena began to expand its footprint in Maharashtra, going from strength to strength. The BJP soon recognized the wisdom of seeking an alliance with Bal Thackeray, formally marking the dawn of coalition politics in Maharashtra. In this third phase of post-independence politics in the state, the Congress Party's hegemony, both before and after the states' reorganization, was thus displaced by coalitions.

The Congress had been displaced from power in most of the other states of India much before the Shiv Sena and the BJP seized power in 1995. But the success of the Shiv Sena and the BJP was not complete because the two parties had to seek support from 45 Congress rebels to make up their numbers in the assembly. A few years later, in 1999, Pawar broke away from the Congress Party again but had to seek an alliance with it to continue dominating Maharashtra's political landscape for the next twenty years and more. Thus, the Congress, in many ways, continued to exert its influence on the government, the most notable example of this being the defeat of then Deputy Chief Minister Gopinath Munde's plans to destroy the party's domination over the sugar cooperatives.

The Congress's political domination of western Maharashtra largely depended on the zoning of its sugar cooperatives. As stated earlier, no farmer was free to take his sugarcane to a factory in another zone to crush and produce sugar. Munde tried his best to break this practice and de-zone the cooperatives, which was fiercely resisted by many rebel Congressmen in his own Cabinet. He also tried to set up some private sugar factories, a move that was shot down through a combination of sabotage within the Maharashtra government and Pawar's bid to exercise his influence over a succession of union governments between 1995 and 2000.

In 1986, when Pawar merged his Congress (S) with the Congress (I) led by Rajiv Gandhi, his party was facing a severe cash crunch. The two years (1978–80) that he was chief minister and headed the first coalition government in Maharashtra (which included the erstwhile Jan Sangh) had not made him very influential. It was his second and third terms as chief minister, in 1988 and 1990 respectively, and his stint as union defence minister in P.V. Narasimha Rao's government starting in 1991, that saw him become one of the most influential leaders of the Congress Party.

Pawar had contested against Rao for the office of prime minister after the assassination of Rajiv Gandhi in 1991 and the subsequent Congress victory at the Centre. In 1998, Pawar had helped the fledging Sonia Gandhi secure 42 of the 48 Lok Sabha seats from Maharashtra (which included three of the Republican Party of India), which had led to his being installed as leader of the opposition in the Lok Sabha. All these acts added to his aura.

Believing that he could sway the Congress cadres to support him, he split the party in 1999 but was outsmarted by Sonia Gandhi who offered to resign if anyone in the party had problems with her or her foreign origins. Pawar's faction was then reduced to a rump, but he made sure that he got the maximum number of supporters from western Maharashtra through a sometimes judicious and sometimes unfair use of the cooperative banks headed by his supporters. As most of the sugar barons were dependent on loans from these banks for their business activities, they chose to safeguard their business interests by compromising their political interests, and willy-nilly aligned with Pawar's NCP.

However, far from sweeping Maharashtra as he had done at the head of the Congress in 1998, Pawar just managed to retain his core seats in western Maharashtra and discovered he had not added much to his strength since the split he had engineered in 1978. The 1999 assembly elections pushed the Congress into the lead over the Shiv Sena and the BJP. Since there were few rebels to support the Shiv Sena and BJP coalition this time, the Congress and the NCP together had the numbers to form the government in Maharashtra.

The 1999 assembly elections ushered in the second major phase of coalition politics in the state (not counting Pawar's Progressive Democratic Front government of 1978–80, which was a ragtag coalition of ideologically disparate parties) with the NCP dictating terms, though notionally the power and the chief minister's office was vested in the hands of the Congress. However, this was the period when there was a dearth of Maratha leadership in the Congress, and the NCP was almost entirely peopled by Marathas. A gap began to open up between the peasantry in the Maharashtra hinterland and the rural elite. While the hegemony of the Congress over Maharashtra was long broken, the Marathas continued to hold the state's reigns in a tight grip, one way or the other. Disappointment began to run deep among other communities in the state.

Barring Sushil Kumar Shinde, who hails from the Dalit community, the succession of chief ministers beginning with the Shiv Sena-BJP regime in 1995 to 2014 have been Brahmin (Manohar Joshi, Devendra Fadnavis) or Maratha (Narayan Rane, Vilasrao Deshmukh, Ashok Chavan, Prithviraj Chavan). Marathas account for a mere 30 per cent of the population, and another 9 per cent if one adds the farming Kunbi community to their numbers (the Kunbis insist on their Maratha origins though some blue-blooded Marathas refuse to include them in their ranks). While Joshi and Fadnavis are urban elites, all the others are from rural areas and are seen as having limited the fruits of power to their own community. There has been very little OBC representation in their Cabinets, which have been heavily tilted in favour of the upper castes since after Y.B. Chavan ceased to be the chief minister.

The unrest among the OBC community (we have to look at Dalits as a separate group because they have been more politically empowered) is, therefore, growing by leaps and bounds. OBCs, who seemed to be content with the status quo even up to the late 1980s when the implementation of the Mandal Commission recommendations had set much of India on fire, are beginning to feel increasingly marginalized. With their seeming decline in power, Marathas, who through the centuries have fiercely resisted being classified as anything but Kshatriyas, are now seeking reservations of their own. Since mid-2016, this demand for reservations has been gathering steam with huge morchas by Marathas across Maharashtra. It has confounded political analysts as Marathas from all ideological streams (the Congress, the BJP, the Shiv Sena and the NCP) as well as social strata (landed gentry, middle classes and landless labourers) have seamlessly come together in huge numbers in almost every district of the state to enforce their demands. Thus, the OBCs and Dalits are afraid the Marathas will cut into their share of the pie. Marathas, for the first time since independence, have been cut out of governance and are feeling the pinch. They were also demanding the repeal of the Scheduled Castes and Scheduled Tribes (Prevention of Atrocities) Act, 1989. It is a demand that threatens Dalits, who have warned of retaliatory agitations. But Marathas, so far content to be seen as upper castes and rulers, now also want a 16 per cent reservation in jobs—that demand makes both OBCs and Dalits wary about their own quotas being cut into to accommodate the historically more privileged classes in government jobs. In response, OBCs are already exhibiting signs of renewed unrest and that is bringing even these communities together, cutting across ideological and social barriers, as with the Marathas.

The disenchantment with the ruling classes had led to the resounding defeat of both the Congress and the NCP, seen as parties more representative of the Marathas, during the Lok Sabha elections of 2014 when Narendra Modi of the BJP, an OBC and considered one of their own, emerged as a clear winner. According to Professor Prakash Pawar of the Shivaji University in Kolhapur, 'Since then, however, the OBCs have been disappointed again that even the BJP-led government has given more representation to upper castes in the Maharashtra government.' This is now a major contributory factor to their distrust of the upper castes and this time the ire is not just against Marathas but also the Brahminical RSS.

The emergence of organizations like the Swabhimani Shetkari Sangathana before the 2014 general elections was essentially a rebellion against the rural elite, but while they succeeded to a large extent in displacing the elite from their ivory towers, there is not much they can do now to seek representation in the government or a larger share of the pie in Maharashtra, though the BJP-led government has done its best to accommodate as many of these interests as possible. However, given the rural distress in the state, the SSS has bowed out of the NDA (in August 2017) citing the BJP's inability to address farmers' issues—most farmers in the state are Marathas. 'If an election is held tomorrow, anything could happen,' says Professor Pawar. 'They could go back to the Congress in large numbers; the Marathas could even migrate to the Shiv Sena.'

Professor Pawar saw the isolation of Marathas in every region of the state and perhaps that is why they finally reacted with huge but silent and very disciplined, non-violent morchas to make their presence and importance in society felt. Large sections of Marathas are looking for a credible alternative force that could keep them as the ruling elite for several decades more and the Shiv Sena, with its emphasis on Chhatrapati Shivaji Maharaj and the Marathi ethos, could emerge as the front runner. At the same time, the disappointment of the OBCs with political parties that are unable to break the domination of the Marathas and other upper castes runs deep. 'It will depend upon which party gets the reading right and its act together ahead of the others. The unrest is deep and the social churning unpredictable,' says Professor Pawar.

Thus, Maharashtra is in a deep state of flux. As journalist and political commentator Kumar Ketkar puts it, 'No political leader today has a sense of history or of the future. Each leader is trying to get the best for his own. And it cuts across the parties. The state can only go downhill under these circumstances.'

4

...But Not Everything That's Nice

A distinction must be made between
'Hindu' and 'Hindutva'.

In 1995, soon after the Shiv Sena and the BJP first assumed power in Maharashtra, they introduced a bill in the legislature proclaiming a complete ban on cow slaughter in the state. Mumbai houses Asia's largest abattoir at Deonar and this move caused panic within large sections of society, among them not just those dealing in the trade but also consumers who were upset at the government interference in their food choices.

Bal Thackeray was then the self-declared remote control of the government and many butchers' associations made a beeline for his residence to petition him to withdraw the bill. One had not heard Thackeray pontificate much on cow slaughter before the bill was introduced in the assembly, and he seemed rather easy to persuade. When the government did not take any action on turning the bill into law, journalists questioned Thackeray about his government's intentions. The Shiv Sena chief was very sharp in his responses: 'Before you talk to me about cow slaughter, please bend down and look underneath the animal, and you will discover it has no udders.'

That rather unrefined statement was Thackeray's way of acknowledging that cows were not really being slaughtered at

Deonar or elsewhere because a previous government had banned such slaughter in 1976. Only uneconomical bulls and non-milch animals were allowed to be culled, and what India knew as beef was mostly from the water buffalo, male or female.

Vinoba Bhave's Sarvodaya activists had been keeping vigil at the gates of the Deonar abattoir for years, and one senior activist acknowledged that the slaughter of such animals would never end in India for, as he put it, 'After gold it is the leather trade that brings India maximum returns in terms of exports. So long as they have that market animal slaughter will not stop in India.'

In the years since, India has overtaken even Brazil as a leading beef exporter. So it came as a great surprise to the world when, without much ceremony, the old 1995 bill, which had been allowed to fall through the cracks, was dusted off by the new government in 2015, and the president of India gave his assent to a complete ban on cow slaughter in Maharashtra. This now meant that one could not even slaughter uneconomical bulls or calves, not even old animals that had ceased to produce milk, and that possession of beef would result in a non-bailable offence punishable by five years in prison.

This law caused a furore across the country and instantly put many enterprises out of business. In a nation where more than 60 per cent of the people are non-vegetarian, the move was non-inclusive and grossly intrusive. The sample registration baseline survey of 2014 by the Registrar General of India revealed that at least 71 per cent of Indians over the age of 15 are non-vegetarian. Earlier a 2006 *The Hindu*–CNN-IBN State of the Nation survey showed 31 per cent of Indians as vegetarian and another 9 per cent as 'ova-vegetarian', that is consuming eggs. Muslims were the obvious target of the move, but government officials seemed to have forgotten that traditionally, large sections of Hindus, particularly Dalits, (including adivasis and nomadic tribes) depend on beef for their nutritional and protein needs.

According to a Dalit leader agitating against the ban on cow slaughter in Maharashtra: 'One kilo of dal will last a family of five for, at the most, one meal in the day. At five times the price of beef, that is far too expensive. On the other hand, one kilo of beef will stretch to three or even four days for the same family who can then also sustain themselves on stew and soup from the bones. Where is the comparison then between dal and beef? Vegetarianism is only for the rich and privileged. The poor have to eat only what they can easily afford.'

The beef ban has been the most obvious manifestation of the resurgence of a Hindu identity in not just Maharashtra but across India (beef has been banned in Haryana too). It does not sit well with the overall socialist ethos of Maharashtra, which has existed since Chhatrapati Shivaji Maharaj's time. But as Professor Prakash Pawar told me, 'Once upon a time when you said, "I am Hindu", it meant you believed in a particular way of life but you were not against any other person. You went to a temple but you had no problem visiting other places of worship. And you certainly had no issues with people believing in gods other than yours. There is a concerted attempt now to change the meaning of the word Hindu. What is happening today is an assertion of "Hindutvawad", not Hinduism. But there are forces in the ascendant in the country who would want to merge being a Hindutvawadi with Hinduism. It will be a sad day when "Hindu" comes to represent exclusion, divisiveness and imposition of one's illiberal beliefs on others.'

The rising fortunes of the Hyderabad-Telangana based All India Majlis-e-Ittehad-e-Muslimeen (AIMIM) in Maharashtra since 2014 has added to these concerns of social scientists. The situation was quite different in the times of Shivaji. Although Maharashtra was at the forefront of the movement for self-rule at that time, Shivaji had no qualms in trusting and relying upon Muslim generals in his army. An easy coexistence with the general Muslim population prevailed even among the common masses at that time.

Following in that tradition, Bal Thackeray had no hesitation, at one time, in teaming up with the Indian Muslim League to have a mayor from his party elected to the Bombay Municipal Corporation (BMC). He had even addressed meetings with IUML President G.M. Banatwala in the 1970s. Distrust between local Hindus and Muslims was a later import to Maharashtra from North India, brought in by migrants from the communally troubled northern states.

But now this distrust has been magnified by what Professor Pawar calls the 'Hindutvization' of the Hindu identity. With the failure of the Congress and the NCP to protect their interests, the minorities have been looking for a group or leader who might help them in the assertion of their own identity, without having to face the consequences of majoritarian impositions.

The shift in the socio-political formulations in Maharashtra was very apparent in the elections to the Aurangabad Municipal Corporation in 2015. Mughal Emperor Aurangzeb's grave lies in Aurangabad and, for years the Congress Party had soft-pedalled the minority population in the city, offering election tickets mostly to Muslims while ignoring the Maratha and Hindu sensibilities. The advent of the Shiv Sena in the 1980s neatly split the communities between the two parties with the Sena always having an edge over the Congress.

But in 2015, the AIMIM emerged as a major challenger to the Shiv Sena and pushed the Congress to third position by taking maximum seats in the civic body after the Shiv Sena. However, in a subsequent assembly election in Bihar, all the AIMIM candidates lost their deposits. So the turbulence is being seen as a shift in the Maharashtra polity rather than a general enchantment of the minorities with the AIMIM. Social scientists believe such polarization, fuelled by acts like the beef ban (and the controversy over the chanting of 'Bharat Mata Ki Jai', which brings to the fore a Hindu-Muslim divide), could lead to further fragmentation of society.

However, Professor Pawar's concern about a renewed divisiveness in Maharashtrian society is not just about religion. The caste issue has raised its ugly head again and there is a concerted attempt to stifle liberal thought even among upper caste Hindus, as is evident in the killing of rationalists like Govind Pansare, Narendra Dabholkar and others who were shot dead by unknown assailants, established after a partial headway in the investigation—in Dabholkar's case they were extreme Hindu bigots belonging to the Sanatan Sanstha—while these old men were out on their morning walk (in case of journalist Gauri Lankesh, a frail, unarmed woman at her gate). All the political parties are guilty of fomenting this division. In the run-up to the assembly elections in Maharashtra, when it became obvious that either Nitin Gadkari or Devendra Fadnavis, both of them Brahmins, could become the chief minister, Sharad Pawar openly asked the people, 'Do you want Brahmins to once again crush you under their rule?'

He was harking back to the Peshwai period when, after marginalizing Shivaji's descendants, the Peshwas had discarded the warrior king's inclusiveness and begun the restoration of the hierarchy of varnashrama. According to Jayant Lele, 'By far the most damaging legacy of the Peshwai and the one that contributed the most to the resentment of the local and regional Maratha elites towards Brahmins (particularly Chitpavans) was the decay of a cultural tradition that had been shared by the masses across the boundaries.'

Maharashtra has always had a rich 'Sant' tradition, with saints who militated against caste divisions in society. Even Sant Ramdas, during Shivaji's time, did not quite succeed in equating Maharashtra Dharma with varnashrama. The saints—Dnayneshwar, Tukaram, Namdeo—who followed, established a 'varkari' tradition in which the masses found an equal share in society. But the Brahmin Peshwas seized this tradition and, through the use of state power, replaced it 'with a highly Sankritized idiom' that, as Lele points out, opened a wide gulf between the common masses and the ruling elite. This was the reason why the British managed to overcome the Peshwas with relative ease (for the masses would not rise to the Peshwas' defence or revolt against the British) and though, in the medieval era, Sant Ramdas's attempt might have been to reinforce Maratha-Brahmin supremacy, by now there was no love lost between the two communities.

The biggest manifestation of this in the modern century has been the controversy surrounding the award of the state government's Maharashtra Bhushan Puraskar to Babasaheb Purandare, a noted writer of ballads, who has done pioneering work in popularizing the legend of Chhatrapati Shivaji Maharaj. Much of the Shiv Sena's interpretations of Shivaji's reign have been influenced by Purandare but, for several years, the Marathas have been resentful of Purandare's attempts to give a 'Brahminical' twist to Shivaji's origins.

Maratha groups had forced the Congress-NCP government in 2008 to drop its sports award, the equivalent of the national Dronacharya award, in the name of Dadoji Kondadeo who has long been regarded as Shivaji's guru. Kondadeo was a subedar in Shahaji's army, entrusted with the responsibility of educating Shahaji's son and turning him into a fine warrior. But he was unacceptable to latter-day Marathas because he was a Brahmin.

So, when the BJP-Shiv Sena government decided to give the Maharashtra Bhushan award to Purandare in 2015, it created a gulf between the Brahmins and Marathas all over again. The NCP, which had appropriated the Maratha legacy, was in the forefront of opposing the government move and succeeded in unnerving the chief minister to such an extent that Devendra Fadnavis even threatened to throw his opponents off a cliff—a medieval punishment for opponents in Shivaji's time that did not endear the Brahmins to the Marathas. There has been a persistent demand for the government to take back the award, and even Maratha

Congressmen have since joined this battle against the return of Brahmin domination in the state.

While the 'upper castes' battle it out between themselves for domination in the state, the gulf between the various communities settled in Maharashtra has been widening. The non-Marathi speaking groups in Mumbai and the rest of the state, whether they are the urban elite or migrating masses from backward areas, are driven by economic interests. However, Maharashtrian society appears to be slipping back to the times when non-Brahmins in the state rebelled against the assertion of Maratha supremacy. That is essentially because, as Professor Pawar says, rural poverty is migrating to the urban areas where, unlike in the nineteenth century under the British, they do not find any interest groups that might help to change their circumstances.

A peculiar situation exists in Maharashtra where there is even less cohesion among the ruling elite now than when the government was run by a coalition of Marathas belonging to the Congress and the NCP. While the political parties then might have been two separate entities, their interests, both political and economic, merged seamlessly and there was an element of cohesion within the government. Now, although superficially, the Shiv Sena and the BJP seem to be on the same side of the fence in terms of socio-ideological formulations, politically, there is a wide gap between their goals and ideals.

This chasm most significantly continues to manifest itself in a Gujarati versus Marathi divide, which has a bearing on the economic interests of the people, for many rural migrants escaping into the metropolis are found to be running away from moneylenders who hail from the Gujarati and Marwari communities settled in the hinterland. The fact that these communities continue to be economically dominant perpetuates the traditional prejudice of the masses from the times of Mahatma Jyotiba Phule against the 'shethjis' (moneylenders or job-givers in the cities) and 'bhatjis'

(Brahmins or the priestly class common to both the rural and urban areas). The conflicts between Maharashtra's communities are thus multilayered.

Under British colonialism, apart from the thriving Parsi, Gujarati, Marwari, Sindhi and Muslim classes, Marathi society was divided into urban working masses of all communities. These communities took advantage of British liberalism and neutrality to rise above their caste and class origins. Concerted efforts were made to integrate the peasantry in the hinterland and the landless labourers—not including the extremely remote and backward tribes in the hills and inaccessible areas of the state—with the mainstream.

Affirmative action, to a large extent, has improved the lot of even those who were once cast out of society and banished to its fringes. But sadly, despite two centuries of pioneering work by social reformists and concerted efforts by elected governments, Maharashtra in the twenty-first century seems to be slipping back into the broad divisions that existed in the nineteenth century. The erosion is due entirely to what Ketkar has described as the self-centredness of politicians of all parties who care little for the consequences of their intemperate actions in the present. Future generations might have to pay a heavy price for the petty self-interests of modern-day political forces.

5

A Matter of Habit

Untouchability is not yet a thing of the past.

*N*amdeo (name changed) was a peon at one of the news organizations I worked for in the 1990s. Ramalingam was a clerk in charge of collating information from the various press releases that arrived at the organization, and preparing a list of daily events. The senior editors could then simply glance through the list and assign the events to different reporters. An easy camaraderie used to prevail in the corner occupied by the clerks—today they would probably be known, rather blandly, as office executives or even news coordinators—and the peons who felt more comfortable hanging out with them than with the more senior employees of the news organization.

Imagine, then, our shock and horror when, one day at lunchtime, as they all sat down with their tiffin carriers brought from home, Ramalingam pulled out a banana from his lunchbox and flung it onto the floor. We were close enough to see his action and were startled into asking, 'Why are you throwing a perfectly good banana away?'

There was general embarrassment all around their lunch table as Namdeo bent down and picked it up. No one can describe our horror as he began to peel it in order to eat it.

'Hey, that's unhygienic!' someone shouted. But this was more than just a matter of hygiene, as we soon discovered. It was a matter of habit. As Ramalingam squirmed and Namdeo looked sheepish, the truth came tumbling out from those at the lunch table who had been troubled by this regular lunchtime ritual but had been unable to do much about it. As we began to probe, it turned out Ramalingam was not just asserting his hierarchical superiority over a lowly peon, which was bad enough, he was also underlining his Brahminism and the latter's alleged 'untouchability', more than fifty years after independence when such acts were outlawed and severely punishable under the law.

Namdeo was a Dalit and he could have easily brought a non-bailable offence to bear against Ramalingam, but he chose to put up with this daily humiliation without protest. 'Raahu de na, saheb' (Let it go, sir), he pleaded in a low voice as general outrage spread through the office, and more and more staff members, attracted by the loud voices, came to the clerks' corner to find out what was going on.

One outraged young woman employee snatched the banana from Namdeo's hands and flung it back on the floor. Then she stood over Ramalingam and ordered him to pick it up. 'Now hand it respectfully to Namdeo.' He wouldn't. So she forced him to take a bite out of the banana himself whereupon he ran in the direction of the men's washroom, presumably to throw up and rinse his mouth clean with soap and water.

For months, many of those who had witnessed the incident were disturbed by this manifestation of untouchability in the 1990s. It made me realize that nothing had changed between the time Dr B.R. Ambedkar had been working as a law officer for the Maharaja of Baroda and the 1990s, when India was fast liberalizing and attempting to take its place in the world alongside the Asian Tigers and the Chinese Dragon.

I recalled a very poignant story about Dr Ambedkar who,

while working as a highly qualified, foreign-educated law officer in Gaekwad's palace, was victimized by the relatively unlettered peon simply because of his origins. According to this legend, the upper-caste peon in Gaekwad's office used to fling legal papers at Ambedkar from the door, preferring not to step in, lest he be soiled. He would not even fetch water for Dr Ambedkar. Instead, a pot and tumbler had been placed inside his office so that he could help himself.

Discrimination such as this led Dr Ambedkar to conclude that Hinduism was not designed for liberty, fraternity and equality of all human beings and therefore, he wrote these values into the Indian Constitution. But it was a sad reflection on the continuing biases in society that an incident such as that between the clerk and the peon should happen in the modern metropolis of Mumbai in the mid-1990s. In a city with a liberal and supposedly evolved workforce that was supposed to represent the fast-paced, resurgent, post-liberalization India.

But this was not an isolated case. Around the time when a statue of Dr Ambedkar was desecrated in the Mumbai suburb of Ghatkopar in the mid-1990s, a professor from the University of Bombay told me that discrimination against Dalits was common on the campus. Of course, there had been no untoward incidents of students or teachers being driven to suicide for being Dalit. But acceptance of them among both faculty and students was low, socializing was taboo and visits to their homes by their upper-caste 'friends', classmates or colleagues was virtually non-existent. The Dalits tolerated such covert social boycott silently.

Namdeo's appeal to his more enlightened colleagues to brush the incident under the carpet and refrain from talking about it was surprising, but it is what Professor Ramesh Kamble of the Sociology Department at the University of Bombay describes as the 'privatization of pain'. He is referring to the silent suffering of the deprived classes who, despite the laws governing their equalization in society, still find themselves marginalized and discriminated against, and deprived of their rights. They tend to bear the humiliation stoically with a fatalism that has been ingrained in them over the centuries.

Maharashtra has always been at the forefront of the upliftment of Dalits. Shahu Maharaj of Kolhapur, in the early twentieth century, had introduced affirmative action in his administration—it is from him that Dr Ambedkar, after having lost his fight to introduce separate electorates for Dalits, drew inspiration and introduced reservations for the deprived sections in the Constitution.

Shahu led by example, making it a point to stop at the tea stall of a Dalit each evening, work closely with them in his office, sit down for meals with his Dalit staff and make no bones about accepting water from their pots. The conflict between him and Tilak arose largely from his reformist and liberal tendency. Tilak, a fierce nationalist, was a conservative on social reforms, and the conflict in Maharashtrian society between the two streams of thought ended only with the death of these two individuals within months of each other. However, Dr Ambedkar lived long enough to realize that despite affirmative action, it would be nearly impossible to change the mindset of upper caste Hindus.

'Religion must mainly be a matter of principle only. Not a matter of rules. The moment it degenerates into rules it ceases to be a religion [...],' he had said, and this was particularly relevant in the villages where strict rules governed societal norms. People from the Mahar caste, though among the balutedars, were in constant conflict with the Brahmins and Marathas over their rights and duties. Many of those who belong to the Scheduled Castes today performed crucial duties in the villages, but their primary importance to Brahmins and Marathas was as scavengers.

In an earlier century, Mahatma Jyotiba Phule had militated against caste and gender discrimination in Hindu society. He set up the Satyashodhak Samaj in 1873, which denounced the caste system and focused on the upliftment of the depressed classes. It is Phule—whose family belonged to the Mali caste and were florists to the Peshwas—who is credited with coining the word 'Dalit', which means crushed or broken because that is what these oppressed sections of Hindu society had become.

Phule was a pioneer of education, both of women and of the traditionally oppressed classes. He believed that these sections were kept deliberately uneducated, illiterate even, and that a deliberate fatalism was encouraged by the upper caste emphasis on varnashrama to keep them serving their masters. His Satyashodhak Samaj found immense support from Shahu Maharaj, and Dr Ambedkar was probably inspired by Phule's ideals to give the call to all Dalits to 'educate, organize and emancipate' themselves.

It is a testimony to the pioneering work of all these forces in Maharashtra that the general lot of Dalits has improved considerably across India. No other state has had such inspiring reformists through the centuries. In fact, Bahujan Samaj Party leader Mayawati borrowed liberally from Phule, Shahu Maharaj and Ambedkar when she was the chief minister of Uttar Pradesh. All these efforts should, by now, have succeeded in equalizing society and polity to a large extent. But, though Dalit groups have become part of many socialist movements across the decades and exercised much influence on governments in the past, their strategies have been greatly flawed and they have slipped back several paces in the modern centuries.

Dr Ambedkar, convinced of the futility of attempting to equalize Hindu society, converted to Buddhism with lakhs of his followers in 1956. That instantly led to the equalization of the most backward classes of Hindu society, and the upper castes in the villages particularly hated this development. After their conversion to Buddhism, these sections were no longer obliged to follow the rules and be confined to the places marked out for them in society. And they did not have to stick to their traditional jobs on the fringes of society. Suddenly, the upper castes did not have the manual force to carry out important activities like scavenging, removing waste and dead bodies, etc. and neo-Buddhists began to meet the upper castes on their own terms.

In the early years after independence, the Congress, which dominated governments across India, saw the utility of co-opting Dalit society into power structures within the state and at the Centre. This was relatively easy because the party had a background of inclusion and had witnessed Mahatma Gandhi's efforts to eradicate untouchability, even though Ambedkar may have disputed these methods. The Congress struck a chord with the vast Dalit masses across the country, and not only in Maharashtra.

However, Dr Ambedkar, who was part of the first government of independent India led by Prime Minister Jawaharlal Nehru, died too early. Only months before his passing away in December 1956—and barely weeks after converting his followers to Buddhism—he had set up the Republican Party of India to give a political voice to the Dalit masses. Sadly, more than half a century later, that party is highly fragmented with innumerable factions led by men who look out only for their own interests, instead of the interests of their oppressed compatriots.

'Dalit "unity" is not the prerogative of Dalit leadership,' explains Professor Kamble. 'In fact it is the dominant ruling political interests that decide the questions of whether to unite, or when to unite, for Dalit leadership. The question of Dalit unity or disunity is the making of the dominant ruling political interests. So, the role that the Dalit political leadership can play, as representing the political interests of the "Dalits", is decided not by the Dalit leadership or the concerns of the Dalit masses but by the dominant political elites and their political interests.'

For example, there was a long-standing demand, going back to the 1970s, to name Marathwada University in Aurangabad after Dr B.R. Ambedkar. Many Congress governments baulked at the measure but then, looking at the intensity of Dalit agitations for the move, Sharad Pawar, who had started the process in his first term as chief minister in 1978, gave in to the demand in 1994. It is not a coincidence that he quickly co-opted firebrand Dalit leader Ramdas Athawale into his government and made him social welfare minister. Athawale went on to become a Member of Parliament, first as a representative of his own faction of the Republican Party in alliance with the Congress, then as an NCP ally.

He had no problems switching sides in 2009 to contest a reserved seat on a Congress ticket. He lost and that propelled him towards the Shiv Sena which, however, could not accommodate his electoral interests. Now Athawale does not have any qualms about representing the BJP in the Rajya Sabha (he is now a minister in the Modi Cabinet). Athawale had lost from the temple town of Shirdi in the 2009 Lok Sabha elections for ridiculing the saffron tilaks of the Hindutvawadi parties. Now he sports one of his own.

As Tushar Jagtap, a Dalit activist and former member of the Bombay University Senate, says, 'The Republican Party got fragmented because Dalit leaders were never interested in unity or upliftment of the masses. They were only looking out for themselves. That left Dalits on the fringes and these leaders have become the furthest fringe of the mainstream.'

Athawale's case is a perfect example of what Professor Kamble describes as the 'self-serving political interests of the mainstream'. 'The Dalit leadership exists because they fulfill interests of the ruling political castes. Any other orientation by the Dalit leadership leads them to either being ousted from the political canvas or made redundant. Of course, they could be "included" in power without any actual power.'

That is perhaps what was attempted by the RSS—whose star has been in the ascendant since 2014—at its Shiv Shakti Sangram in January 2016. The BJP's resounding defeat in the Bihar assembly elections in November 2015 was attributed to its chief Mohan

Bhagwat's proposal to junk reservations for the deprived classes in favour of a more merit-based society. Merit, however, is evident when all sections of society have equal opportunities; a return to domination by the upper castes, in case reservations are dropped, would once again relegate Dalits to the fringes of society. So it was not surprising when the RSS attempted a course correction by dusting off some unknown members of Jyotiba Phule's 'family' and presenting them to the world in their new avatar as BJP supporters.

However, that effort instantly fell flat when, within days, Dalit activists exposed the fact that Dattareya Phule, and his brothers and cousins paraded on stage by the RSS, were not descendants of Jyotiba Phule but of his brother Rajaram Phule, who had ostracized Jyotiba for his pioneering work on Dalit upliftment and women's education. Phule did not have children of his own and thus the attempt to create a dynasty for India's and Maharashtra's first Dalit reformist pioneer was the RSS's strategy to be seen as including Dalits in its power structure.

Appropriating Phule was a dire need as Prakash Ambedkar, the grandson of Dr Babasaheb Ambedkar, after a few initial flirtations with saffron parties, had decided that he was placing himself left of centre and he would have nothing to do with the existing political dispensation in the state. In fact, he had been needling the RSS for months over its 'shastra' (arms) puja, pointing out that the RSS was essentially a Brahminical organization that should not be dealing in arms, which was an occupation for Kshatriyas (he forgot the Peshwas, though, who were Brahmin warriors, known as the 'Sword of the Chhatrapati'). Prakash Ambedkar has been concerned that such an exhibition of arms worship might send the wrong message to the masses, encouraging them to take up weapons; those vulnerable to attacks will not just be the Muslim community whom the RSS targets but Dalits too, who have traditionally not been able to defend themselves against the upper castes, armed or unarmed.

Ambedkar was one of the three MPs of the Republican Party of India—the others were Professor Jogendra Kawade and the late R.S. Gavai—who had successfully contested an election to the Lok Sabha in 1998 from general seats. Their success was entirely due to the efforts of Sharad Pawar who was hard put to persuade the 'savarnas' to vote for Dalits; usually the reverse is an easier task. This was another classic example of co-opting Dalits to the power structure without actually giving them any power. As Professor Kamble says, 'The political careers of various Dalit leaders is testimony to this.'

Athawale, Ambedkar, Kawade and Gavai are by no means the only ones who have allowed themselves to be patronized by mainstream parties in return for personal gratification. Even Dalit leaders once inimical to the Congress or the Hindutva parties have chosen to submerge their identities and marginalize themselves. They have compromised not just their own but also their communities' interests.

The Dalit Panthers, for example, were a force that stormed into existence in the 1970s, promising hope for a better future for Dalits. Of course, they believed in (rather rusty) arms and violence, patterned as they were on the American Black Panthers, which rose around the same time in the United States to fight for the rights of African-Americans. But they soon ran out of steam, ending up as the first Dalit allies of Bal Thackeray and the Shiv Sena when, with their violent and militant methods, they could easily have supplanted the similarly inclined Shiv Sena in the affections of at least the Dalit masses in the state. But, instead, they adopted the Sena traditions of the Ganpati and 'dahi handi' celebrations, and formed their own teams in the name of Babasaheb Ambedkar who had forbidden idol worship or support of any traditions that excluded one community from the other. This was their means of mainstreaming themselves, though that led to the renewed submergence of their individual identity and rendered them rather unseen and faceless in traditional Hindu society.

But perhaps the biggest blow against the continuing emancipation of Dalits in Indian and Maharashtrian polity has been the economic liberalization of India. It is not only Dalit movements but all social movements—women's movements, workers' movements, peasant movements—that are in a state of crisis today as a result.

Professor Kamble says, 'For social movements, including the Dalit movement, to remain politically relevant, they need to succeed in collectivizing "pain", they need to make the pain collective, as well as create the hope that collective actions will lead to effective intervention in transforming pain. However, the ascendance of neo-liberal material, social and cultural forces since the 1990s has succeeded in making the pain "private". The privatization of economic institutions has led to privatization of pain; with the privatization of pain and anxiety, the question of escape from the pain has become the "private" domain of the individual. This has undermined the efficacy of social movements, has made them irrelevant and redundant. Again, privatization of pain and anxiety has led to a paradox; one has been "included" in the market-led material/cultural forces and yet feels alienated from them at the same time.'

Professor Kamble adds, 'For Dalits who have perennially been at the material and social fringe, the privatization of the institution of state, as well as indifference exhibited by the state in terms of providing basic social goods, has had far-reaching consequences. The state as a public institution ought to recognize the claims of Dalits and other marginalized sections over basic resources and a life of dignity. The "privatization" of the state means the state's turning into an agency that makes the fulfilment of private interests as its priority, and disregards the public membership of the institution. This vacuum then is filled by the NGOs, and with numerous "campaigns" instead of "movements".'

Professor Kamble's theory is reflected in practical terms in the suicide of a Dalit student, Rohith Vemula, at Hyderabad Central University in January 2016. His pain was very private, though the discrimination against him was not. He was discriminated against because he chose to be different and not part of the mainstream. He wanted his own identity and not one decided for him by the more privileged sections of society. But his suicide resulted in ensuring that his pain—and that of others like him—did not remain private. It set off a fresh churning in society across India. As Professor Prahlad Jogdand of Bombay University said, 'I have hope that this would be the turning point in giving Dalits a new presence in society. Look at how people drove Dalit leaders like Balasaheb Mungekar (Congress) and Ramdas Athawale (BJP) out of Hyderabad, labelling them as stooges of the mainstream parties, preferring to conduct their movement without any political support and you will know what I mean.' (Mungekar is a former vice chancellor of Bombay University and an ex-member of the Planning Commission under the United Progressive Alliance [UPA] and Athawale is minister for Social Justice in the Modi government.)

Professor Jogdand believes that this time it will not be the mainstream political parties that will define the Dalit identity but society at large. His was a prophetic statement, considering a few months later in July 2016, there was a leaderless Dalit uprising in Gujarat after some of them were beaten up by members of the upper castes for just doing their jobs—skinning dead cows. The movement unnerved both the Gujarat and Union governments and there have been concerted efforts to win back the Dalits with not much result.

Now, however, there is a major ongoing tussle between Athawale, firmly on the right and Ambedkar, left of Centre, over Rohith's mother who has since then converted to Buddhism, which confirms Professor Kamble's theory that Dalits in India can exist only at the will and patronage of the upper castes. Athawale's attempt, at the BJP's behest, to felicitate Rohith's mother in 2016 was just another manifestation of such patronage. Professor Jogdand says, 'Maharashtra is now astir with a churning in society that will soon become apparent in the near future. The people will rise and define their identity themselves. I would not write off the Dalit movement just yet.'

In this scenario, mainstream political parties will have to pay more than just token lip service to Dalit upliftment across India. If they do so, there could well be a tectonic shift in the social and political formulations in Maharashtra, which has been the pioneering state in Dalit upliftment through the centuries. The state could well be the first to break the (bad) habit of patronizing the Dalit masses and continuing to keep them subservient to the interests of the upper castes, and the mainstream political parties defining those castes.

REGIONS

Justice will not be served until those who are unaffected are as outraged as those who are.

—Benjamin Franklin

Anyone who knows history [...] will recognize that the domination of [...] government by any one particular [...] faith (or group) is never a happy arrangement for the people [...]

—Eleanor Roosevelt

6

From Mills to Malls...and Wells

Liberalization of the Indian economy
has been the bane of farmers.

S eema Telange was fifteen years old when she first learnt of her father's indebtedness. The man was on the verge of bankruptcy and close to committing suicide. He had borrowed funds from a private moneylender to sow his crops during a hard season, when the monsoon had failed and banks were unwilling to extend more loans than they already had. But the crops failed again the following season and the moneylender was calling in his loan, failing which he would sell off her father's land to the highest bidder.

This practice has become common in the killing fields of Vidarbha—because of their cumbersome procedures, banks are unable to give loans to farmers in time for the sowing operations. These farmers then invariably head to the local 'sahukar' to seek a quick loan. The private lender hands over the money with alacrity because he knows the banks will release the farmer's funds as soon as the red tape has been cut. The private lender then grabs the money from the farmer which, in any case, is not adequate to cover the high interest rate at which he has borrowed from the sahukar. Moreover, if the farmer's crops fail, he is not able to pay back either the capital or the loan amount or the interest on it.

Many farmers in the cotton districts of Vidarbha—and to some extent in Marathwada—have lost all their land in this manner because they deposited their original title deeds with private moneylenders who sometimes did not even wait for the repayment before selling off the land. Since unlicensed moneylending is a crime, these unscrupulous sahukars put a distance between themselves and the farmers even before the harvest season by mortgaging the papers to unrelated land sharks. Sometimes they sell off the farmer's land to someone who might not be interested in farming at all. In that case, the farmer is ousted from his land and, if he is lucky, he ends up as a farm labourer on his own ancestral property. By and large, though, the preference is for the commercial expansion of the agricultural land. The farmer then might end up as a construction worker on his own land, or is rendered homeless if the new buyer prefers to throw him off the land altogether, which has become the norm in recent years.

Seema's father was on the verge of such an ouster when she decided to take matters into her own hands. She examined the papers, put together a scheme for repayment and marched to the moneylender's home with determination. She went down on her knees before the man when she realized he was preparing to sell off her father's farm. 'Have a heart,' she pleaded with him. 'Think of what might happen to his family.' As this man was an exception among moneylenders—he did have a heart—he accepted Seema's terms of repayment. The papers were eventually returned to the family and Seema succeeded in saving her father's life.

But not all farmers are as lucky, or have such understanding and resourceful children. They do the best they can by their families, but once their children discover how their fathers—or even mothers, in the absence of a paternal head—have mortgaged their land to the banks or private moneylenders, there are usually remonstrations and anger in the family, followed by the suicide of the farmer. Sometimes, there is more than one suicide in the family.

When Seema woke up to the reality all around her, she decided she was not going to follow the normal path of a young farm girl's life, but be of good use to her compatriots. She put marriage and domesticity on hold and descended with both feet into the black cotton soil of Vidarbha to fight for other farmers like her father. She got a law degree and petitioned the courts to get corrupt moneylenders to return the farmers' lands. Most of these private moneylenders were politically connected, and used their clout to get policemen to turn away farmers when they arrived at the police station to lodge an FIR. Under these circumstances, only the courts offered a solution. So successful was Seema in her selfless devotion to their cause that some years later the farmers in her village elected her to the local zilla parishad to represent their cases politically.

However, no political dispensation really understands farmers' issues, according to Professor Ghanshyam Darne of the Savitri Jyotirao College of Social Work in Yavatmal. He has been fighting against moneylenders through the Sahukargrast Shetkari Sangharsh Samiti for years with marginal success. 'No government has any policy for the farmer. All their policies are only oriented towards the corporates or the middle-classes. There is even interference with the market forces to benefit the middle-class consumers, which is why the farmer dies without any succour,' he says.

Professor Darne gives the example of the rising prices of toor dal in the winter of 2015. 'The government encouraged farmers to grow more toor dal and promised remunerative prices for the same. But by the time the farmers were ready to harvest, the government had got so unnerved by the middle-class outrage over the rising prices that they decided to import the pulses. Here in the fields, the farmer was preparing to take his crop to the market and in Mumbai, dal was already being offloaded by the container. Prices instantly fell, the farmer could not even recover the cost of his seeds. It was the same with the soya bean crop in the rabi season. Where does the farmer go, except towards inevitable suicide?'

The government continued with the policies through 2016 and 2017, encouraging farmers to grow more toor daal but, in panic at the rising prices, contracted with the government of Mozambique for supply of the pulses for five years. Domestic farmers were left stranded and were not just denied minimum support prices to cover their costs but also faced the prospect of their gunny bags of pulses rotting round the market yards in the state.

The fact that farmers are being encouraged to grow crops other than cotton in this dry farming region of Maharashtra is itself a big departure and a desperate measure in desperate times. According to Professor Srinivas Khandevale, an economist and former professor of Nagpur University, the soil is fit for nothing else but cotton, and does not lend itself well to cash crops like soya bean or pulses. Indeed, that was why the British had selected Marathwada and the Central Provinces and Berar for the production of cotton for their mills in Manchester following the failure of the American cotton crop in the mid-nineteenth century.

So rich was the black cotton soil and so excessive was the production of cotton in Vidarbha, that the move by the British to settle cotton farmers in Vidarbha even led to a change in the political economy of Maharashtra. Textile mills were set up in their Bombay Province to cater to this rich produce from the hinterlands. We have already seen in earlier chapters how this affected the communities, demography and eventually the political formulations in the state. However, at the time the British decided to set up textile mills in Bombay, there was a huge demand for cotton fabric the world over, including the British and Indian armies, which needed cotton cloth for their uniforms. To meet these demands, some captive mills were set up by both the government and private parties in Vidarbha.

'But now those mills have turned into malls,' says Professor Khandewale, remarking on what has happened not just in Mumbai but also in Nagpur and other cotton-growing districts of the region. 'It is the economic demands of the time. Once upon a time it was profitable to produce yarn and cloth in these mills. Now there are other activities that give them better returns. And this has affected the economy of the cotton districts, having a bearing on continuing suicides of farmers.'

The lack of local demand for cotton and yarn means farmers have to export their cotton produce to other centres in India, which adds to the production costs. Moreover, market prices are not pegged to the farmers' production costs and the government's remunerative prices are by far too minimal to offset the losses. The cotton-growing areas of the state are rather dry and there is an absence of 'protective irrigation', which can lead to crop failures, adding to the farmers' misery.

But it is also the Indian government's failure to negotiate a good treaty for its farmers within the World Trade Organization in the 1990s that has led to the recurrence of suicides through the decades. The United States is one of the world's main producers of raw cotton. While the world treaty was being negotiated, Americans forbade developing countries like India from offering subsidies to their farm sector, saying this would create imbalances in the market forces. However, the Americans continued to offer heavy subsidies to their own cotton growers. As a result, it is easier for the American farmer to produce cotton that is exported to countries around the world at competitive prices. The lack of similar subsidies for the Indian farming sector is one of the major causes of the growing and continuing distress in the cotton counties of the country, according to Professor Khandewale.

The liberalization of the Indian economy has taken an inevitable toll on the farmers. Sometimes whole families have been sacrificed to the free market economy. For example, about forty years ago, Shyamrao Bhoyar was the sarpanch of Amla, a small, nondescript village in Wardha district. He had a flourishing milk business, but his major source of income was his 16-acre farm on which he used to cultivate cotton. The returns were lucrative and he lived a life of relative luxury for those times.

However, circumstances changed in 1991, more so in the last two decades, when the government began to open up the economy. Market pressures and the fierce competition in the free market economy took a heavy toll on the farming community. Farming families found they were unable to cope in the resultant agrarian crisis. Like many farmers who gave in to the pulls and pressures of the liberalized markets, Shyamrao committed suicide in February 2011 at the age of sixty-four.

Shyamrao's thirty-eight-year old eldest son, Kawdu, who could not understand how his father had overstretched himself, thought he would be better at cultivating the family land. But within a couple of years, he also committed suicide—by swallowing pesticide—because of crop failure, crippling debts and the inability to get remunerative prices for his produce. The family's plight worsened when Shyamrao's youngest son Umesh, thirty-four years old at the time, killed himself by jumping into a well in November 2015. He, similarly, could not cope with the low price of raw cotton in the market and the mounting pressure from private moneylenders—he had defaulted on a bank loan of ₹97,000 and had no one to turn to and nowhere to go.

Shyamrao's sixty-four-year-old widow Kamlabai now lives alone with Sumit, Umesh's nine-year-old son, and despite her grief, moneylenders continue to harass her. Both her daughters-in-law, Varsha and Rukma, in their early thirties, abandoned their marital home after their husbands' suicides, so Kamlabai is the only one whom creditors can chase for their money. Kamlabai, who now works as a casual farm labourer, says she has no option but to end her life as well. 'We eat only once a day. How can I repay loans?' she asks.

The Bhoyars' story illustrates how farmers are unable to break even in a market-driven economy, and get caught in a vicious cycle for generations. The pressures of high agro-input costs and low remunerative prices for the produce are some of the primary reasons for the growing desperation among the cotton growers in the region.

However, the 'mills to malls' phenomenon has contributed to farmers' misery in other ways, for which the farmers themselves are responsible. Suicides, of course, are a by-product of the growing liberalization of the times but the uncontrolled materialism arising from this liberalization is entirely the farmers' doing. Earlier, says Professor Khandewale, the farmer was content with a bullock cart and a bicycle as modes of transportation. Now he must have a tractor, and a motorcycle, as well as a television set and a mobile phone. He also wants the best leather shoes, instead of the humble Kolhapuri chappals (which are in any case being driven out of the market due to lack of leather arising from the beef ban) that he would have earlier managed with throughout his life.

'These might seem trivial but these lifestyle costs add to his overall incapacity to sustain himself on minimal produce which is compounded by droughts and then unseasonal rains with the global changes in weather. Where does he then go, except to the well on his farm?' asks Professor Khandewale.

Practically every sociologist and economist agrees that the government needs to do more than just declare relief packages for these farmers. According to Shivaji Patil, one farmer I spoke to, 'What I get from that (relief) package is not even worth the cost of my travel to the urban centre where the cash is being disbursed.'

After the unseasonal rains in 2014, when large areas of western India were deluged by a hailstorm and practically every standing crop was destroyed, the then government declared a package of ₹4,000 crore for the farmers in the state. 'I got a thousand rupees,' says Patil, 'which was half as much as it cost me to go to the tehsil office to receive the payment and stay overnight until my turn came. That did not even buy me any seeds and it certainly did not cover the costs of my damaged crop. Others who were wiser than me did not even bother to venture to the headquarters for their measly share of the compensation. At least they saved on the travel!'

A subsequent government, which promised adequate compensation, also failed to bring succour to farmers because, as Professor Darne says, there is always a four-month gap between policy declaration and its implementation. 'Farmers are encouraged to sow the crop and they borrow in the hope that soon their debts will be repaid. However, by the time the funds do arrive, middlemen have got into the act—the farmer must harvest his crop and park his produce somewhere. Traders get in between and mop up the government compensation when it does arrive by taking the farmers' produce from their godown to the procurement centre. The farmer does not get even the minimum compensation that is due and returns to the cycle of loans and indebtedness for the next crop season.'

Professor Khandewale says governments are wrong to say farmers commit suicide because of emotional fragility or mental weaknesses. 'No one can bear grief alone. There has to be the publicization of this personal distress to prevent the farmer, male or female, from going over the edge.' Like Congress Vice President Rahul Gandhi did in the case of Shashikala and Kalawati, two farm widows from Yavatmal district. Kalawati Bandurkar and Shashikala Ringne became the faces of the agrarian crisis after Rahul Gandhi visited their homes in 2008. They claim that the concern shown by Gandhi and the benefits that followed in the form of support from government agencies changed their lives.

Sixty-three-year old Kalawati, a poor farm widow whose husband Parshuram committed suicide on 23 December 2005, feels her life is stable today thanks to financial assistance from diverse sources after Gandhi's visit. Gandhi had visited her house in Jalka, a nondescript village in Yavatmal district, during a tour to study the agrarian crisis in Vidarbha and mentioned her plight during a speech in the Parliament. This prompted Congress workers and NGOs to flock to her doorstep with financial help. Kalawati gets a monthly financial dole of ₹15,000 after an NGO deposited money in a bank.

The money has enabled Kalawati, who has seven daughters and two sons, to get all her daughters married. She is now looking after her grandchildren. Her two sons, Pritam and Balram, are studying in a local college and school, respectively. Pritam, who is studying science in Class XII, wants to become an engineer. Increasingly, in the villages of Vidarbha, education and professional degrees are the route to escape the eternal cycle of debts and suicides. Kalawati, who owns four acres of land, says, 'I always help my daughters and sons-in-law through my limited resources.'

Unlike Kalawati, Shashikala of Sonkhaas village in Yavatmal district is a landless labourer and works as a farm hand. 'How can I forget Rahul Gandhi? We were hungry and there was no electricity in my house when Rahulji visited my place. Now we eat well and live well. Yes, we got the electricity connection within ten days of Rahul's visit,' she says with a twinkle in her eyes. 'That day Rahulji just stopped by my doorstep and asked if he could come in. I invited him in. He sat on a shabby cot. I offered him a glass of water. He talked about my family, earnings and other details,' she says.

After that casual visit, Shashikala's fortunes changed and she was even able to educate her three sons. One of her sons, Mahindra (22), got a job in the Central Reserve Police Force as a constable while her other son, Yogesh (21), has been serving as a guard in the Forest Department since February 2015. Her youngest son, Jayendra (20), is in third year of graduate college in Yavatmal.

'An NGO made a fixed deposit in a bank from which I get twelve thousand rupees every month. Moreover, a former Lok Sabha member, Naresh Pugalia, gave a lakh and a half rupees for the education of my children. Another NGO gave me two lakh rupees to help me build my new house,' she says.

On an average, three farmers commit suicide in the Vidarbha region per week because of the unprecedented agrarian crisis. Over 60,000 farmers have ended their lives in the region since mid-1995 (according to National Crime Records Bureau) due to crippling debts and crop failure. But it is not feasible for leaders to visit all the families and publicize their grief. The government has to find other means of helping the region's farmers and their families. Kalawati, who has given her four-acre land on lease because she could not farm the land, is unable to offer a solution for the problems plaguing the region.

'No one in this region is able to cope with farming pressures due to the high costs of seeds and other inputs required, and the low price the farmers get for their produce. The only reason I am now better off is because of the financial help from Sulabh International, an NGO,' she said.

The Maharashtra government should have been able to better deal with the situation. It has failed essentially because every political party in the state has a vested interest in the continuation of the farmers' distress. Unlicensed moneylenders have worked out a system of political gratification. One election season, while I was sitting with farmers in a village in Yavatmal district listening to their tales of woe, news arrived that the ruling party had awarded a moneylender's brother the ticket to the constituency where these farmers were registered voters. The faces of the farmers crumpled and their distress was clearly visible. Many farmers in that village had lost their farms to this moneylender and knew that it did not matter whether the man won or lost the election, he would continue to harass them with impunity.

In another instance, a moneylender's family killed a farmer in anger when he refused to repay his loan. For once, the police registered an offence against the powerful scion of the family but then had to let the man go because the chief minister (Vilasrao

Deshmukh) himself called the police authorities to request that they be lenient with the man. He was pulled up for this act by the apex court some years later, but by then it was too late for the farmer and his family.

It is this moneylender-politician nexus that Professor Darne rages against when he says, 'Politicians who are supposed to be the social workers here do nothing for the farmers except garner their votes. It is corporates and self-interest that have taken them over and so every which way the farmer is surrounded by distress.'

But where there are fewer vested interests, there is hope. Journalist and social activist P. Sainath points to Andhra Pradesh where in 2004, the local government made a 'one time settlement' with moneylenders. They called a meeting of both farmers and their debtors and paid off the loan sharks with the warning that any further attempt to fish in troubled waters would be punished severely. The moneylenders then crossed the border into Maharashtra, where the government belonging to the Congress Party, which also ruled Andhra Pradesh at the time, was not motivated to resort to similar tactics because of the nexus between high officials and moneylenders.

Even Kerala, then ruled by the Congress Party, did better. 'It publicized all the farmers' debts,' Professor Khandewale points out. Unlike in Maharashtra, where a Congress leader's private visit made public the debt and grief of just two farm widows. As a result, everything was on record and moneylenders could not harass the farmers or claim more than they were owed. The government also called a meeting of farmers and lenders and worked out a systematic plan for the repayment of loans. It offered financial support to farmers so that they could pay off their debts. 'Suicides reduced instantly and we do not hear of much from Kerala or Andhra Pradesh as we continue to do in Maharashtra and Vidarbha,' says Professor Khandewale.

It might be the era of malls and materialism, but the state

governments owe it to the people to take care of their agricultural interests. 'It is not just the lack of a concerted agricultural policy. Even our education system is geared to turning more and more rural children into office workers than into farming technologists,' he says.

As technology overtakes the world at a pace that is difficult to keep up with, Professor Khandewale laments the lack of technological training for farmers. 'Smartphones and computers will help only so much in keeping connected with the rest of the world. What the farmers need today is simple technological innovations in pest control, in waste disposal, compost management. But no one is willing to invent these simple technological processes that will limit the farmers' labour and increase yields. Why would the farmers' children then want to continue on the land? Not just cotton farming, agriculture on the whole is an activity on its way out as governments increasingly cater to urban interests and treat farmers as a mere vote bank.'

Even in the US, whose farm subsidies are hurting Indian farmers, landowners are mostly corporate entities, but Khandewale believes such corporate farming might be a long time coming to India. In the meantime, however, one needs a visionary, perhaps like Bhausaheb Vikhe Patil, to unite cotton farmers into a cooperative. Why has that not happened so far, especially when western Maharashtra has led the country in cooperative farming in the sugarcane sector?

A conversation that I had with Professor Darne during a local election might hold the answer. Farmers were in distress all across the district yet they were unwilling to vote for the candidate who understood their problems and promised to reduce their distress. 'They will vote only for a candidate of their caste. Caste is all that matters to them even if they are in pain and dying. It is only when the two chief rivals put forward a candidate of the same caste does the better man stand a chance of winning,' Professor Darne explained.

Unlike in western Maharashtra which is dominated almost entirely by Marathas of all social strata, Vidarbha is not so homogenous. A fair section of Dalits and Buddhists are also farmers as are Kunbis, who count themselves as Marathas in spite of being denied that status by the blue-blooded royals of western Maharashtra and Marathwada. Therefore, there is no cohesion and unity among farmers even though each one faces the same situation because of misplaced policies and the vagaries of nature.

Is there any hope, then, for the cotton farmers of Vidarbha? Only if governments orient themselves to rural needs and necessities, says Professor Darne. 'They are out of sight and thus out of mind, every which way.' By the time a farmer makes news, he has already committed suicide. He no longer has any use for government remorse after he is dead. Government compassion, while the farmer was struggling for a living, might have helped to keep him alive. Until government officials change their mindset, farmers will continue to drink alcohol laced with pesticides or throw themselves into wells whose water table has dropped to a point that cannot be reached even by a pail and a long rope.

7

The Romantic Notion of a Separation

*The laid-back attitude of its leaders has kept
Vidarbha backward.*

In the winter of 2014, as Maharashtra was headed for an assembly election that would eventually bring the BJP to power in an alliance with the Shiv Sena, Union Minister Nitin Gadkari was lamenting the lack of passion for statehood among the people of the region. He was speaking on live television and when someone asked him about his party's position on a separate Vidarbha, he said, 'You must agitate. Take to the streets. But I notice every time there is a demand, some fifty persons gather somewhere, shout some slogans and return. Nothing more happens.'

For years, Gadkari was against statehood for Vidarbha but he has recently changed his public position in line with his party's policy regarding smaller states. On live television, he stopped just short of inciting the people to violence. But he did say, 'Agitate like the guys in Telangana did. If there is enough of an outcry, we will persuade the Congress to cooperate with us as we cooperated with them vis-à-vis Telangana.'

But no one was motivated enough, either then or later. Within a few weeks of that television show, the BJP came to power in Maharashtra on the strength of its enormously good showing in

Vidarbha. Without the seats from Vidarbha, the party could not have formed a government or indeed, installed a chief minister in Mumbai. This commercial capital of India has always been of significance to all political parties; the rest of Maharashtra shrinks in importance without Mumbai and its substantial economic potential.

So the BJP had to place any separation plans on hold and get to the business of governing Vidarbha as well as Maharashtra. Now the people of the region have even lesser reasons to demand statehood, for, as many ordinary citizens claim, Vidarbha and Nagpur have never had it so good. They have a high performing minister in Gadkari as their MP and, for the first time ever, they have a chief minister who belongs to an urban Nagpur constituency.

Unlike in the 1960s when Vasantrao Naik, despite hailing from Yavatmal, was beholden to Maratha politicians such as Yashwantrao Chavan from western Maharashtra for his survival, and hence focused his development efforts on that region, Devendra Fadnavis, who was installed as chief minister in October 2014, has no reason to ignore his home constituency.

Says senior journalist Sarita Kaushik, 'I do not believe in this bogey that Vidarbha could not develop because of western Maharashtra. The simple truth is that no politician from Vidarbha was so far motivated enough to do things for the people.'

A case in point is that of seven-term MP Vilas Muttemwar from the Congress (five times from Nagpur and twice from Chimur), who has been a minister in different union governments. He was laid-back and unmotivated, simply because Nagpur kept electing him to office against all odds, and took his constituency and the people for granted. Yet when the then Chief Minister Vilasrao Deshmukh, who hailed from the backward region of Marathwada, came up with a policy for integrated road development for Nagpur, the city went from being an overgrown village to ranking as among the top ten cities in the country. There has been a noticeable change in the circumstances of Nagpur, the winter capital of Maharashtra, since then. So, says Kaushik, 'There is no other argument for the separation of Vidarbha than the lack of development. But that problem will not be solved by a separation. You need committed leaders who will focus on the ground, not sit back with complacence.'

But that is precisely the continuing problem, according to former Maharashtra minister Nitin Raut who hails from the region. Raut's argument for a separate Vidarbha is that even BJP leaders from the region have become complacent. According to Raut, despite having both an MP as a union minister and a chief minister from the city, Nagpur still failed to make it to the top twenty smart cities, the flagship programme of the National Democratic Alliance (NDA) government at the Centre.

'That is because the city is bankrupt. Its municipal corporation is out of funds, they are borrowing from the Nagpur Improvement Trust (NIT) to fund projects, including waste disposal. It did not make it to the top cleanest cities because you can find garbage lying all over as there is not enough money to pay the workers. Soon NIT will be out of funds altogether and there will be nothing for development. There is that recognition even among the governments at the state and the Centre and that is why nothing gets done. Had I been chief minister in place of Fadnavis, I would not have lost that golden opportunity. I would have instantly declared funds of a thousand crore rupees for Nagpur. I would have planned the projects later. That would instantly have brought up the city's profile and given an impetus to the development of the region,' says Raut.

For years, Congress leaders treated Vidarbha as their fiefdom without seeming to realize the need to give the people of the region something in return for re-electing them to the Lok Sabha and the state assembly decade after decade. In 2004, Muttemwar was the only Congress candidate elected to the Lok Sabha from Vidarbha. All the other seats were won by the Shiv Sena and the BJP, though the government at the Centre was formed by his party.

Despite being made a minister, there was not much to show on the ground for his five-year term, so he thought he had lost the 2009 elections. He was fast asleep as the counting was in progress when he was rudely shaken awake by a party functionary who asked him to rush to the counting centre where he had gained a substantial lead over his BJP rival.

Muttemwar won that election too, but in 2014, there was no doubt he would lose against Gadkari who had been nursing the constituency for at least three years before elections were due. Muttemwar was a member of the Parliamentary Committee on Urban Development between 2009 and 2014 when the committee was discussing the implementation of various metro projects for cities across Maharashtra. He allowed Pune to get a major share of the funds.

It was Muttemwar's party colleague and former member of the Rajya Sabha, Avinash Pande, who threw a spanner in the works and demanded a metro service for Nagpur on the grounds that it was the second capital of Maharashtra. Pande was backed by Raut in the state cabinet, but the project remained on paper until the UPA government was voted out of power and the NDA government came in, with Gadkari as its transport minister. 'I am glad that Gadkari has actually taken that project off the ground. I have no qualms in giving credit where it is due,' says Pande whose position on a separate Vidarbha is conditional on development. 'Not before we catch up with western Maharashtra,' he says.

That reality may not be a long time coming with Gadkari in the Union Cabinet and Fadnavis at the helm in Maharashtra, hope the people of Vidarbha. So, Gadkari might have to wait for some time to see the people take to the streets in their demand for a separate state, if, of course, they are still discontented about the pace of development.

There are many experts who believe divorcing from Maharashtra before it is developed will instantly condemn Vidarbha to a 'third grade' state. As Pande told me, 'I am for a separate Vidarbha but not before we are equal to it because, as a politician today, when I say I am from Nagpur, which is in Maharashtra, I immediately get a four-star rating, if not a five-star one. If Vidarbha will no longer be part of Maharashtra, it will immediately condemn us to a one-star rating or even below, bringing us even behind Chhattisgarh or Jharkhand.'

The separation of these regions from Madhya Pradesh and Bihar respectively, he says, is a case in point. There has been no development in these regions since they became separate entities, and their officials have also lost clout at the Planning Commission level for allotment of funds. 'Today even if you are part of a backward region of Maharashtra, for the youth, being a part of Maharashtra means they have a gateway to the rest of India. Mumbai as their state capital gives them that advantage. Without Mumbai, that gateway would be shut. We would be just a "bimaru" state (common political parlance for sick states comprising Bihar, Madhya Pradesh, Rajasthan and Uttar Pradesh). And that is something that we don't want.

'The only reason why Vidarbha will be in the news as a separate state then will be for farmers' suicides in Yavatmal and Naxalite attacks in Gadchiroli. We can do better than that as part of Maharashtra,' concurs Kaushik. The proponents of separate statehood, however, believe Vidarbha, with its high number of thermal power plants and its enormous forest cover, could be economically self-sufficient. 'We are rich in minerals, coal, forests and electricity. Agriculturally we are self-sufficient with cotton. A separate state is sustainable,' says Naresh Pugalia, a former Congress MP.

But, according to experts, that is a fallacious argument because those rooting for Vidarbha on the basis of self-sufficiency and sustainability do not understand the devolution of finances. It is true that Mumbai draws most of its electricity from Vidarbha's thermal stations, but it pays Vidarbha handsomely in return. The problem has always been the utilization of those funds. Complacency has led to a situation where, even with all the electricity from its thermal power plants at its disposal, Vidarbha has no industries to speak of that could utilize that excess power.

Vidarbha's situation is similar to West Bengal's at independence. West Bengal was left with empty jute factories while all the production of jute was in Bangladesh (then East Pakistan), instantly leading that state to bankruptcy. West Bengal has never recovered and one has to only look at Assam, rich in oil and forest cover, to understand the point the opponents of a separate Vidarbha make. The revenue from the forests goes into a central pool and Vidarbha's allocation of that would be miniscule, perhaps even less than Assam gets from its forests and oil reserves. And despite its rich natural resources, Assam is undoubtedly an undeveloped state. As are Jharkhand and Chhattisgarh.

We read in the previous chapter how the soil in Vidarbha is unfit to produce anything much beyond cotton (and oranges). Without captive textile mills, which no longer exist in Vidarbha, the farmers would be worse off than at present when the Maharashtra government feels obliged to offer a remunerative price to cotton growers. But, says senior journalist Praveen Bardapurkar, Vidarbha is also a major market for steel, timber, coal and other minerals apart from cotton. 'Those markets will disappear because the entrepreneurs of Mumbai then will set up markets in their own territory. In fact, it would be advantageous for them to open shop in or around Mumbai. The political economy does not make a case for a separate state.

'Moreover, there are at least five districts of Vidarbha that do not want the hegemony of the Nagpur division—Akola, Amravati, Washim, Buldhana and Yavatmal. They are strictly not part of Central Provinces and Berar, they come under Warad and should this separation take place, there would soon be a clamour for a separate Warad state,' says Bardapurkar. Having observed the politics of the region for close to thirty-five years, he says the demand for separation comes mostly from Hindi speakers or at times from some prominent local politicians, whenever they are sidelined by their political party.

Pugalia says, 'We have been consistent in our demand since the 1970s.' But then he is what Bardapurkar calls a 'Hindi bhashik', overshadowed by Marathi speakers. However, the divide between Hindi and Marathi speakers is not strictly straitjacketed. There have been locals like the late Jambuwantrao Dhote, a former firebrand Congressman, who was a consistent proponent of a separate Vidarbha. He even formed his own political party when he found the Congress would not concede his demand. 'But, whereas as a Congress candidate he won with margins of one lakh or more, he could barely get twenty thousand votes as a Vidarbha proponent. He lost every election and faded out for his refusal to give up the demand for a separate Vidarbha,' says Bardapurkar.

Leaders like the late Dr Shrikant Jichkar, a former minister of state for finance in the Maharashtra government, had called for a referendum in case any government wished to hive off Vidarbha from Maharashtra. That is a demand now being raised even by the RSS. There is a precedent for this—under the late Prime Minister Mrs Indira Gandhi's regime, Goa voted in a referendum—officially referred to as an 'opinion poll' as there is no Constitutional provision for a referendum—for statehood rather than integration with Maharashtra. But the idea of a referendum is not very popular with most proponents because they know the people would vote overwhelmingly against statehood.

'If I start a morcha at my city's biggest and most populated chowk (Indira Chowk in Gondia), I will hardly get ten people willing to march for a separate Vidarbha,' says former union minister Praful Patel. Today's fight for a separate Vidarbha, thus, is an intermittent movement by a handful of malcontents from various fields and communities, who believe they might do better in a separate state once they are free of the domination of politicians from the rest of Maharashtra. The youth, however, still look to Mumbai and Pune for jobs and other opportunities, and are unmoved by the demands for a separate state.

But there is also the argument that statehood would result in instantly pitting the 'Hindi bhashik' politicians and entrepreneurs against the majority Marathi speakers, who they dominated before Vidarbha broke away from the Central Provinces and Berar to integrate with Maharashtra. The Hindi-speaking entrepreneurs were immediately dwarfed by their counterparts in Mumbai, and have never been able to regain their influence on political authority, as they might have in the years before the reorganization of states. 'It is mostly people like these who are seeking a separation. It is not a sheer issue of development,' says Bardapurkar.

Indeed a white paper on Vidarbha, written by Dr Jichkar in the 1990s, clearly states that the Marathi-speaking people of the region who had fought hard to integrate with the rest of Maharashtra were determined to remain one with the state even today. Writing in the white paper titled *Public Finances of Maharashtra*, Dr Jichkar says, 'Regional claims need not be denigrated but regional viewpoint should not precurse forces of disintegration (of the state). The concepts of dispersal of economic forces, decentralization of economic entrepreneurship, demands to remove backlog, desire to possess a state etc., have their rational expectation. None of them, however, should go toward the disintegration of the nation.'

What was needed was a 'revolutionary' stance to liberate the economy from the false theory of growth as a categorical imperative of politics, he said, adding that the social choices in politics were 'obvious'. 'If we can dissolve the contradiction within a macro level of the Indian economy, the contradictions on the micro level like the region would be smoothened and may disappear...'

The native Marathi-speaking former advocate general of

Maharashtra, Shreehari Aney, however, begs to differ. Despite holding office in Maharashtra, he had been advocating for a separate Vidarbha and says, 'I wouldn't do it if I didn't believe in the viability of statehood.' According to a paper that he has written, titled 'Vidarbha Gatha', every micro and macro level problem that Vidarbha faces is on account of politicians from western Maharashtra who have denied Vidarbha its due share. There is some reluctant acknowledgement that Vidarbha's own politicians have done little to benefit their region when in power but 'Vidarbha Gatha' is the cry of a child from the heart. Anyone who ignores the region is sure to fall by the wayside, he believes, like the Shiv Sena did for not doing enough for Vidarbha when it was in power between 1995 and 1999.

But the Sena, opposing Vidarbha, did much better in 2014 and is unlikely to concede the state even today. In fact, Sreehari Aney had to resign his job as advocate general under pressure from the Sena when he went a step further and advocated for a separate Marathwada on the same grounds. That, however, was a trick, but no one fell into the trap. Aney believed that if the people of Marathwada could be persuaded to demand statehood, 'a separate Vidarbha would become inevitable'. Not only did that strategy boomerang on him, it left the people of Marathwada cold. As Atul Deulgaonkar, a writer and activist from Marathwada said emphatically, 'We simply cannot afford it. Vidarbha is different. For us everything comes from Maharashtra.'

As far as Vidarbha goes, Aney believes that all the politicians who call for a separate state and then forget about the issue when elected to office will soon be reduced to nothing. In reality the reverse is true—those demanding a separate Vidarbha have almost always been at the end of their careers and then faded away altogether.

There have been two state reorganizations involving Maharashtra—one in 1956 when the Gujarati-speaking areas of

India, mainly Kutch and Saurashtra, were included in Bombay State; and the second in 1960 when the Government of India conceded the states of Maharashtra and Gujarat. 'Vidarbha, too, was offered that choice in 1956 but when a second reorganization took place, they were flatly denied statehood,' rues Aney.

Maharashtra's politicians would not concede the demand for statehood and Vidarbha gave in for a time after the first chief minister of the unified unilingual state, Y.B. Chavan, made a resounding 'zukta maap' speech in the assembly, promising full justice to Vidarbha. 'Zukta maap' literally means tilted balance or scales, and Chavan promised that these scales would be tilted heavily in favour of Vidarbha. But Aney's lament is that the reverse has happened.

That is a sore point with the former advocate general whose grandfather, Bapusaheb Aney, a Congress MP in the 1950s, was at the forefront of the movement for a separate state of Vidarbha at that time, and won his seat on both a Congress ticket and the Nag-Vidarbha Andolan Samiti platform in later years. Aney believes the issues raised then still hold true more than seven decades later. He quotes Dr B.R. Ambedkar, who in 1955 had described Bombay as a 'monster state' and advocated that it be split into four—Bombay, western Maharashtra, Central Maharashtra and Eastern Maharashtra.

Arguing against the organization of states on linguistic grounds, Dr Ambedkar had said, 'All that one can think of is that the (States Reorganization) Commission has been under the impression that one language one state is a categorical imperative from which there is no escape... In fact one state, one language should be the rule. And, therefore, people forming one language can divide themselves into many states...' That is the basis on which RSS ideologues like M.G. Vaidya, too, are advocating the splintering of the state into four parts today—Central Maharashtra will include Khandesh, Mumbai will include Konkan and Eastern Maharashtra will remain intact with all its districts of present-day Vidarbha, leaving Maratha territory of western parts and Marathwada to band together.

While there is a risk of the disintegration that Dr Jichkar warned about, there are no takers today for statehood in any of the regions suggested by Dr Ambedkar. Even in Vidarbha, there are a mere handful of people, from both the Hindi-speaking and Marathi-speaking groups, who support statehood for the region. Both groups differently propagate the case for a separation. If Pande, a native Hindi speaker, is not for Vidarbha until it is developed, Vijay Darda, owner of the *Lokmat* group of newspapers, and a former Rajya Sabha MP from the Congress, is passionate in his defence of a separate Vidarbha state. 'They (the rest of Maharashtra) have looted us, cheated us, betrayed us, deprived us, denied us, stolen from us,' he says emphatically. 'But the problem is that those who when out of power keep demanding a separate Vidarbha, quite forget about it while in power and give the demand a quiet burial.'

As a Congress MP, he could not persuade any of his leaders to make Vidarbha a separate state, but like many others he had hoped that after the BJP passed a resolution for smaller states in its Bhubaneswar executive meet in 1995, the inevitable would happen when they came to power. 'But it didn't,' he says dejectedly. 'I told Advaniji (the then deputy prime minister) then, "You are simply giving in to the blackmail by Bal Thackeray and the Shiv Sena. You are dependent on them and cannot overrule them."'

To a certain extent that remains the situation even today. Thackeray's heir Uddhav is equally opposed to a separate Vidarbha and the BJP continues to be dependent on the party to run its government in Maharashtra. Nothing has changed. The BJP might find it difficult to persuade even Raj Thackeray of the Maharashtra Navnirman Sena (MNS) to concede—Raj Thackeray has already threatened the RSS, saying Maharashtra is not their birthday cake to cut into as many pieces as they wish. The threat of violence looms in the air, rather more violence than Gadkari had advocated while making the case for a separate Vidarbha.

'*Rajya ke tukde karne se vikas kabhi nahin hota hai,*' (You do not need to break a state into pieces to ensure development) says Hemant Gadkari, general secretary of the Maharashtra Navnirman Sena. This is so very visible in the other states that have been similarly broken up. You need just three things for development— leaders with good intention, bureaucrats with the ability to implement decisions promptly and an alert public who will enforce those policies.

'The demand for a separate Vidarbha comes from leaders after they lose their cars with red beacons,' Hemant Gadkari says disparagingly, pointing to the examples of Vilas Muttemwar and Ranjit Deshmukh, at one time the two leading Congress politicians from the region. He believes the Gadkari-Fadnavis duo is the best thing that could have happened to Vidarbha, and will bring development to the region without having to separate it from Maharashtra. 'If they bring us the funds and the policies, if they lay irrigation pipes so that cotton farmers get adequate water, they will stop committing suicide and the region will once again be flush and thriving. As a party, we have a blueprint for the development of Vidarbha within Maharashtra, but unfortunately we are not in power. But we are prepared to share our plans with the ruling BJP, which is now in power both in the state and at the Centre. Maharashtra *ke tukde karne ki zaroorat nahin hai.* What is the guarantee that even after the split the politicians will work for the region's development?' That seems pretty final and insurmountable.

A similar argument comes from young entrepreneur Rahul Kale, who runs a nationally successful cosmetic business in Nagpur. Kale endorses Dr Jichkar's views against a separate Vidarbha, and says most of the region's people have sentimental and historical reasons for not seeking to separate from the rest of Maharashtra. Those who wish for statehood suffer from a misplaced romantic notion that a separation will lead to development, progress and every material quality that they lack today. But that is not strictly true. 'We have to see where we came from and where we are today.'

Undoubtedly, Vidarbha, which was part of the Central Provinces and Berar, and Marathwada, which was part of the Nizam's Hyderabad State, as well as the Konkan, which was already part of Bombay Province, are somewhat backward compared to Mumbai, Pune and western and southern Maharashtra. Kale feels that we must compare Nagpur and Vidarbha to places like Betul, Balaghat and Seoni in Madhya Pradesh, which are contiguous with Nagpur, have the same climatic conditions and had the same per capita income (PCI) and human development index (HDI) at the time of the states' reorganization. 'Where are we today and where are they?' he questions.

So despite complaints of neglect of the region, the HDI and PCI of Vidarbha are way ahead of those of these neighbouring districts of Madhya Pradesh, and also those of Chhattisgarh. Kale agrees with Kaushik and Hemant Gadkari that it is the attitude of the local leaders and entrepreneurs towards the development of Vidarbha that is of greater consequence than what the leaders of Mumbai and western Maharashtra might do for Nagpur. 'We are always just waiting for a miracle. Nothing gets done at the local level.'

His case in point is that of Nagpur's Butibori, Asia's largest industrial estate. It was inaugurated in the 1970s, on the same day as the Baramati industrial estate in Pune, by the same chief minister who flew in a special aircraft from Pune to Nagpur to do the honours. But the attitude of the leaders of the business and political community here fell short of expectations. For today, Baramati is chock-a-block with industries while Butibori is virtually a non-starter as an industrial hub.

Two-and-a-half decades later, another chief minister decided Nagpur should have an integrated development hub and set up the largest special economic zone, the MIHAN (multimodal integrated hub and airport at Nagpur). There were no takers until 2016 when Baba Ramdev decided to develop 400 acres within MIHAN for a centralized unit of his Patanjali products. 'So who profited, invested or became a stakeholder in this crucial project, except for real estate speculators?' Kale asks. 'In fact, speculation is the only thriving industry here... Are we industrious, entrepreneurial and prepared to put in enough effort? Or do we just want to make a quick buck from speculation?'

The answers to these questions sadly are 'no' and 'yes', in that order. That's why Kale believes a separate state of Vidarbha will sink into the quagmire sooner than Chhattisgarh and Jharkhand did with their coal and mineral mafia. And the benefits of development will accrue to just a few powerful and rich families as they did in Chhattisgarh, or just a few politicians as in Jharkhand, with the human development index and per capita income sinking below those of these two states.

So the response of a majority of the people to the case for a separate state is 'Thank you, but no thanks.' They would rather be somewhat 'undeveloped' compared to their fellow compatriots from Mumbai and western Maharashtra than drop below even the one-star rating that Pande fears will happen if Vidarbha separates from Maharashtra without prior development. Love for Vidarbha will fly out of the window and there will be no room for romance at all, he fears.

8

On the Edge of a Desert

It is not just the water wars in Marathwada that are toxic.

Ranjit Babulkar's family had no warning of what he was planning to do that evening. He was not at home when they woke up that morning. They thought he might have left early for his farm to survey his drying produce for the nth time—an unseasonal hailstorm in March that year had destroyed the standing crops days before harvest and the next season proved equally unfruitful as Marathwada received barely 20 per cent of its due rainfall in June. All hope that Babulkar could recoup his losses from the previous season vanished with the deficit rainfall.

As the family went about its household chores, devastating news arrived—Babulkar had been found hanging from a tree on his own farm. It was an ugly sight to see him swinging from the dry branches of the tree on his farm in the Kej Taluka of Beed district. He didn't have the money for a less gruesome death—pesticides were expensive and the wells were too dry to ensure a proper drowning. Babulkar's family was shocked into a dry-eyed grief. Fortunately, the government handed the family a compensatory cheque within days, and they used this money to sow a fresh crop for another season. However, the cycle of unseasonal hailstorms in the summer and a dry spell in the monsoon continued unabated for two seasons, and Babulkar's family members were at the end of their tether.

Even the deer were dying by the dozens in the miniscule forests of Marathwada during those four summer seasons from 2012 to 2016. Carnivores had migrated to other forests in search of water and there was no ecological balance anywhere in the region. There still isn't—even an ample rainfall in 2016 and 2017 proved too much of a good thing. Crops were destroyed by flooding as the retreating monsoon, awaited eagerly by farmers, proved devastating by bringing more showers than were necessary both years. For the farmers of Marahwada, nature can never get it right—it gives too much or too little. Both are damaging to their interests—and their crops.

Water is a source of life, but it has also become a source of power in Maharashtra, and the worst sufferers in the political game involving water are the people of Marathwada. There were large districts like Jalna, Beed and Latur that received water just once a month during the summer months in 2016, while the luckier districts like Aurangabad, the divisional headquarters, got water perhaps once every week. During the 2016 monsoon, these districts received too much rain in the last spell of the season and roads, farms and houses were submerged. The year 2017 brought some hope in the form of dams filled to capacity but excessive flooding still played havoc. 'Because of such extremes, the entire region is on the verge of both desertion and desertification. If things go on the way they are today, in just about two or three years one might see Marathwada as a large desert to rival Rajasthan, with no people settled here at all. Marathwada will become the ghost district of Maharashtra,' says environmental activist and writer Atul Deulgaonkar.

Traditionally, Marathwada has always been the orphan land of Maharashtra. It was under the rule of the Nizam of Hyderabad, but successive nizams hardly paid any attention to the development of the region. It is not a coincidence that even today Marathwada, along with Telangana, which in its entirety was the realm of the nizam, and the districts of Bidar, Gulbarga and Bijapur in North Karnataka, continue to be among the most backward regions of India in an otherwise oasis of development south of the Vindhyas. Unlike Vidarbha, which had stalwarts as leaders before and after the integration of the region into Maharashtra, Marathwada was always deprived and denied the fruits of association with Maharashtra. Nagpur, along with Raigad in the Konkan, is counted among the 'Most Forward Districts' (MFDs) of the state, despite belonging to a backward region. But there is not a single district in Marathwada—including Aurangabad, which is fairly industrialized—that is not counted among the 'Most Backward Districts' (MBDs) of Maharashtra.

'Marathwada is the other ugly face of a progressive Maharashtra,' says Professor Sudhir Gavhane, formerly of the Babasaheb Ambedkar Marathwada University and now Dean of Liberal Arts at the MIT Univeristy of World Peace in Pune. 'The per capita income and human development index here are even lower than those of Bihar, and if you separate areas around Pune and Mumbai from Marathwada, the entire region comes under the most poverty-hit districts of the country.'

Marathwada, along with Vidarbha, was among the most centrally placed regions in the country and its importance did not escape the notice of Muhammad bin Tuglaq who, in the fourteenth century, shifted his capital from Delhi to Deogiri (present-day Daulatabad) as he believed the kingdoms of the south could be better controlled from the Deccan. But certain ludicrous policies such as the forced migration of all his subjects from Delhi to the Deccan (most of them died on the way) and the uncontrolled minting of coins—which emptied his treasury—forced Muhammad bin Tuglaq to abandon the region to other dynasties, both Hindu and Islamic. But now, says Professor H.M. Desarda, noted economist, a former member of the state Planning Commission and a visiting professor at the Gokhale Institute of Politics and Economics, 'The policies of this government are becoming madder than Muhammad bin Tuglaq's.'

That is because, until good monsoons arrived in 2016, no one seemed to have a clue about how to tackle consecutive droughts (since 2012) and subsequent flooding and deluges following the good monsoons. 'The region received just 20-30 per cent of rainfall in 2015 (not much higher in subsequent years, despite the deluge), but I notice even that much is enough to reap a rich harvest of cash crops like grapes and soya bean,' says Professor Desarda. In fact, that is exactly what many farmers have started growing. They were harvesting sweet lime (mosambi) and grapes in Jalna, bananas in Latur, soya bean in Beed, etc. All these crops, however, were washed away in the deluge during the 2016 and 2017 kharif season. The farmers are back to where they were before, their only hope being that with the dams now full, they will not have to suffer during the rabi season in March–April. That is, provided there are no unseasonal hailstorms, which have been a matter of routine for at least five years now. Says Deulgaonkar, 'As a concerned farmer, I have been talking to meteorologists in the US and Australia who are spot on with their forecasts. They hold out no hope. This situation is dismal and we may once again have to face unseasonal hailstorms in March–April.'

So far as the drought goes, instead of maximizing the farmers' efforts, the government, in its misplaced enthusiasm to solve the issue of drought permanently, was hell-bent on dredging river beds and nullahs with the intention of widening these water sources. 'They are messing up the ecological balance of the region, which has taken centuries to evolve, and now I am afraid that even in the instance of a good rainfall (B. Venkateswarlu, vice chancellor of Vasantrao Naik Agricultural University in Parbhani believes good rains will aid these government efforts), these kinds of activities would interfere with the aquifers and destroy the water conservation chances of the region,' says Desarda, who has been on a massive campaign for land, water and employment across the region for months. His words have proved prophetic.

'The weakness of our drought mitigation measures and lack of meaningful water harvesting and water resource planning and policy stands exposed. Indeed, it is more than a failure of rains. Monsoon can be truant or excessive, but this highlights the lacuna in the agricultural and water resource management strategies over the years. Despite pumping in billions of rupees and building more than one third of large dams in the country, Maharashtra is so vulnerable. This calls for an alternative approach to water resource planning, in particular decentralized storage and rainwater harvesting,' he says.

'The government, through its "Jal Shivur Yojana" is messing with natural aquifers', says Desarda, who has always criticized the policy of dam-building for water conservation. Storing water in dams subjects it to evaporation in the summer. This causes rivers to dry up and it also displaces thousands of villagers from their fertile land. 'The recent policies are adding to the ecological imbalances,' Desarda says.

But it is not just the mismanagement of water conservation methods that is threatening to turn Marathwada into a desert (or ocean, as it happened during the 2016 deluge). It is also the politics of the state. According to Dr Bhalchandra Kango, the national general secretary of the Communist Party of India, 'The entire politics of Maharashtra is sugar-based. Western Maharashtra, of course, has a large number of sugar factories, but now every politician worth his name in Marathwada too wants his own sugar cooperative. And sugarcane is a very water intensive crop, depleting the groundwater resources very fast. The region already has seventy sugar factories and thirty more will be coming up this year. The government keeps giving permission for these factories despite knowing well how it damages the ecosystem.'

He is right. A good rainfall in 2016 encouraged both the promoters and the government to press for more licences to be given out to new factories. The destruction of the kharif crop and fear of unseasonal hailstorms during the rabi season also compelled farmers to go in for the water intensive sugarcane crop—a real money-spinner—again to recoup their losses. While the decision was understandable, it can only end up worsening the cycle of depleting water tables and lack of irrigation to other, less water intensive crops. According to Deulgaonkar, despite the good monsoon, the additional sugar factories mean there will not be enough water for all farmers and particularly those not growing cane. As Dr Bhalchandra Kango says, 'There might be work for farm labourers for a season and some employment for factory workers. But eventually the addition of the new factories will deplete the resources and they will all have to migrate to greener pastures.' This migration, however, has already begun. Not just students who prefer to study at colleges in Mumbai and Pune, but professionals from the region are migrating to other cities of Maharashtra and Hyderabad in search of jobs and a comfortable life that is not dependent on the vagaries of the weather so they do not have to worry about where their next meal, or bottled water, will come from.

Ah, yes, bottled water. The entire business of bottled water is precisely what is contributing to the lethargy of Maharashtra's politicians to address the water resource problem in Marathwada. For the first time in nine years, the 2016 monsoon helped to bring dams up to full capacity so that for at least two years, people might have no drinking water issues. But that dependence on nature is not enough. According to Pradeep Purandare, who has filed two public interest litigations in the Bombay High Court to compel the government to formulate its water laws, 'Most politicians have set up their own bottled water plants and none of them is, therefore, motivated to solve the water scarcity in the region. The rich survive on bottled water, the poor are simply dying of thirst and disease.'

Purandare says Maharashtra's water laws have existed on paper for years, but they have not been 'populated' because if these laws were to be specified and formulated down to the articles, a number of politicians would lose their hold over the people. The sugar-specific politics of the state means politicians of western Maharashtra have always had control over water resources. Marathwada doesn't have any rivers of its own and has always been dependent on western Maharashtra for its water supply.

While the medieval rulers of the region did little to develop Marathwada, Deulgaonkar points to existing pipelines beneath the ground connecting Ahmednagar to Aurangabad, which indicate that the Islamic kings did endeavour to take care of the basic needs of their people. But the control of the modern-day Jaikwadi dam, which is the main source of water supply to Marathwada, vests in the hands of politicians from western Maharashtra. Even as recently as 2013, when Marathwada was reeling under a second consecutive drought, these politicians chose to stop the water supply to the region in order to keep their sugarcane fields flush and flourishing.

There can be no greater example of the callousness of these politicians than the crass response of Ajit Pawar, then deputy chief minister of Maharashtra, to the demands of farmers who had been fasting for the release of water from the Jaikwadi dam in 2013. 'Should I now urinate into the dam to irrigate their fields?' Ajit Pawar, who had at one time been irrigation minister for over a decade, asked very publicly. This comment did not go down well with large sections of the people, including the Congress Party, his allies in government.

It must be remembered that water was the source of the major students' agitation in Marathwada in 1974—apart from a call for development of the region, the establishment of schools and colleges and a demand for industries, the agitators had pressed for the completion of the Jaikwadi dam. The agitation had led to a change of guard in the state. Vasantrao Naik, the longest serving chief minister of Maharashtra to date, was replaced by Shankarrao B. Chavan who hailed from Marathwada. People believed Naik was doing little for their region, which had been reeling under the effects of the drought of 1972–73. S.B. Chavan had been through the anti-nizam agitation and Mrs Indira Gandhi believed he would do justice to Marathwada. He did not betray that faith, and even today is regarded as the sole politician of the region who did his best for Marathwada.

In 1986, when Chavan returned as chief minister for a second time, he had the gumption to take on politicians from western Maharashtra full throttle, and mooted an eight-month season for the sugarcane crop. 'The existing four months in the year should belong to farmers from other districts so that they can draw upon the state's water resources,' he said. But when Sharad Pawar replaced Chavan as chief minister in 1988, he quietly allowed sugar farmers to draw water round the year.

The complete depletion of groundwater resources in Marathwada is said to be the result of this short-sighted and highly self-centred policy. 'No one was interested in putting the water regulations on record because then they would not have been able to play fast and loose with water. Had those laws been properly formulated, we would have had recourse to the courts and would have ensured an equitable distribution,' says Purandare who is now hoping that the courts will take action on his public interest litigations in this regard. For good rains or not, the lack of irrigation facilities renders water a point of perpetual dispute between the regions.

Unlike the case with Vidarbha, Marathwada saw more than one powerful chief minister from the region, but barring S.B. Chavan, who headed a Congress government, the others were mostly dependent on leaders from western Maharashtra, notably the NCP. Hence, they had to cede to pressures in their attempts to bring full-scale development to Marathwada. Even these politicians, however, chose the route of sugar politics and set up their own sugar factories in a region where the groundwater resources were not suitable for sugarcane cultivation. It is no wonder then that the region is facing major ecological imbalances and heading towards complete disaster.

Dr Kango says, 'Water is essential to development. Without water there can be no industry or ecology and hence no development. I wonder how much longer it will take the planners to realize this crucial fact.' However, water, a common resource for all, is not the only problem that Marathwada is facing. In 1974, when students agitated for growth and development, the communities were united. Today, they are highly fractious and divided owing to the short-sighted policies of various governments and leaders. Muslims, Marathas and Dalits are the major communities in the region and each is suspicious of the other. The decade of the 1990s contributed in various ways, inadvertently or deliberately, to the fissures in society whose fault lines are now clearly visible.

In the 1950s, Dr B.R. Ambedkar and S.B. Chavan were among those leaders who had agitated against the Nizam of Hyderabad for the inclusion of Marathwada in Maharashtra. As mentioned elsewhere in the book, after that task was accomplished, there was a long-standing demand from Ambedkar's followers to name Marathwada University after him. It was a demand fiercely resisted by upper-caste Marathas and, indeed, most governments—then led by the Congress Party—baulked at the very thought. But when Pawar returned to the state as chief minister at the head of a Congress government in 1993, he gave in to the demand and renamed the university after Babasaheb Ambedkar. Marathas resisted the move bitterly so to pacify both communities, the university was named 'Babasaheb Ambedkar Marathwada University'. But did it work?

As the most prominent Maratha leader of the state at the time, Pawar had complete confidence in his ability to persuade fellow Marathas to be magnanimous to Dalits. But he had reckoned without Bal Thackeray. Thackeray was not a Maratha leader and had no feeling of fellowship for Marathas, but saw in the renaming of the university a brilliant political opportunity for himself and his party. The Shiv Sena needed to grow out of the confines of Mumbai and become a larger force in the state. Until the mid-1980s, the Shiv Sena was in danger of extinction, but the rise of Hindutva forces enabled its revival. Thackeray also exploited the Maratha disappointment with Sharad Pawar to the party's advantage.

The 1980s was also the decade of the Mandalization of the polity, and although there was always a dispute about whether the Marathas were upper-caste Kshatriya or belonged to Other Backward Classes, Pawar, without a process of consultation with the community, deemed them as economically and socially forward and turned down random suggestions of reservations for the community. All these factors came together in one crucible—that of Marathwada. Other regions of the state were by and large unaffected by this churning.

Thackeray positioned himself not just as a leader of Hindus (at this point of time too extreme for even the rising BJP) but also of Marathas in their battle against Dalits. All three communities of Muslims, Dalits and Marathas had until then placed their faith in the Congress and other parties on the left. The late 1980s and 1990s, however, saw a shift in their loyalties, which even Pawar could not fathom until the Congress suffered a massive defeat at the hands of the Shiv Sena-BJP alliance in the 1995 assembly elections.

Thackeray did not care much for the Dalit vote bank, but the late BJP leader Gopinath Munde was clever enough to sense the mood of the Other Backward Communities in the wake of the Mandal agitation. Thackeray married the anti-Dalit sentiment of the Marathas to his own brand of Hindutva, and the late Pramod Mahajan did the rest by forging an alliance with the Shiv Sena to keep these vote banks from splitting. Today, the polity and society of Marathwada is split among these three communities and there is a new entrant—the All India Majlis-e-Ittehad-e-Muslimeen (AIMIM)—which has been able to make some headway in the region, essentially because of the recent split between the Shiv Sena and the BJP. The AIMIM managed to have a single MLA elected from Central Aurangabad in October 2014, but it did far better in the municipal elections in 2015, replacing the Congress substantially in the affections of the Muslims.

But, says Abdul Kadeer, a senior journalist with the *Dainik Bhaskar* in Aurangabad, 'The enchantment of the Muslim youth with the Owaisi brothers (Asaduddin and Akbaruddin) is over. The AIMIM is losing base even in its native Telangana and they will not do as well in Maharashtra again.' The Muslims in the state are beginning to feel the heat of the anti-Muslim rhetoric of the ruling forces, and they have also wised up to the AIMIM's game plan. Soon after the Aurangabad Municipal elections, in which his party was the main rival to the Shiv Sena, Akbaruddin Owaisi had crowed, 'Can you see what we can accomplish together if the BJP and the AIMIM join hands with each other? We could beat the Congress out of existence!'

That statement frightened members of Akbaruddin Owaisi's own community. It was compounded by older brother Asaduddin's suo moto challenge to RSS chief Mohan Bhagwat who had said students in India should be asked to chant '*Bharat Mata Ki Jai*' to inculcate the nationalist spirit in them. Muslims believe that even those people who do not object to the chant have been unnecessarily bracketed with orthodox Muslims who might not want to deify Mother India. In the process, they have all been rendered highly vulnerable to bigots who have targeted them in the name of patriotism and are out to prove that every Muslim is a traitor to India. Dr Kango says, 'They will soon be looking for protectors of their interests. At the moment security is more important to Muslims than anything else.'

Obviously, the AIMIM, seen to be on the opposite side of the

Hindu right, is not the protector Dr Kango is referring to; and it may or may not be the Congress. But Pawar certainly seems to be hoping it will be his own NCP. It is a hope that may be belied, for no other leader is responsible as much as Pawar for contributing to both Marathwada's water depletion and the destruction of its communal harmony. And this has as much to do with the disharmony among the castes and religions as it has to do with unrest within his own community.

The Marathas, who were earlier a privileged and content lot, were largely farmers, but the countrywide rural distress is beginning to affect those privileges and interests. They are now in the forefront of the agitation for reservations, because the agrarian crisis is of such immense proportions that they see themselves as worse off than even the Dalits and Muslims (who were also provided with reservations by the Maharashtra government in 2014). The Bombay High Court struck down reservations for Marathas (the BJP government allowed the ordinance providing reservations to Muslims to lapse), and the Maratha community is increasingly embittered at having to deal with the rising graphs of the Dalits in the region, who end up as collectors and tehsildars and become superior to the upper castes while the farmers continue to sink into poverty.

'Since there are hardly any private industries to speak of in the region, students from Marathwada increasingly look for government jobs, particularly in the state public service commission, and this is where reservations will enormously benefit them,' says Dr Kango. 'When they don't get those jobs, emotions simmer and thus the region is enormously divided on communal and caste lines. In the last two decades, we have seen large numbers of riots, which did not take place between religions and castes for centuries together.' So it is not just the natural ecology of the state that is now highly disturbed, even social harmony is at peril. But Dr Kango is not as despondent as the others. 'There is a silver lining to every cloud,' he says. 'An opportunity rises out of every disaster.'

In terms of the natural disaster, Dr Kango believes a paradigm shift is already happening—agro-based industries are beginning to appear, and if governments act as facilitators and refrain from destroying the ecology further, the region could thrive again. As for community amity, that might take a little longer. Mending the fractures will require some inspired leadership, which at present is lacking in the region. There are no local leaders worth their name except, perhaps, former Chief Minister Ashok Chavan, who has his limitations as an opposition leader. Those in government like Pankaja Munde, daughter of Gopinath Munde, have been described as 'childish and immature' by Deulgaonkar and others, and Ashok Chavan agrees with that view—despite her father's legacy, Pankaja Munde does not have enough of a grip over the administration to get things going, he says.

'My wells had sunk so deep that I was drawing water that was a thousand years old,' says Deulgaonkar. 'Most other farmers were doing the same—can you imagine the toxicity in those waters? The ill-effects could show up anytime soon. It is difficult to escape such toxicity completely.' But it is not just the waters that are toxic. Society itself is in danger of ending up with high levels of toxicity, the ill-effects of which might be even more difficult to combat. 'When there is no water at all, toxins in whatever water is available will have to be put up with,' says Venateswarlu. 'The health consequences are not then an immediate priority.'

But the same cannot be said of communal toxicity. The health of social and communal relations is in urgent need of prioritizing. These relations cannot be allowed to remain toxic indefinitely. The rains might wash away the toxicity in the well waters but who or what will do the same for communal relations? The region already sits on a geological fault line. But it is the social fissures that are in more urgent need of addressing.

9

A Land More Blessed

Western Maharashtra has always ruled the roost.

When the young Shivaji decided not to follow his father's footsteps to become a vassal of the Muslim rulers of Bijapur—Shahaji was a high officer in that court—he chose to settle on the strip of land that had been granted to his grandfather by a previous Muslim ruler. The land was close to the borders of the Mughal empire's territories in the Deccan plateau, squashed between the Mughals on one side and Bijapur on the other. Embarrassed by Shivaji's independent streak, according to Dennis Kincaid's definitive history of Shivaji, *Shivaji, The Grand Rebel*, his father entrusted him to a Brahmin tutor and steward called Dadoji Kondadeo at the age of thirteen. He had full faith that Kondadeo would watch over his rebellious son.

Dadoji set about working the wild tracts of land that, at the time, seemed rather untamed and primitive. Kincaid says these lands between the borders of two kingdoms had been 'crossed and recrossed' several times over the decades by many mercenary armies, and most of the villages had disappeared. There was hardly any cultivation worth the name and 'fewer men to cultivate' whatever bits of land had not been surrendered to wilderness. In fact, much of the land had turned into a jungle, overrun by wolves and vegetation, and it must have been a difficult task to tame it. Yet, it seemed, Pune and its environs were blessed. Gradually, it returned to habitation—Dadoji first tackled the wolf menace by offering rich rewards for each wolf killed, then tempted the men who took on the task to stay on and cultivate the land at nominal rentals.

The last Muslim army that had crossed Pune had caused widespread devastation—all the houses had been pulled down, all the fields flattened by donkeys drawing ploughs, and the Muslim king had planted an iron rod in the middle of the town to mark his conquest before abandoning the territory. Dadoji responded by harnessing a pair of white bullocks to a plough made of pure gold, before restarting cultivation in the villages to encourage the people to get over their fear and superstitions. Gradually, a peaceful and industrious habitation came up in Pune—it defines the character of the region and the city even today.

Dadoji even banked the Mula-Mutha rivers flowing through Pune and raised a palace, called Rang Mahal, beside it for Shivaji and his mother. Later, when Shivaji's descendants moved the seat of power to Satara, their prime ministers, the Peshwas, chose to stay on in Pune, building another palace, the Shanivarwada, in their name. In the medieval centuries, Pune thus became the de facto capital of India and, in many ways, continues to be the de facto capital of Maharashtra even today.

The Peshwas had made a hereditary office of their prime ministership and remained at Shanivarwada even though Shahu Maharaj, Shivaji's grandson, chose to shift his capital to Satara. All the battles against the various kingdoms in the north and the south were launched from Pune. So when the British annexed the territories of the Marathas in the early nineteenth century, Pune had the advantage of proximity to Bombay Province which, as a port city, had replaced Surat as the commercial capital of British India.

Pune was always a great centre of learning and intellectual

discourse given that stalwarts of the reformist movement like M.G. Ranade, Vishnu Shastri Pandit and others, came from the region. It was also the karmabhoomi of Bal Gangadhar Tilak, who was not just a pioneer in the freedom movement before the advent of Mahatma Gandhi but also a leading educationist and a journalist. He was among the first to recognize the value of dissemination of information among the people and started two newspapers, *Mahratta* (in English, now defunct) and *Kesari* (in Marathi, still thriving). Pune was also the crucible of cataclysmic changes in the Maharashtrian society of the nineteenth and early twentieth centuries. The city and the region was, as in ancient times, the confluence of Brahminical and Maratha life streams, and this continues even into the modern century.

The region of western Maharashtra is doubly blessed, placed as it is so close to Bombay (Mumbai) on the one hand and advantageously located in terms of natural resources, on the other hand. It has both the Godavari and Krishna river basins that flow down south, giving the region control over the waters. The first rains from the Sahyadri ranges always come to western Maharashtra.

However, although Shivaji's preferred capital was Raigad in the Konkan, various settlements in western and southern Maharashtra were later the capitals of the Maratha kings and the Peshwas. Thus, a large proportion of Maratha leaders hail from western Maharashtra, rather than Marathwada which, of course, has a good proportion of them, though there is hardly any Maratha presence in Vidarbha.

Having been edged out by the Brahmin Peshwas in prominence during the latter days of Maratha rule, the Marathas were simmering for a century or more against this upper caste domination of their territory. Tilak's conflicts with Shahu Maharaj of Kolhapur compounded the situation through the late nineteenth and early twentieth centuries. However, the advent of Mahatma Gandhi and the rise of the Congress during the freedom movement was a great opportunity for the Marathas to assert themselves. In some ways, it was Shivaji's Maharashtra Dharma that propelled them towards Gandhi whose politics was all inclusive—denying the untouchability of Dalits, as had Chhatrapati Shivaji, and including Muslims in the mainstream, as had the Maratha warrior King in his army. It was not difficult to see which way the wind was blowing, and the earliest Maratha leaders like Yashwantrao Chavan knew exactly which side they would be on once the British quit India.

Other men, both Maharashtrian and Gujarati, were chief ministers of the undivided Bombay State, but there was always a feeling among the Maharashtrians that the Marathi-speaking parts of the state (at that time just Konkan and western Maharashtra) were unlikely to get justice under the domination of the Gujaratis in the state Cabinet. However, it was the left and socialist parties, and not the Congress, which were at the forefront of the movement for a unified Maharashtra. Pandit Jawaharlal Nehru fiercely resisted the bifurcation of the state and initially the areas of Kutch and Saurashtra remained with Bombay State while Vidarbha, which was also rebelling against similar domination by Hindi-speaking people, and the Central Provinces and Berar, were formed into one whole. At the time, central leaders had promised that if the arrangement did not work out, both Gujarat and Vidarbha would be free to form their own states.

The Congress was virtually the sole ruling party in the decades after independence, but the party's resistance to a bifurcation of Bombay State began to take a toll on its fortunes in western Maharashtra where socialist parties began to gain on the Congress in the electoral sweepstakes. An unnerved Nehru was then persuaded by Chavan to cede Bombay to Maharashtra, and was installed as the first chief minister of a complete Maharashtra state.

Certain sections in Vidarbha have, however, always held this against the Congress leaders in both Maharashtra and at the Centre for, despite Nehru's promise, Vidarbha was not allowed to exercise its choice to separate, like Gujarat did, and form its own state. Today, many of these people blame the western Maharashtra region for all their woes, as we have seen in earlier chapters.

But politicians from western Maharashtra vehemently deny these allegations. Their argument is that there is a difference between the enterprise and industriousness of Vidarbha and Marathwada and that of western Maharashtra which has, in many ways, helped itself rather than simply depending on government largesse for its development. With the advantages of its rivers and early rainfall, the region, of course, has managed some good farm economics, though it is not completely free of the perils of drought and deficit rainfall.

In fact, there are large tracts in the districts of Solapur, Sangli, Satara and Ahmednagar that are as drought-affected as Marathwada and Vidarbha, but farmers manage to survive because they don't depend solely on sugarcane for their livelihood. They also have milk sweetened by the sugar from their cooperatives. During a year of deficit rainfall when even a lush region like western Maharashtra suffered from a water shortage, farmers found a way out for such lean times—they set up milk cooperatives. Strangely, although Maharashtra was the pioneer in the cooperative movement in sugarcane farming, other regions of the state, with the exception of some sections of Marathwada, did not really take to it. 'These regions have been depending on just one crop (cotton or soya bean) for survival,' says Radhakrishna Vikhe Patil, former agriculture minister of the state and now leader of the opposition in the Maharashtra assembly.

'Vidarbha in 2015 got more rain than even some districts of western Maharashtra where also we have got unseasonal hailstorms in April and May. And then a gap of 48–52 days between one shower and the next during the monsoon months. That kind of rainfall does not behove well for crop survival. But what saved the farmers here was dairy farming. We produced 20 lakh litres of milk with just about 250 mm of rainfall. Various districts in Vidarbha got 900 mm and yet they produced only 70,000 litres of milk. What stops them from doing better?'

'It is not right to blame the leaders of western Maharashtra alone for their backwardness,' says Vikhe Patil. For Vidarbha has had the longest serving chief minister in Vasantrao Naik and even Marathwada had a galaxy of leaders from the region ending up as chief ministers. 'So it is just a blame game for the lack of their own enterprise.'

However, as former finance and rural development minister of Maharashtra, Jayant Patil says, perhaps the impression of injustice to Marathwada and Vidarbha arises because of the 1990s decision of the Shiv Sena-BJP government to set up the Krishna Valley Development Corporation (KVDC) to harvest water from the Krishna River, according to the directives of the water tribunal, within a specific period of time before the project was abandoned a few years later. The KVDC was then mostly seen as benefitting western Maharashtra, and it perpetuated the impression of injustice to all the other regions of the state. 'However, on the governor's orders, we stopped that work in 2003, but that impression prevails,' says Patil, who agrees with Vikhe Patil that setting up irrigation facilities and an equitable distribution of water to all regions is one of the primary solutions to end the feeling of injustice among the people.

'Unfortunately,' says Vikhe Patil, 'we have not learnt how to conserve the water. Much of the rainwater flows into the sea and I believe if we develop the harvesting systems for this water and develop the Godavari basin, large tracts can be irrigated. The successive droughts have been so bad that, in 2015, even Konkan, which is a seaside region of Maharashtra, has faced dryness. There are no ways out of such natural calamities unless you make provisions for the future well in time during good seasons.'

Even with regard to cotton, which is grown in Marathwada and

Vidarbha, Vikhe Patil wonders why entrepreneurs in these regions cannot set up spinning and ginning mills, which are currently located mostly in western Maharashtra, adding to the costs of farmers as they have to transport their produce to the buying centres. But the regions must move away from just cotton and soya bean and diversify into orchards (where Vidarbha has an advantage with its oranges), or other cash crops that are not water intensive, are easy to harvest and transport and could benefit from industrial enterprise—like food processing. 'There is a citrus research institute in Nagpur. So, why have oranges not had better yields and why do they have to be transported to other parts of the country for processing?' Vikhe Patil asks.

The lack of such enterprise, however, affects even western Maharashtra, as Ramrao Patil, a farmer from Solapur tells me. 'I grew a lot of bananas last year and, even with a deficit rainfall, I got a reasonable crop. I was happy that I would recover my costs when I first harvested the fruit. But there was so much banana that the market could take only so much and prices fell rapidly. Ultimately, there were no takers and I had to cut large bunches and abandon them by the roadside for anyone to come and take them for free.'

That story is eerily similar to what happened to the orange growers of Vidarbha in the 2015–16 season—the fruit was so lush on the trees that the orange growers invited wayside travellers into their orchards to pluck the oranges for free and take as much as they wanted. The farmers, however, managed to recover their costs since the price of oranges moves according to the availability of the fruit in the market—at the end of a lush season, consumers can get them for as little as ten rupees a dozen, at other times it can be ten times that price.

If agro-industries existed, the banana farmers of western Maharashtra and the orange growers of Vidarbha could have been saved the losses they incurred in a bountiful season when there was excess crop despite unseasonal hailstorms and a deficit rainfall. Ramrao says his bananas could have been preserved and processed, but neither the government nor private entrepreneurs seemed interested in doing this. That is the story of Marathwada, too, and also of Vidarbha where the orange crop is abundant four years out of five, but there are no industries to process them locally (that could, however, change with the arrival of Baba Ramdev's Patanjali in Nagpur, which has promised to drive most other brands of orange juice out of the market in a few years).

Long ago, a group of entrepreneurs had set up the Nagpur Orange Growers Association, which produced and bottled orange juice, jam and marmalade under the brand name of NOGA. But NOGA received little government support and was soon driven out of business by the market leaders. 'It was an attempt at forming a cooperative, however small. Why couldn't the government stand by such enterprise?' asks Ramrao who is not hopeful that such support will come to western Maharashtra either in the near future.

He believes there is general government apathy towards all farmers. If western Maharashtra seems an oasis in a desert of backwardness, it's because the leaders of the cooperative movement have contributed, to a large extent in their individual capacities, in setting up schools, research institutions, roads and other facilities in their respective districts.

Dr Kango agrees in part with this assessment. He points out that if large portions of western Maharashtra's districts are underdeveloped; it is entirely because of the selfish motives of the politicians who have ruled the region for decades. 'They should have chosen the district as the basis of backwardness and developed entire regions but then that would bring them no credit in their individual capacities. It was more electorally beneficial to make the taluka as the basis of development, so every leader worth his name brought a lot of facilities to his own taluka, which also brought him votes. That resulted in talukas which did not have a minister or otherwise powerful person elected to office remaining backward and contributing to the overall lack of development and distress of farmers on par with those in Vidarbha or Marathwada.'

Vikhe Patil does admit to the fact that western Maharashtra may have been allocated more irrigation projects and dams than other regions but, in bad years, even these dams and rivers run dry, which happened during the period 2014–16. 'All dams were below the half level mark at the start of the monsoon season in 2015. All the water that we have should be in safekeeping for drinking purposes. So even with somewhat better irrigation facilities, farmers in western Maharashtra did not get their share of water for growing sugarcane in 2016.'

Global climatic changes are a reality now, so innovative ways are required to manage the vagaries of the monsoon, says Vikhe Patil. 'If we can combat this factor, it will go a long way in helping all regions out of distress.' In the absence of these measures, even the farmers of western Maharashtra are not confident of getting government support in a lean season.

In 2015, farmers harvested their sugarcane earlier than scheduled and turned the crop into cattle fodder, as there were no guarantees that the factories would have the capacity to acquire their complete sugarcane crop and crush it in time. Similar doubts prevailed in 2016. Each factory with a 2,500 tonne capacity to crush cane requires five lakh litres of water per day, and with the sinking levels of water in the dams in western Maharashtra, it is doubtful if even sugar factories in western Maharashtra will be able to work uninterrupted in the next few years in the absence of sufficient monsoon rains—just one good and surplus monsoon, as in 2017, is not sufficient.

According to both Jayant Patil and Vikhe Patil, other regions of the state should stop indulging in a 'blame game' and refrain from trying to project politicians from western Maharashtra as villains all the time. Western Maharashtra definitely is fortunate in the manner in which it is placed geographically and ecologically, but that is an advantage only in times of bountiful rains. Bad times bring equal distress to all regions, and any difference in outcomes is due to local enterprise. 'In the future, however, irrigation facilities must be stressed upon for all regions along with water conservation. Sadly, despite the distressing situation for three consecutive years, governments' budgetary allocations for irrigation have been miniscule and this is bound to affect the future of farmers in the coming years in all regions of the state,' says Patil.

So, while nature does not discriminate between regions and people, humans certainly do. The flushness of western Maharashtra is owing in large measure to some early discriminatory policies of the state's leaders, but voters from Vidarbha and Marathwada who got more than one chief minister from their region, believe they should have had the gumption to stand up to politicians from western Maharashtra and benefit their own regions.

To accuse the leaders of western Maharashtra of looting and cheating other regions might be an over-the-top reaction of those wishing to cover up their own inadequacies. In any case, the change of government in 2014 has shifted focus from western Maharashtra, the fiefdom of the all-powerful Pawars, to Vidarbha, which has given the state a chief minister again and a powerful and enterprising union minister. Marathwada, however, continues to be an orphan in this regard. The next few years should see the disappearance of the existing imbalances, and all the regions of the state are likely to be back on an even keel. With the blessings of the rain gods, of course!

10

Up in the Mountains So High

A placid people of Khandesh make
for the richest and poorest in India.

When Sonia Gandhi finally decided to enter politics in 1998, she chose Navapur in the Nandurbar district of North Maharashtra as her launch pad. Sharad Pawar, then the unspoken soul of the Congress in the state, was surprised at the response Sonia got to her first public meeting. The fact that she was not able to deliver her lines perfectly in Hindi did not seem to matter to the people of North Maharashtra who had little knowledge of pure Hindi anyway. They did not even fully understand spoken Marathi. Their lingua franca was a mishmash of Gujarati, Rajasthani, Hindi, Magadhi and Marathi, a language called 'Ahirani', which set these adivasis—mostly of Bhil origin—far apart from any other adivasis anywhere else in Maharashtra.

Khandesh was the name given to the northern districts of Maharashtra by its Islamic rulers, the earliest being the Faruqui dynasty. Later, in the sixteenth century, the Nizam-ul-mulk was sent as viceroy to the Malwa region of Madhya Pradesh but ended up annexing the territories and setting up his own dynasty. During the states' reorganization of 1960, Burhanpur, which was the capital of Khandesh, was annexed to Madhya Pradesh and the remaining two districts of Dhulia and Jalgaon, which the British had divided into East and West Khandesh, were integrated with Maharashtra.

In the 1990s, the Maharashtra government bifurcated Dhulia to carve out a new district of Nandurbar. That is about all that successive governments in Maharashtra seem to have done for the region. Although the Tapti River flows through Khandesh into Gujarat where it joins the Arabian Sea, there are no irrigation facilities, for the river bed is too deep to lend itself to canaling, and the people depend mostly on natural rainwater for farming in the high mountainous regions of these districts.

In 1998, though, there were miles and miles of these abandoned tribal people making their way to Navapur to hear Sonia Gandhi speak. The adivasis were delighted that she had chosen their district to launch her political career. They did not stop coming even after Sonia Gandhi's helicopter had taken off at the end of a very successful rally. Seeing the tribals making their way to the rally grounds prompted Sonia to circle the region thrice in her helicopter and wave out to the disappointed people far below. She seemed quite reluctant to head back to Delhi.

When the United Progressive Alliance (UPA) decided to set up the unique identification scheme, the first Aadhaar card was handed to a tribal woman in the Khandesh region of Maharashtra. If Sonia Gandhi had not selected Khandesh for her first public appearance and unveiling of the Aadhaar card—one still does not know why she chose it—Khandesh might have slipped from the consciousness of most people, even in Maharashtra.

Khandesh is situated in the Tapti-Purna valley, tucked away amidst the Satpura range of hills to the north, the Ajanta-Satmala hills to the southwest, the Sahyadri range to the south, Vidarbha to the east and Marathwada to the west. Its socio-cultural influences are more Gujarati and Rajasthani than Maratha or Marathi. The adivasis are mostly of Bhil origin, descended from Rajasthan. None of the region's historic events seem to have affected their placidity—

they were subjugated by different kingdoms, including the Mughal subedars, the Nizam of Hyderabad and later the Marathas who included the Scindias of Gwalior, the Holkars of Indore and the Gaekwads of Baroda in Gujarat. The British, who seized control of Maratha territories, later divided the region into East and West Khandesh, to which the tribals responded with acceptance and resilience. Many freedom fighters hailed from the region and Khandesh also threw up distinguished poets and littérateurs.

'That placidity of the common folk is because they were rather cut off from the mainland and in a way they were living in the dark ages all this while. There was no connectivity and not much modern-day communication,' says Sanjay Zende, a senior journalist working with the *Maharashtra Times* in Dhule. 'It is only of late that they are rising to national consciousness because of the arrival of the Internet and television. Before this nothing mattered to them except their undisturbed way of life.'

There is a distinctive ethnic division between East and West Khandesh, defined by non-tribals and tribals respectively. The mountain ranges, inaccessible and highly underdeveloped, have reported a series of malnutrition deaths among children, and maternal and child mortality rates continue to be high, yet there are few protests about government inattention and lack of development from the people of West Khandesh. East Khandesh, on the other hand, is mostly home to people of Jain, Gujarati and Marwari origin. Hence, they are a traditionally entrepreneurial class and cannot be labelled as deprived or backward. The fruits of their labour, however, have not been passed on to West Khandesh or Dhule and Nandurbar, perhaps the two most backward districts in the entire state of Maharashtra.

Zende says it is in the nature of the people not to protest. They are typically content with the slow pace of development. 'It is not as though nothing is happening. Development is coming in dribbles and they are okay with it. Anyone wanting more chooses to move away to the more developed areas of Nashik, Jalgaon (which is the most advanced district of Khandesh), Pune and Mumbai rather than press governments for more funds and programmes for their region. You can call it a character flaw or a drawback but that is how the people here are.'

But with increasing access to the Internet and smartphones, the people of Khandesh are beginning to emerge from the darkness into the light and are catching up with the rest of the world. This has resulted in some discontentment and disappointment. One major issue is that despite the existence of socially and economically advanced communities, at least in East Khandesh, the region has never been considered good enough for state leadership. Pratibha Patil, who was leader of the opposition from 1978–80, was passed over for chief minister by Mrs Indira Gandhi who first chose Abdul Rehman Antulay and next opted for Babasaheb Bhosale, a Maratha leader from western Maharashtra.

History has repeated itself with Eknath Khadse, who is a Leva-Patel, one of the richest communities originating in Gujarat. He is one of the tallest leaders of the region, and the people of Khandesh had believed that if the BJP came to power, they might finally succeed in getting a chief minister from their region, given that Khadse is the most senior leader in the state unit of the party with experience of governance during the Shiv Sena-BJP regime from 1995–99. However, he, too, was passed over by central leaders in favour of the comparative novice Devendra Fadnavis. Later, despite allegations of corruption against several ministers in the Maharshtra Cabinet, the party chose to axe only Khadse. And that, says Zende, has not gone down well with the people of both East and West Khandesh.

'It wouldn't have mattered earlier. But now it does because awareness is growing and they are also reacting to the demands of other regions for more growth and development. Until that happens,' says sociologist Dr Pramila Patil, secretary of the Jawahar

Shikshan Prasaran Sanstha at Dhule, 'the proportion of the poor in these regions will always remain around the national average—that is on par with states like Bihar, Jharkhand and Orissa and, in some years dipping even below the national average.'

That pulls Maharashtra down by several notches, but do the people of the prosperous districts of the state and its leaders care? Dr Patil has serious doubts. 'The thing is, it is not as though we do not have good educational institutions or intellectuals from the region,' says Zende. 'We have had poets, writers, reformists, freedom fighters, sportspeople making a mark on the national scene. But they have chosen to migrate to Mumbai or Pune or even Nasik and left little stamp of their personalities on the Khandesh region per se. They have no sense of belonging to their own region. It is a fact we have to live with but hopefully things will change soon.'

Until then, the best the people of the region can hope for is that it does not take them as long to come into the twenty-first century as it did to catch up with the twentieth century.

11

Hendry-Kendry by the Sea

Beautiful Konkan is fast becoming a dangerous chemical zone.

*D*espite the fact that India is surrounded by seas on three sides, ironically none of the native kings in medieval times ever thought of setting up their own navy. Even the Mughals and other Islamic dynasties depended on Arabs and European seafarers for trade and the movement of goods across the seas, which brought many European powers to the Indian coast in search of riches. Among these were the Dutch, the Portuguese and the British, all of whom fought amongst each other for the control of the Konkan coast.

But there was one power that they all found difficult to combat, the Siddis, who were of African descent and nominally owed allegiance to other Islamic powers in India, notably the Adil Shahi kingdoms and the Mughals. But even though the Siddis were vassals, their seafaring powers were such that most of these kings were entirely dependent upon them. In fact, they strived to keep the Siddis friendly and content so that the sea routes to Mecca and trade in luxury goods was not interrupted.

Shivaji, whose capital was in Raigad on the Konkan coast, however, was the first of the indigenous kings to realize the value of naval power. He became a thorn in the side of both the Portuguese and the British, who sometimes attempted treaties with him and at other times tried to obstruct his efforts at building a formidable navy of his own. They were well-aware that the grant of sea power to Shivaji's rather primitive fleets would render their trade and control of the islands in the Arabian Sea vulnerable. The British were particularly incensed by the Siddi's control of the island of Andari (Hendry). They were also unable to prevent Shivaji from fortifying the nearby island of Khanderi, which the British referred to as Kendry. 'Hendry-Kendry' thus became a term symbolic of the British inability to conquer its enemies, and affected their complete control of the islands they later inherited from the Portuguese in the form of dowry, brought by Catherine of Braganza in 1662 when she married Charles II, king of Britain from 1662 to 1685.

However, despite the obstructions from the British and the Portuguese, Shivaji soon built a series of sea forts, including Vijaydurg and Sindhudurg in the Konkan. Although his ships did not equal those built by the Siddis or even the European powers, one can today describe him as the father of the Indian navy. One of modern-day India's naval training ships is named INS Angre after Kanhoji Angre, a formidable naval commander during the time of Shivaji who conquered many sea powers and seized many islands from both the Portuguese and the British on the Konkan coast. The Indian Navy has also named its training ship in Lonavla as INS Shivaji, in tribute to India's original naval power.

The city of Mumbai, a part of the Konkan region of the state and Raigad, towards which the Maharashtra government is attempting to extend the environs of Mumbai to accommodate its rapidly expanding population and infrastructure, is among the 'Most Forward Districts' of the state. Sadly, though, one cannot say the same of the other coastal districts of the region. The people of the Konkan are by and large dependent on fishing and horticulture, yet successive governments over the decades have turned these beautiful sylvan districts of Maharashtra into a chemical zone, which is affecting both fisheries and horticulture.

'When I was a child, we never had to buy fish,' says Anwar Hussain, a native of Ratnagiri district. 'You felt like eating fish, you just put your boat out to sea and cast the net. There was always so much fish caught in the nets that you could distribute plenty to the whole village and there would still be enough left over for the evening. But now that is no longer the case. The fish are coming up dead in the nets. Sometimes, the quantities are so poor, you barely have enough to feed the family, let alone distribute to your neighbours.'

As with most regions of Maharashtra, the complaint of the Konkanis is that politicians from western Maharashtra perpetrated injustices on their region, or those belonging to the Konkan did more for western Maharashtra than for the coastal regions of the state. Unlike Khandesh, which has never had a chief minister in Mantralaya, Konkan has had three chief ministers lead the state government—Abdul Rehman Antulay in the 1980s and nearly two decades after that, Manohar Joshi and Narayan Rane of the Shiv Sena in quick succession between 1995 and 1999. There is an eerie similarity between the complaints of the Konkanis and those of the people of Vidarbha and Marathwada, thus negating the protestations of politicians from western Maharashtra who claim they have done no injustice to other regions of the state.

The Konkanis blame their leaders for the undue attention given to western Maharashtra during the Shiv Sena-BJP rule of 1995–99. Both the Sena chief ministers were from the Konkan and yet their focus was on the Krishna Valley Development Corporation (KVDC) in western Maharashtra, while they could have brought much-needed development to their regions for far less than the cost of the KVDC. The Konkanis question why none of the chief ministers of Maharashtra, from any party and from any region, has been able to do anything for his own constituency and has focused on western Maharashtra instead. When Antulay did try to shift the focus from western Maharashtra, politicians from that region—notably Sharad Pawar—conspired to displace him under false charges of personal corruption. It took him twenty years to be acquitted by the courts, but by then it was too late.

In the early days of Congress rule in unified Maharashtra, the government of Vasantrao Naik sanctioned several chemical factories for the Konkan region, which affected its ecology and, more particularly, its numerous estuaries and fisheries. 'There are many rivieras in the Konkan districts where mountains meet the sea, which have enormous potential for development. Shipping, tourism, fishing and horticulture should have been the focus of various governments, yet when these chemical factories were to be set up in the 1970s in western Maharashtra, its politicians flatly refused to risk their region's ecology and pushed those factories towards the Konkan. Recent governments are insisting on the development of a nuclear power plant at Jaitapur. Why are they not harnessing hydel power to generate electricity when there is plentiful water in the region even during a severe drought in the rest of Maharashtra?' asks Hussain Dalwai, a former Maharashtra minister and Rajya Sabha MP from the Congress who hails from the region.

Because of the ethos of Maharashtra Dharma, Konkan, which was settled by many of Shivaji's followers, had a socialist bent of mind. For many years, politically and electorally, the region supported socialist parties like the Peasants and Workers Party and the Congress. However, the short-sighted politics of socialist leaders like Madhu Dandavate, who sought support from the Shiv Sena in Mumbai for local elections, completely turned the politics of the region on its head. For the Sena support did not come without a price tag—Bal Thackeray demanded a toe-hold in the Konkan and got a substantial foot in the door in return, which changed the political equation of the region in the 1970s and 1980s.

With the lack of employment in their home districts, most wage earners from the Konkan made their way to Mumbai, and the growing influence of the Shiv Sena in the city had its inevitable effect on the coastal districts of the state. Thackeray, however, had a unique style of entrusting the regions to his lieutenants and not interfering in their shenanigans on their home turf. Thus, for many years former Chief Minister Narayan Rane had the responsibility of delivering the Konkan to the Shiv Sena, which he did through alternating fear with favour.

After he fell out with Thackeray, though, it appeared that the foundations of the Sena in the Konkan would become weak, but it did not take long for critics to realize that the peoples' loyalty lay with the party and not with the individual. Therefore, the Sena continues with its political domination of the region denying a toe-hold now to its ally, the BJP, while the Congress lurks furtively behind, with Sharad Pawar attempting for years to make inroads into the Konkan with little success. 'But it is also the short-sighted politics of Pawar that has contributed to the strengthening of the Shiv Sena,' says Dalwai.

That is another tale of an attempted Maratha domination of the people, which even Shivaji did not undertake. Pawar was unwilling to cede control to other communities, and while with the Congress, he put up his own caste candidates against the dominant castes of the region—such as the kurmis and agris. As a result, these communities swung towards the Shiv Sena. While Shivaji might have built and captured many forts in these coastal districts, he never attempted to interfere in the the social milieu of the region and its dominant communities and the traditional castes continued in their defined positions for centuries after Shivaji. Since the Sena professes to uphold Shivaji's dharma, it was easy to shift loyalties to Bal Thackeray's party.

'But it is not as though the people have given up their traditional socialist mindset,' says Dalwai. 'However, there is no leadership worth the name anywhere to draw them back to the socialist ethos.' Today, however, what moves the people of the Konkan is the question: Who has their best interests at heart? The answer is: Perhaps no one.

Although the Konkan Railway, started by Dandavate when he was the railways minister in the 1990s, did open up this earlier impenetrable region to the masses, it still needs more roads and transport services to make the capital city accessible to the villagers. Just like in the other regions of the state, the people also want agro-industries for large-scale food processing. Despite the messing up of ecological balances, Konkan still has fish in plenty and produces fruit in abundance—for example, mangoes of many varieties including the world-famous alphonso, banana, coconut, jackfruit, cashew and spices.

Konkan's rivieras and its sylvan beaches adjoining those in Goa could be a major tourist attraction, as could the Olive Ridley turtles, which hatch on the beaches every year and make their way to the sea, and have become a very popular sight. But have successive governments cared? Instead there have been environmental violations on these beaches by bauxite miners who could have damaged the ecology beyond repair if the people had not taken the matter into their own hands, thrown out the contractors and decided to save the turtle habitat through their own efforts.

Dalwai says the people want to preserve their Hendry-Kendrys—that is their heritage, including the forts that Shivaji built along with other monuments, many of which are falling into neglect and ruin. They want more tourist resorts, more roads, more rail connectivity to Mumbai—not just a passing-through of trains to and from South India—and of course, the protection of the traditional fishing habitat instead of the mechanized fishing successive governments have been encouraging. This way more people like Anwar Hussain will be able to cast their nets into the sea and make a fresh catch whenever they feel like it, instead of buying what is naturally theirs at exorbitant market prices.

'But all they are getting is a nuclear power plant,' says Dalwai. 'And they are genuinely afraid they may have to face another Fukushima in the near future.'

GATEWAY POLICIES

Founders never leave our memories for they leave indelible footprints on our minds. They give us the reasons to look back and ponder. They give us the reasons to look forward with the hope and aspirations to beating their footprints of distinctiveness. Their mistakes are our lessons and the reasons to reason.

—Ernest Agyemang Yeboah

To win the big stakes in this changed world, you must catch the spirit of the great pioneers of the past, whose dreams have given to civilization all that it has of value, the spirit that serves as the life-blood of our own country—your opportunity and mine, to develop and market our talents.

—Napoleon Hill

12

Crushing the Cooperatives

Cooperative institutions have become synonymous with corruption.

'Pandit Jawaharlal Nehru came all the way from New Delhi to Pravaranagar (in Ahmednagar district) to see my grandfather,' Radhakrishna Vikhe Patil tells me with a touching childlike pride. Vithalrao Vikhe Patil, as is now widely known, was the doyen of the cooperative movement in Maharashtra. And Pandit Nehru was surprised that a mere farmer 'who was just a fourth class pass' could think up an institution as enormous as a cooperative, which would not only work unerringly for the interests of farmers, but one day would end up defining the politics of the entire state.

The cooperative movement in Maharashtra, which has been the subject of several studies, initially existed primarily in the area of sugarcane farming, as mentioned earlier in the book. Only recently has it been extended to dairy farming, an activity that has saved the lives of farmers in the bad years of drought and failed crops. This is largely the reason why politicians from western Maharashtra, and particularly those from the Congress, have been able to dominate the state and most of its other regions. But Vikhe Patil believes that the cooperative movement has not been allowed to realize its full potential.

The cooperative sector was a major cause for rivalry between Sharad Pawar and the Vikhe Patils, notably Balasaheb Vikhe Patil, Vithalrao's son, and this enmity between the two had a lasting impact on the politics of the state. 'Ever since Pawar took over the reins in Maharashtra, he did not allow the cooperatives to become autonomous bodies. He always wanted overall control, so that he could dole out favours and drive fear into the cooperative leaders' hearts as and when he wished,' says the grandson of the man who was among the first Padmashrees in the country for attempting to do just that—make the cooperatives autonomous and independent of political interference. But that was not to be.

Radhakrishna is not far wrong. The fact that Pawar has continued as the uncrowned king of Maharashtra even after ceasing to be chief minister, and even after the resounding defeat of his party in the state elections in 2014, can all be traced back to his family's grip on the cooperative institutions of the state. A cooperative farming unit does not just comprise farmers who are organized into a group and are working together towards their collective prosperity. In both the sugarcane and dairy sector, there is enormous need to generate funds for cane crushing factories and chilling plants, and this is something that comes, again, through the route of cooperatives—in the banking sector.

Maharashtra is one state where there is a plethora of cooperative banks, which maximize their funds by playing the markets. And they are all controlled by an apex cooperative bank. For years, Pawar's nephew, Ajit Pawar, at one time the finance minister of the state, controlled the Maharashtra State Apex Cooperative Bank, amounting to a direct conflict of interest. But no one seemed to notice, or they did not want to raise objections because Ajit was highly democratic in the disbursal of funds from this apex cooperative bank. Leaders from all political parties, including the Shiv Sena, the BJP and the Congress, benefitted from this largesse, which he distributed according to his whims and fancies, without taking precautions as to collaterals. There was no consideration as to procedures and the laws of the land, something that went against him when the Reserve Bank of India superseded the bank and put a halt to its activities in 2011.

This is also how Sharad Pawar formed his NCP—mostly through subtle coercion with the aid of the apex cooperative bank. When Pawar split the Congress, Ajit was the chairman of the apex bank and most of the cooperative stalwarts who later joined the NCP thought hard about their loyalties before joining Pawar. For their politics depended much upon their business interests (that is their factories), which were entirely dependent on loans from the apex cooperative bank.

In later years when the NCP was ruling Maharashtra, the Pawars could keep the opposition quiet essentially because of their control of their apex bank—until the advent of Prithviraj Chavan as chief minister in 2010. Strangely, despite belonging to a family of Congress stalwarts from western Maharashtra, Chavan had not developed any interest in the cooperative sector and, therefore, had no reason to be beholden to the Pawars. Without any fear or favour, then, he decided, with the help of the then Union Finance Minister Pranab Mukherjee, to have the apex cooperative bank superseded. That made him very unpopular with the Pawars, with Ajit going to the extent of describing him as 'the worst chief minister of Maharashtra I have ever known'. It once again led, inevitably, to a change in the political equations in Maharashtra.

The superceding of the bank instantly deprived the Pawars of their power to control the fortunes of the state. Pawar, at the time, was the union agriculture minister, but he could do little to persuade the UPA to reverse this decision. It was inevitable then that the NCP would cut its ties to the Congress and seek greener pastures. With the BJP under Narendra Modi growing by leaps and bounds, it decided to chart a fresh course and offer support to the minority government of the party in Maharashtra.

Now even the BJP has cottoned on to the modus operandi of the Pawars' control of Maharashtra. The government, no longer dependent on the party's support, is insistent on passing a law that will deprive any director of any cooperative bank accused of misusing its funds, the right to contest the board elections for two terms—which means ten years. The Congress had earlier barred directors from contesting such polls for one term. 'Which is five years and good enough to deprive anyone control of the cooperatives in good measure,' says Chavan who has been the only Congress leader who had the courage to go so far in order to curtail the powers of the Pawars, and ended up being hated by the NCP.

Ten years can be a very, very long time in politics. At the time of writing, the Pawars were putting up a bitter fight by bringing forward a stay from the courts against any further action in the matter. If the courts uphold the government's decision, it could lead to a paradigm shift in Maharashtra's politics, whose effects might be visible sooner than expected.

The Shiv Sena-BJP government, which ruled Maharashtra from 1995–99, attempted to curtail the Congress's grip over the cooperatives by dezoning them, as we have read in Chapter 3. However, a unified Congress put up a bitter fight and, far from breaking the monopoly of the various modern-day feudal lords, even leaders from the Shiv Sena and the BJP ended up setting up their own sugar and milk cooperatives and banks in various regions of the state. They failed because they had not learnt, from the Congress and the NCP, how to connect with the common people they intended to serve, and instead ended up being just private manifestations of political greed. Many of these non-Congress institutions thus soon shut down. But the movement, though pioneered in western Maharashtra, did not quite succeed in other regions like Vidarbha and Marathwada, perhaps because of the ecological advantages of western Maharashtra.

Radhakrishna Vikhe Patil does not agree with this perspective.

'There were at least twenty such cooperatives in Vidarbha. Why did they fail? Not because of lack of water but the sheer mismanagement of the directors who could not bring themselves to handle the sector professionally. Even with regard to milk cooperatives, I can say they are very half-hearted. Compare the milk production and rainfall in 2015 in Ahmednagar in western Maharashtra with that of Amravati in Vidarbha the same year and you will see what I mean. Why should that be so?'

He answers the question himself: no one is seriously interested in nursing and nurturing cooperatives any longer because of the enormous interference of the government in the sector. Reading between the lines, this means people are sick of the interference of the rural elite in their daily business, and have themselves induced the decline of their own sugar mills and cooperatives. 'They have sold out to the private sector where zoning does not matter and to many farmers this is a better option. But that has killed the cooperative sector.'

In reality, the issue is more complex. The cooperative sector is today synonymous with power and corruption—the power comes from the financial muscle they gather and that muscle is used to cow down the general voters, says Chavan. 'Cooperatives today are set up specifically with the purpose of selling out to some or the other political leader. I don't wish to name names but it is not too difficult to find out how many former chief ministers and ministers have deliberately bought out cooperatives across western Maharashtra and Marathwada. That is why no one in government was compelled over the years to clean up the cooperatives and now it has become synonymous with a certain kind of politics that the NCP particularly follows.'

Meanwhile, the livelihood of the poor farmer is affected by the lack of an assured market, even in those years when the rainfall is good and there is a bountiful crop. Thus the parties that set up cooperative farming to benefit the common people have themselves defeated the purpose—today they are less benefactors of the people and more businessmen looking out for their own interests. Chavan is not far wrong in declaring Congress and NCP leaders as 'essentially businessmen' if one takes the example of just one such enterprise that goes under the name of 'Dynamix'.

Although Sharad Pawar has little to do with it on record, it is a cooperative of farmers in Baramati that has captured a huge chunk of the dairy segment, and not just in the state of Maharashtra. It is a robust rival to the best in the industry, including the Amul Cooperative of Gujarat. It doesn't just supply milk to supermarkets and other outlets, but also produces cheese, butter, yogurt and other dairy products at its plant in Baramati, as well as bottled fruit juices, iced teas and every other preserve possible for companies such as McDonald's, Britannia and Nestle.

Women are at the centre of this cooperative and their daily earnings are paid into an all-women's bank, but the control of the entire enterprise is in the hands of Pawar's cronies. Pawar had realized very early in the day that in a globalized world, it would not always be possible to protect the farmers against predatory multinational corporations. He had once told me: 'The multinationals will most certainly come into India however much you resist. And they will not come to India for charitable purposes. They are here to make profit. So, I thought I would make sure that they will not be able to do business without taking us along. No multinational company now can make profits in India without passing on a portion of it to the local people.'

But it is debatable how much of these profits actually goes to farmers and how much goes to the rural elite. 'Unfortunately, the political system in India, of first past the post, is such that the only way to survive in politics is to make loads of money and not get caught with your hands in the till. This is true not just of Maharashtra but across India. And one way to make loads of money with low risk is this cooperative sector,' says Chavan.

Mahadeo Jankar, president of the Rashtriya Samajwadi Party—which represents the Other Backward Classes—and now a minister in the Maharashtra government says, 'If anyone even believed that the cooperative sector was for poor farmers, they were fools. It is only the rural elite, the Pawars, the (Ashok) Chavans, the Patils, the Kadams and the Deshmukhs who set up cooperatives in western Maharashtra and Marathwada for their own children. The poor farmer ended up just as a watchman or peon in those factories.'

Jankar's party and the Swabhimani Shetkari Sangathana of Raju Shetti (who has now exited the NDA for allegedly failing to protect farmers' interests) emerged as alternative groups for farmers a year or two before the 2014 Lok Sabha elections, and put tremendous pressure on the then Maharashtra government to give a better deal to farmers who, they insist, have been exploited by the rural elite for decades. 'Even in western Maharashtra there are at least seven to eight talukas that are drought prone. I can show you at least 48 villages even in Baramati (the Pawars' home turf) where there aren't any drinking water supplies. How does that sit with the rural elite who call themselves leaders of farmers?'

Although Jankar targets the rural elite as a whole, his ire is particularly directed at the Pawars. The two farmers' parties formed an alliance with the Shiv Sena and the BJP during the Lok Sabha polls, and such was the people's ennui with the rural elite that the Congress got no seats at all in the region and the NCP managed barely four seats, including the one that Jankar contested against Pawar's daughter, Supriya Sule, from Baramati.

What enrages Jankar is that even the BJP seems to be following the Congress-NCP model, manifest in Union Transport Minister Nitin Gadkari's embroilment in the Purti scam, which was an attempt to set up what he describes as a 'social enterprise' in Vidarbha in exactly the manner that the Pawars did in western Maharashtra. 'They do nothing for the peasants and workers. They keep benefitting the rich while the poor farmer remains where he has been for all times.'

Jankar is particularly incensed at the way BJP leaders like Modi and Arun Jaitley have been cozying up to Pawar. 'I had hoped that the BJP-led government, of which I am an ally, would chart an independent course in a manner that would benefit the common and poor farmer,' says this leader of shepherds whose party has been making remarkable headway not just in Maharashtra but also in neighbouring Gujarat. 'But now the Jaitleys and the Modis are all taking advice from the Pawars, which means just more of the same. I am holding my silence for now, not just because I am part of the alliance (and now minister in the state government), but because they have had very little time to study and repair the damage done by the rural elite over decades. If they do not make a course correction very soon, I am prepared to strip down their pretensions and expose even this government as I and Raju Shetti had done with the previous one.'

Strong words, but in view of the continuing rural distress across India, parties like the RSP and the SSS, which represent interests other than those personified by the national parties like the Congress and the BJP, are fast gaining ground across regions and states. Indeed, there might be some truth to the suspicions of these parties. The motives for the BJP-led government's attempts to clean up the cooperative sector may not be purely altruistic. There is a more significant reason behind the move to break the back of the cooperative sector—the BJP must make inroads into western Maharashtra so that they are not dependent on Vidarbha or the Shiv Sena, as at present. It is very likely that the Shiv Sena will do better in the next elections, at least in Mumbai and its surrounding areas, and the BJP's core strength in 2014 has come from its seats in Vidarbha.

The BJP is in favour of statehood for Vidarbha, but it cannot afford the separation because that could result in its losing control of Maharashtra, which is a far more significant state than Vidarbha would be after bifurcation. The Congress example, wherein the party lost control of both Telangana and Seemandhra after splitting Andhra Pradesh, also presents them with a hard choice. The Shiv Sena is a strong rival in both the Konkan and Marathwada regions, but western Maharashtra is out of reach for both parties. Despite the unusual sweep across the state during the 2014 elections, it continues to remain the turf of the Congress, and even more so of the NCP. Breaking the back of the cooperative movement here would level out the playing field in many ways, which might be good for the state.

But in these petty political battles, farmers' interests are sacrificed every time. For the fear remains that the situation could be like an 'Animal Farm' with one set of politicians replacing another like in 1995–99, and everything else remaining the same.

13

Speaking for the Poor

Two Gandhi topis and one employment guarantee scheme have done wonders.

$\mathcal{M}$andakini was just five and her brother was three years old when their mother deserted their father and sought work in the nearest city. Maharashtra was going through a severe drought in the early 1970s and Sonabai's husband was an alcoholic. As adivasis, anything they garnered from the forest fetched very little returns and Sonabai was afraid that her two young children would simply die of hunger. She thought she would seek employment in homes in the city, but this work paid very little. Then someone told her about the need for construction labourers at a building site coming up some kilometres from the city. The pay was less for women than for men, but it was far more than she could make as a domestic help.

However, Sonabai was worried about her two young kids—she could not abandon them and neither could she bring them to the site, which was too far for a daily commute from the village, especially with two children. Her problem was solved when the site officer told her she could apply for shelter at the camp that had been set up close to the construction site. While housing was now no more an issue for Sonabai and her children, schooling still was.

She chose to keep Mandakini at home and sent her son to school.

The choice was clear for Sonabai—she didn't have enough money to educate two children, and educating a girl child was not a priority for her. So, Mandakini ended up being completely unlettered. She minded her younger brother until he was old enough to go to school. But with no firm parental hand to guide him, he was half-hearted about his studies. 'I had to choose between earning a living or sitting outside his school all day to keep him in class. I knew what was more important,' says Sonabai, now full of regret that she could not do better by her son. For he ended up as a petty thief when he grew up and is frequently in and out of jail even today.

Nearly two decades after Sonabai made those hard life decisions, Mandakini (now called Manda) was married off to an older man, and history repeated itself as her husband also blew up every paisa he earned as a mason on alcohol. Manda had four children and did domestic work to sustain the family. She had two sons and two daughters and soon realized that she needed to do something to improve their future prospects. She did not want them to be illiterate like herself. Moreover, she did not want her sons to turn to robbery and dacoity like her brother, who by then had had several brushes with the law and could not find a regular job.

After considerable thought, Manda 'sacrificed' her first-born son to the Goddess and, like her mother, separated from her husband. This was no blood sacrifice, however. Manda simply decided to abandon her elder son to the care of his father even though she knew that wouldn't be good for the boy. But her husband would never have let her go with her two daughters and youngest son, then barely six months old, if she had not surrendered the custody of her eldest son to him. Manda has not seen her husband or son since the day she left the family home, but she believes her sacrifice was well worth it.

For that decision enabled Manda's older daughter to study

up to class VI before getting married to a carpenter who has his own modest business. The couple has two daughters who go to school, which is now free for girls in Maharashtra. Manda's younger daughter completed her schooling and is training to be a nurse. Manda managed to salvage her daughter's lives by doing the same kind of road works that her mother had done several years ago.

But construction work played havoc with her health, and she was forced to return to being a domestic help. Domestic work does not pay too well and therefore, Manda was not able to raise the college fees for her younger son, who wanted to enrol in a commerce college. He is too educated to follow in his mother's footsteps, and anyway, she will not have him do such menial labour. She is worried that her sacrifice all those years ago will come to nought if her younger son, who now hangs out with his friends at roadside dhabas, ends up as a vagabond.

Nearly thirty years apart, both Sonabai and Manda were the beneficiaries of the Maharashtra government's employment guarantee scheme. But while Sonabai's generation could have benefitted only in Maharashtra, Manda's generation was luckier as the scheme had by then been extended throughout India and began to have a lasting effect on the fortunes of the poor everywhere.

That is because when the Congress unexpectedly raced ahead of the BJP in the 2004 Lok Sabha elections and its United Progressive Alliance formed the government at the Centre, it came up with a unique scheme for the poor. At the time, the Congress Party controlled at least 14 states across India. Sonia Gandhi, the party president and chairperson of the UPA, held a conclave of her chief ministers soon after forming the government at the Centre, and asked each state to present at least one scheme that defined the state. She said she would choose the scheme best suited to the Centre, and this scheme would be implemented all over the country.

It goes without saying that Maharashtra was the winner with its Employment Guarantee Scheme (EGS), which opened the gates for the poor in the rest of India. Maharashtra had many other pioneering schemes, but Vilasrao Deshmukh, who was chief minister of the state at the time, presented EGS to his party president, confident that it would become the stellar scheme of the UPA. EGS had been Maharashtra's social safety net for the poor for at least three decades before the Centre adopted it as the Mahatma Gandhi National Rural Employment Generation Scheme (MGNREGA).

The drought of 1972–74 was very severe throughout the state. Much was made of the recent spell of drought in Marathwada because of the widespread media attention, but the situation was much worse in the 1970s. At that time, India was recovering from the 1971 war with Pakistan to liberate Bangladesh, and faced a severe water shortage. Water was scarce not only in the villages but also in the cities where water cuts were imposed—at that time bottled drinking water did not exist.

Villages across Maharashtra were in the grip of drought and cattle were dying by the hundreds. People were migrating in search of work, but there was none to be found anywhere in the state. One evening in those dark days, two of the last Gandhians in the Congress—they were still wearing khadi kurtas, dhotis and Gandhi topis and had not switched to the safari suits that had become synonymous with politicians in that decade—came together over dinner and began to discuss ways to resolve the crisis. These two Gandhians are the real unsung heroes of the Employment Guarantee Scheme, which has now been declared by the United Nations as the best rural security scheme anywhere in the world.

Those two heroes need not have bothered to find a solution to the prevailing crisis since it wasn't their responsibility. But it was an era when Congress rule was supreme and Congressmen had not yet begun to place self above the party. Their names were V.S. Page and T.S. Bharde and they were the chairman of the Maharashtra Legislative Council and speaker of the state assembly respectively.

Their hearts truly spoke for the poor. They took their idea to then Chief Minister Vasantrao Naik who jumped at it, and it was officially adopted as government policy at the next Congress shibir (camp), which was a frequent Congress activity at that time.

In the 1970s, Maharashtra, like the rest of India, was still developing and much work needed to be done on building infrastructure, including roads, government housing, airports as well as institutions, research centres, etc. Page and Bharde were of the view that infrastructure should be developed in advance, even if it was not immediately required, to provide jobs for hungry villagers. The benefit of this development would be that when such infrastructure was actually required, it would already be available and time and effort would not be wasted in building the facilities.

Why not start right away, they declared, so that villagers could be given employment. Thus, in the 1970s and 1980s, infrastructure was developed throughout the districts of Maharashtra—brand new buildings, roads that were used only by bullock carts, airports that became just picnic spots etc., came up as the government successfully battled the hunger crisis arising out of the severest drought the country had faced until then.

Even Deshmukh, who was then the Zilla Parishad president in Latur, jumped to take advantage of the scheme. Marathwada had poor rail and road connectivity and it would take years (2008) for the first train to roll out of Mumbai to Latur. Until then the people of Latur district, which in 2015 experienced its worst-ever drought and then complete inundation in 2016, had to motor down to Solapur or Hyderabad and take either a train or a flight respectively, from those cities to reach Mumbai. There were only three airports in Maharashtra at the time—Mumbai, Pune and Nagpur—of which Pune's airport was protected since it was under the control of the Indian Air Force.

Deshmukh made sure that whenever the skies opened up, his constituency of Latur would have an airport ready and waiting. It took three decades for the first flight to take off from Latur, but when it did, not much work was needed to get the airport ready. It had been built to civil aviation specifications under EGS and the same workers, labouring under the same scheme for decades, made sure that the tarmac was kept in perfect shape for private and smaller government aircraft to land in Latur. The first commercial flight took off from this EGS-built airport barely a few years ago, in 2010.

Thus, MGNREGA did not come as a novelty to Maharashtra and its politicians. The state government first introduced a 2 per cent professional tax for all salaried employees in the state, whether in public or private enterprises, to raise funds for the scheme. Many people were outraged, for at the time no one understood this concept of social responsibility. Some people even petitioned the courts, pleading that they could not be taxed twice for the same income.

The Bombay High Court examined the government's case closely and ruled in its favour, stating that the more fortunate urban salaried class owed it to their rural brethren to alleviate their misery. The Maharashtra government, for years, kept a separate account for the funds raised through this professional tax. The drought ended in 1974, but the government continued to budget for EGS separately, and when Deshmukh presented it to his party president in 2004, the scheme was still in active use in Maharashtra. Deshmukh told me that both Sonia Gandhi and the then Prime Minister Manmohan Singh had been impressed by this concept of guaranteed employment to the rural masses in times of distress.

The scheme was modified by the UPA to work even in normal times and ensure at least a hundred days of employment to one person per family across the country. Unlike the opposition to the scheme by various political parties nationwide when it was first introduced at the Centre, Maharashtra's political parties had wholeheartedly supported this brainchild of the Vasantrao Naik government in the 1970s. Their only condition was '*paije tithe kaam, kaamache daam ani thithech vishraam*', meaning 'whoever wanted work should be given it, paid a fair wage for it and also be offered shelter close to the place of work', so that they would not have to travel to and from their villages. The shelter was important because this development work, which was akin to killing two birds with one stone (alleviating rural distress and contributing to nation-building at the same time), was not always available to people close to their villages.

The government accepted this condition of the opposition and shelters came up close to the places of work. In many instances, the women were given priority over the men and adequate shelters had to be provided for all the women workers to ensure their security. The EGS, in some ways, also spawned the food security scheme in Maharashtra because these women demanded rations instead of cash for their labour—idle husbands were likely to snatch away their money and blow it up on alcohol, but a kilo of rice or wheat and dal would go a long way in feeding entire families. The government institutionalized the system and EGS also began to be known loosely as the 'Food for Work' programme. 'Food for Work' is common parlance in the nation today, thirty years after it first appeared in Maharashtra state's political lexicon with little fuss or formality.

It is surprising that in the thirty years or more that EGS was being implemented in Maharashtra, no other state in India thought of adopting it to tackle their own rural poverty and unemployment. Even after the UPA passed the National Rural Employment Guarantee Act and began implementing its flagship programme from 2005, for some years there was bitter opposition to the scheme, with its critics calling it a waste of money and resources. Admittedly, there was corruption and some leakage, but in the dozen odd years of the scheme, there has been visible alleviation of rural poverty thanks to the hundred days of employment guaranteed to villagers and unemployment dole provided to them in the absence of work. These measures were added to the original Maharashtra scheme for more equitable benefits.

After initial opposition to the scheme, opposition leader L.K. Advani praised MGNREGA in the United Nations General Assembly in 2012. Advani described it as the 'best scheme for rural empowerment', which had helped to break down social inequalities and build rural infrastructure. But his fellow party leader Narendra Modi, then the chief minister of Gujarat, did not agree. Even after he became prime minister he sneered at the Congress, saying, 'Do you think I will put an end to the scheme? My political wisdom does not allow me to do so. This is a living monument to your failure to tackle poverty in sixty years. With song and dance and drumbeat, I will continue the scheme.'

He did continue the scheme but without the song and dance or drumbeat. In the meantime, there was fulsome praise for MGNREGA from both the United Nations Development Programme and the Obama administration in the United States. They described it as the best social security scheme anywhere in the world. Modi then changed his mind and was full of praise for MGNREGA, prompting Congress Vice President Rahul Gandhi to taunt him over his political wisdom in continuing with the scheme. Whatever the political one-upmanship, the fact remains that without the stellar minds of Maharashtra's past generation, the scheme would never have seen the light of day. And the credit clearly must go to the political parties and leaders in the state who had the wisdom to realize the impact the scheme would have on the rural poor.

14

Darubandi

When women get 'drunk' on success.

*P*arvati Mali, so the story goes, was poisoned. Parvati was the sarpanch of Vashi village in Kolhapur district in the late 2000s and was among the first women in this region to raise her voice against the proliferation of liquor dens. But before she could set in motion the process for a shutdown of these dens, some vested interests lured her to a private party and poisoned her food. They say that her alcoholic husband was among those who celebrated.

Sunita Mahadeo Shinde was luckier. She lived to tell her tale. Sunita was the sarpanch of Vathar village when she received petitions from the suffering wives of several drunks in her village who demanded that the local liquor store be shut down. When she started the process to shut it, eleven of the fourteen gram panchayat members moved a motion of no-confidence against her and she lost her job.

'I was thrown out but I made sure the process was complete before that. I may not be the sarpanch anymore but there is no longer a liquor shop in my village, either. We shut down the liquor store one day, they got a new sarpanch two days later. It was a sacrifice well worth making,' Sunita told me during a meeting at her friend's home. Meeting her openly in her home would have put her at risk as she is still among the most hated women in the village. She is unable to move around freely and does not even venture out to the market. Believing there is safety in numbers, she is surrounded by friends and family when she does go out.

Though it has been over two decades since former Chief Minister Sharad Pawar brought forward a law, in an amendment to the Bombay Prohibition Act, that gave women the right to shut down liquor stores across villages in the state, there has been a sudden spurt of 'darubandi' activity all across Maharashtra. Every day brings with it a new tale of a village fighting to shut down its liquor dens. If anti-corruption activist Anna Hazare had paid a little heed to the laws in his own home state in 2012 when he launched an agitation in New Delhi for a Lokpal, he would have had little to protest about. Instead of tying young men to trees and whipping them into giving up alcohol as he avowed, he could have spurred the women of his village to sue for shutting down liquor stores. The task would have been accomplished with less pain and humiliation for all.

It was in 1994 that the Pawar government gave women in the villages of Maharashtra the right to seek closure of liquor shops if more than 25 per cent of them were troubled by drunken husbands, sons or other family members. The collector has to conduct a secret ballot (referendum) among the women, and if more than 50 per cent of them vote for closure, the liquor shop is shut down in an hour. There is no case for appeal.

This, of course, has not gone down well with the liquor shop owners, and they have tried everything they can to avoid being busted. One year in Siddhnerli village in Kolhapur district, one country liquor shop and three beer bar owners teamed up to try their luck with the courts. They filed petitions in every court in the vicinity with a certificate from one of the gram sevaks saying that their shops were outside the village precincts and therefore, a shutdown was illegal. One court ordered a stay. The village women found out about it only a few hours before the voting on the referendum. An angry sarpanch, Suvarna Kamble, then locked down the gram panchayat office saying there would be no development work until these shops were closed. The Darubandi Samiti in this village, comprising more men than women (they jocularly refer to themselves as the 'Darubandi' Party), promptly brought in a 'talati' to measure the distance and found that the shops were not just well within the village borders but also less than 100 metres from the local primary school.

When liquor shop owners are not misleading the courts, they are harassing the women in other ways, says Sulochana Patil, a former president of the Bachat Samiti, of Bhadole village's gram panchayat. 'We voted one year on Gauri puja day. The men had conspired with local officials to make sure that as few of us turned up as possible. But we decided we would rather miss our puja than the voting. Then, they paid five hundred rupees each to the drinking men of the village to steal their wives' voter ID cards. We found these in the liquor store during a raid we conducted the night before. And, of course, physical threats to the women are commonplace.'

But the women manage to stand their ground because they have a good deal of help from the non-drinking men in the village. These men help the women find strength and courage by backing up their activities, filing caveats in courts and making sure the drunks do not interrupt the voting process.

Meanwhile, life has changed for Tanubai Dhondiram Vadd of Bhadole who has spent nearly fifty years living with a drunk for a husband. But while Tanubai's life has improved and she has money to buy clothes and food, the same cannot be said for Aknabai Shivram Chavan of Vathar. The men in her family, including her father-in-law and his father, have been drunks for generations. Her husband died of alcohol and her sons are alcoholics, too. The village shut its liquor store but Aknabai's family has found another outlet in nearby Vadgaon. Vadgaon is covered by a municipal council, not a gram panchayat, and this law is applicable only to villages.

The Maharashtra government has proposed to extend the law beyond the villages to the areas under the jurisdiction of municipal councils, to prevent the men from getting drunk. All this is happening in the midst of fierce opposition from sugar barons, who want an outlet for the molasses generated by their sugar factories, and the liquor mafia, which has been suffering major losses since the darubandi campaign in the villages of Maharashtra took off. There are entire talukas that have become free of liquor shops since the village women of Maharashtra realized what a boon this law was for them and their families.

It is a unique law, which exists nowhere else in the world except Maharashtra, and Bihar Chief Minister Nitish Kumar and the then chief minister of Tamil Nadu, the late Jayalalithaa, who had promised to shut down the liquor shops in their states, need not have looked further than Maharashtra and could have adopted this Maharashtra model of social reform. It empowers women, gives them the right to choose their own way of life, is not patronizing, and does not impose upon the freedoms of the people.

This unique liquor policy is one of Sharad Pawar's landmark achievements. Pawar wanted to attract the votes of women in the 1995 state elections by giving them the power to shut down liquor stores so that the men in their families and villages would stop drinking. The policy was slow to take off—most women did not notice the new liquor policy then—and Sharad Pawar's government was voted out of power, receiving a major drubbing in the assembly elections that year. But, by and by, women realized that they did not need an Anna Hazare to tie drunkards to a tree and beat them up until they fell in line. In the two decades since that policy became law, village after village has held a referendum and banned alcohol.

Although there are whole districts now that are alcohol-free, this status has not come without a struggle. As we have seen, women sarpanches who have taken the lead in banning alcohol in their villages have been threatened by the liquor mafia. The process does not come without the inherent bribery and corruption— attempts are made to influence officials to rig the results, women are threatened on voting day, sometimes tied to furniture in their own homes by their husbands, many of them go into hiding, surfacing minutes before voting commences, even collectors are sometimes threatened from declaring the results. But the policy has succeeded to such an extent that it has become difficult to persuade governments to overturn it. Of course, vote bank politics is involved—no one in government dares to antagonize one half of the population and lose votes. Losing revenue is a far safer bet!

The policy is unique in more ways than one because it has compelled chief ministers to stand firm in their support of women, even at the risk of annoying their own party men and supporters. In the fifteen years of the Congress-NCP regime, run largely by sugar barons, many ministers sought ways and means to maximize revenues as well as their own personal gains. Shutting down liquor stores meant huge losses in excise duties, but the sugar barons also needed to find an end use for the molasses generated in their factories. They tried many tricks to overturn the policy but to no avail.

Sharad Pawar might be remembered for many things not too savoury or sweet, but the rural women of Maharashtra largely associate him with making their lives less miserable thanks to the liquor policy. It has given them a sense of empowerment—and it is not only the women sarpanches and panchayat samiti members who feel this way. Even the ordinary housewife in the village feels she has a right to live her life on her own terms.

There could not be a better policy for the empowerment of rural women whose lives are defined by drink and the resultant penury, than this. It enables them to not only take charge of their once miserable existence, but to also put together more pennies for the future. Even if they are not trained for any work, they can save money by the simple expedient of stopping every paisa earned by their husbands from going into the pockets of liquor barons. Maharashtra, once again, has opened the gateway to progress—one wonders if it will again take thirty years or more for the Centre or the other states to notice. Or is it fear of the liquor mafia and the inability to resist the funds provided by the liquor lobby that stops other states from adopting a similar policy? It would need exemplary courage and commitment, but it can be done, as Maharashtra has shown.

15

Taking the Bull by the Horns

The beef ban has left farmers stomping and raging.

Shankarbhau runs a very successful vegetable business in Nagpur, away from the popular markets and the sabzi mandis. Some years ago, he set up shop in a corner of a posh residential area in Chief Minister Devendra Fadnavis's constituency. His vegetables are fresh, and if you miss going to his stall early in the morning, you are likely to find them sold out. Shankarbhau does not believe in stale vegetables, so you never find slightly soft tomatoes, potatoes with eyes, yellowed coriander leaves or even brittle onions at his stall. His vegetables may be slightly higher in price than those of other vendors, but people do not mind because the quality of his vegetables, sourced individually from farms around the city, is not found in any other stall in the city.

But lately, you do sometimes see rotten tomatoes, yellowing leafy vegetables and soft cucumbers, placed at one side of his stall. These vegetables are not for sale. They are meant for the stray animals that visit Shankarbhau's vegetable stall. There has been a proliferation of cows on the streets of Nagpur lately, and many of these animals (including bulls) somehow find their way to Shankarbhau's vegetable stall. At first, he used to hop off his high perch in the middle of all his vegetables and shoo them away. Then he employed an extra hand exclusively for the job. Finally, he decided it was better to give the animals what they were looking for—food. Shankarbhau has figured out that these animals are all 'anaath' (orphans). No one owns them for they have been abandoned by farmers in nearby villages who can no longer afford to keep them on their farms and feed them through the drought.

When the Maharashtra government decided to completely ban beef in the state—including the meat of bulls and male calves—making even the possession of beef non-bailable and punishable by five years in prison (the courts have since struck down this section), the consumers of beef were not the only ones affected. Farmers were up in arms too.

Cow slaughter was banned in Maharashtra—as it was in many other states—in 1975. But when the Shiv Sena-BJP alliance came to power in 1995, among their first acts—apart from changing the name of Bombay to Mumbai—was to bring forward a bill that sought to ban the slaughter of bulls as well as calves. Mumbai houses Asia's biggest abattoir at Deonar, a northern suburb, and it always did brisk business with truckloads of animals being brought to the city even from the neighbouring state of Gujarat and from as far north as Rajashtan and Uttar Pradesh. When the members of the butchers' association of Mumbai first heard of the total ban on beef, they made a beeline for Matoshree, Bal Thackeray's residence, to plead their case.

They pleaded that they were not slaughtering cows because it was against the law. But bulls and buffaloes were a different matter altogether—the law specified that the progeny of the cow could be slaughtered only on certification of it being unfit for agriculture and that is exactly what they were doing. However, that was only the partial truth. Cows, according to the law, could be slaughtered only after they had reached the unproductive age of fourteen years. But with India competing with Brazil and other markets for beef exports, who, after all, would want to eat the flesh of old animals?

The law about certification had a loophole, however. Farmers across India who did not wish to sustain more animals than they needed would sell them off at cattle markets, and these animals would then be categorized as 'fit' or 'otherwise'.

The animals in the 'otherwise' category were physically fit, but not economical for agriculture. Touts would often break their legs or bust one of their eyes and starve them in the sun and heat to make them look weak and useless. Veterinarians then had few qualms about certifying them as unfit. Once this certificate was obtained by the traders, the animals were taken to cooler environs, their thirst quenched with ample troughs of water, and they were then fed well and, literally, fattened for the slaughter.

Bal Thackeray was aware of this strategy, but he listened to the complaints of the butchers' associations anyway. After gold exports from India, leather exports made for considerable returns. For example, India, even then, was not only among the leading beef exporters, but its cowhide was among the most coveted and made for the most lucrative trade in the business. At that time, there was also a strong suspicion that animal rights activists funded from abroad were working to destroy India's monopoly in the international market. And Thackeray was nothing if not a true-blue nationalist. So he conceded the point to the butchers' associations, and the Maharashtra government did nothing further in the matter.

Thus, bulls and male calves continued to be led to slaughter until the Maharashtra government, now led by the BJP, in early 2015, abruptly resurrected the bill, which had been put into cold storage, and sent it to New Delhi for presidential assent. This complete ban on beef was aimed in particular at the Muslim minorities whose entire communities (the Qureshis) have been in the business of beef trade for generations. It was presumed that all Muslim minorities were consuming beef by the kilos every day.

This intrusion into their kitchens did not go down well with Muslims. It also affected large sections of the non-Muslim population, including farmers, nomadic tribes, other adivasis and Dalits in the state and elsewhere in the country, where the ban has been copied in toto on the lines of the Maharashtra Act, and imposed with strictness and no mercy. According to Prakash Ambedkar, grandson of Dr B.R. Ambedkar and president of the Bharip Bahujan Mahasangh, Muslims have been the least affected by the government's beef ban. 'This was a cheap meat and so preferred by large sections of Muslims. All that they have had to do now is shift to slightly more expensive meat, like goat, lamb and chicken. There has not been much disturbance otherwise in their lives.'

This is not quite true. For poorer Muslims in the trade, there were no options and they have been quietly driven out of business. But the story is slightly different for the reasonably well off. When private abattoirs run by members of their community shut down almost overnight in the wake of the ban, many people in the community were enterprising enough to find other areas of business to sustain themselves. 'But the most affected are the farmers, many of whom are Hindu and vegetarian to begin with. The government has now pushed them to even more penury by effecting this beef ban.'

Ambedkar points to Marathwada, which was reeling under severe drought. Under the circumstances, the ban on the slaughter of bulls now means there is no market for even water buffaloes who are as much milk-givers as cows, but who are otherwise of no use in ploughing fields or for other agricultural purposes. The price of these animals has crashed in the markets.

'There is a particularly beautiful buffalo breed called Khilari. The animal is a very fine specimen, very beautiful to look at and coloured an even grey. So, it is very much in demand in the villages. Before this beef ban, one such animal would fetch a minimum of one and a half lakh rupees in the cattle market. A fine and healthy Khilari buffalo could sell for even four lakh rupees in good times.

But now there are no buyers. No one is willing to pay even twenty thousand rupees for the best breed in cattle. Had the beef ban not been effected, the farmer could have sold just one animal for one and a half lakh rupees and sustained himself through the drought season. Now the farmer is dying in lean seasons and so are his animals,' says Ambedkar.

That is why Shankarbhau finds so many stray and abandoned cows and bulls herding around his vegetable stall. Farmers have driven them to the cities and left them to fend for themselves. There are now noticeably more animals in Mumbai and other cities of Maharashtra. At Shankarbhau's stall, the animals at least get vegetables to eat, even if not fresh or of the best quality. But more often than not, these animals are found browsing around garbage dumps, eating rubbish and bedding down for the night on roads and highways, affecting traffic. Sometimes they are mowed down by heavy vehicles, and there is no one to claim their carcasses. For, the cow vigilantism around the country has ensured that even if people traditionally empowered to skin cows and dispose of their carcasses—like Dalits and Banjaras—try to do their jobs, they may be beaten, humiliated or otherwise harassed or even criminalized by the police, who do not apply their minds to the law and get swayed by the vigilantes.

Ambedkar does not agree that the policy was 'short-sighted'. 'It is not short-sighted. It is rather long-sighted, I would say. It is a purely religiously-oriented policy and it is the RSS's way of not considering anybody, including other Hindus, as their family except for their core supporters and believers in their ideology.'

Beef is scientifically considered to be a 'protein meat' while lamb and other meats are 'fat meats', he says. That is why, for centuries, nomadic tribes, adivasis and Dalits, in that order, were heavily dependent on beef to sustain their protein needs. The fact that the price of dal and other pulses is more than four times that of beef seems to have escaped the government's attention. No wonder, says Ambedkar, that children born since 2015–16 to nomadic tribes and other adivasis are even more stunted and malnourished than usual. 'The mothers have not been getting adequate nutrition while carrying the children and it has also affected their milk, which has led the children to being more undernourished than ever before.'

Even the vegetarian farmers, however, are raging at the Maharashtra government. Balu Shinde, a farmer from Sangli in western Maharashtra, which is supposed to be prosperous but has some talukas affected by drought, says all he needs is one pair of bullocks soon after the monsoon to till his fields. 'When it rains, the soil gets mushy and sometimes it is not possible to run a tractor through that kind of land. That is when I need to harness a pair of bullocks to plough the fields and prepare them for the first sowing. Once the rains have receded, the bullocks are of no use to me. I would otherwise drive them to the post-monsoon cattle markets in September/October and sell them off for a good price. This year and the last I could not do that. Now I am saddled with more animals than I need, and I do not have enough fodder and water for them all.'

Shinde says the government is living in the dark if it believes that the trade and slaughter of such animals will cease completely only because of the ban. 'All that it has done is to drive this business underground. Bulls are still being slaughtered. But it is we who are suffering, we are not getting the right price for our animals. And why should I sell when I cannot even recover half what I paid for them and their sustenance? When I begin to find it impossible to keep them on my farm any longer, I will turn them loose as many others have already done.'

Shinde may be finding it difficult to sustain his animals, but at least he can afford to abandon them in the city. There are other farmers who are not as insouciant. They have very few animals to begin with and have been haunting the depleted cattle markets to get a good price for their cattle. If they don't get it, they fear they won't have any money for seeds in the next season, despite a good monsoon. And without the seeds, they are afraid they will be finished altogether.

'Are these animals more important to the government or do they not care about what happens to farmers at all?' asks Bhaurao Patil, another farmer who is hopping mad at how governmental authority has interfered with farming cycles in the villages. 'As though the rain gods were not doing enough damage to begin with and now this...' he says, swallowing his anger and pointing in the general direction of his cattle.

The sentiments of the farmers have not quite escaped politicians from the hinterland. When the beef ban was imposed, it evoked no protests from the Congress, but the Shiv Sena and the NCP were both troubled—the Sena, perhaps, because they had an understanding of the issue from Bal Thackeray's time. The NCP is a party that is more representative of farmers in the villages, and with Sharad Pawar being a former agriculture minister, the NCP was able to understand the significance of the beef ban and the impact it would have on the farm economies.

In the late 1990s, while speaking to farmers during a massive rally in an idiom they could understand, Pawar tried to tell them what they must do with the non-performing Shiv Sena-BJP government: 'When your bull just sits down and refuses to get up, what do you do? You first kick it or beat it with a stick. Then you get a pin and poke it deep so that it hurts its thick hide and compels him to rise. When even that does not work, you must push a rope through its nose and drag it to the cattle market to sell it off. There is no use keeping an unproductive animal on your farm.'

Then Chief Minister Manohar Joshi was enraged at this remark and responded, 'Send your cow to us and we will show you what our bull can really do!' The farmers chose to sell the bull in the market rather than take Joshi up on his offer. Today, these political metaphors are once again resonating around the villages of Maharashtra, which is something that has not escaped the political grassroots. Now even legislators from the BJP who understand the ground realities are beginning to worry. They are well aware of the distress the beef ban has caused to the farmers, and one of their legislators from Maharashtra, Bhimrao Dhonde, has gone on record to say, 'It is time to reconsider the ban.'

But there is a typical rural-urban divide in the BJP with its leaders saying sufficient funds would be provided to farmers to tide over their distress, and that the government was in the process of constructing goshalas for the abandoned animals. However, there is not much evidence of this construction on the ground. The Maharashtra government did open some shelters for animals in the immediate wake of the ban—250,000 heads of cattle are housed in these shelters across the state but only, as the government says, 'until their owners are ready to take them back'. This may never happen, for according to some estimates, there are around 40 lakh heads of cattle loose across Maharashtra, and it will not be possible to build shelters for them all—the farmers would not have abandoned these cattle if they had any intention of keeping them in the first place.

Now even the Vishwa Hindu Parishad, which had initially taken responsibility for building the shelters, has demanded that the government should do more. Laxmi Narayan Chandak, head of the VHP's Maharashtra cattle shelter unit, has been quoted as saying, 'Nearly seven lakh cows and bulls will starve to death or will be smuggled to slaughter houses. We have to save them.'

But how? Nobody has the answer.

Nevertheless, this is an inadvertent admission of the failure of the government's beef ban policy—far from saving the cow, the beef ban has driven the slaughter underground and, in the process, removed all the existing controls on the statute. These controls ensured that female animals under the age of fourteen were not sent to abattoirs until they were truly economically unviable. The slaughter of their male counterparts was also governed by the existing laws.

Bhaurao says rather cynically, 'When have bans ever worked? You brought darubandi into the villages but has alcohol disappeared from the panchayat areas? Gutkha has been banned but you still get it at five times the price than when it was legal. Similarly with this beef ban, you have driven the business underground. All that has happened is that beef has now become a rarity, an exotic food for rich tables. The traders and the butchers make a fast buck even if they have to do it in a hush-hush fashion. The poor consumer and the farmer who should have really benefitted have been put to extreme trouble and penury.'

Shinde adds, 'The government does not want us to sell the cattle. Okay. But then it has to give us the maintenance cost of each animal that we have to forcibly keep on our farms. Because they have made the law such that we cannot sell at full prices and the merchants take advantage of our distress, then sell the cattle to the abbatoirs at more than double the prices before the ban. Who loses? Just the farmer!'

Ambedkar says that contrary to its purpose, the ban has been the least painful for Muslims, even if it was aimed at the minority community. While Advocate Y.H. Muchala, who has represented the Bombay Suburban Beef Dealers Welfare Association in the Bombay High Court, asks if the ban was meant to cater to Hindu sentiments, Ambedkar points to the lakhs of Hindus who are suffering because of it. 'But probably nomads, adivasis and Dalits are not the Hindus that the BJP wants to people its ranks with.'

It goes without saying, then, that the BJP-led government in Maharashtra did not quite understand either the dynamics or the economics of the beef ban when it passed the law without debate. Other governments, including Haryana, followed. A few months later, a Muslim blacksmith was killed in Dadri in Uttar Pradesh on the mere suspicion that he had stored beef in his refrigerator.

A forensic examination later revealed that the meat belonged to a goat. But the question remains whether the life of the blacksmith was less precious than that of an animal, which was not even slaughtered. Some months later, a Muslim man and a teenage boy who were taking their buffaloes to the cattle market were lynched and hanged from a tree in Latehar in Jharkhand. Then Dalits in Una in Gujarat who were skinning a dead cow were beaten up, tied to a vehicle and paraded through the streets by cow vigilantes. That led to a massive uprising of Dalits in that state and has redefined caste equations in the country. Then in April 2017, Pehlu Khan, a dairy farmer from Rajasthan who was legitimately transporting milch animals from Haryana, was lynched by cow vigilantes despite the fact that he had all the papers to show for the sale. There have been more lynchings even after this. Ambedkar says that the focus of all those incidents was entirely religious and had little to do with other considerations.

For centuries, Maharashtra has taken the lead among Indian states with regard to every reformist and socially progressive measure. However, cattle slaughter and trade is one area where the state has led the country to regression. The rest of India should have locked the door to this particular gateway and thrown away the key.

ALL AT THE CROSSROADS

There are two ways to go when you hit that crossroads in your life:
There is the bad way, when you sort of give up, and then there is
the really hard way, when you fight back...

—Matthew Perry

The whole modern world has divided itself into Conservatives and
Progressives. The business of Progressives is to go on making
mistakes. The business of Conservatives is to prevent mistakes from
being corrected.

—G.K. Chesterton

16

Winking in the Dark

The Congress is fast running out of ideas.

When Congress Vice President Rahul Gandhi visited Mumbai in January 2016, he told a group of editors at an informal chat that he and his party were 'looking for the next big thing' that would both define the Congress in the next decade and also resonate with the masses. 'I am talking to a lot of people to get ideas. We are searching for it. We do not yet know what it could be, but I am sure we will get there soon,' he said.

Congressmen, however, believe that Rahul Gandhi might be talking to the wrong kind of people, and the 'soon' could have been sooner if only Congress Party leaders had not dumped the party's decades old, tried and tested style of brainstorming. In the Lok Sabha elections of 2014, the Congress did astonishingly poorly, winning just 44 seats—it had never before fallen below the three digit mark, even in the worst of times. In the subsequent Vidhan Sabha elections, the party did marginally better, but it still lost half its seats in the assembly. In both these elections, the Congress did not have any dreams to sell to the people, and it had little to show besides its already existing flagship schemes like the MGNREGA, the land acquisition laws that gave farmers a better deal than before and the temptation of food security.

All these schemes were rubbished by the UPA's main challenger, the BJP, and its prime ministerial candidate Narendra Modi. The Congress was already reeling under the burden of big ticket corruption charges. 'I was speaking to Tony Blair the other day,' Rahul told the Mumbai editors. 'I asked him what was the one thing he regretted about his prime ministership. And he had no hesitation in telling me it was the British Right to Information Act.'

The RTI in India was another of the UPA's stellar achievements and, says former Chief Minister Prithviraj Chavan, 'It was the RTI that was responsible for the people's disillusionment with the Congress. All the cases of corruption that were exposed against the UPA government came through RTI applications. Now Modi is trying to crush democracy and suppress the RTI. He knows very well the havoc it can wreak with governments.'

The Congress, founded in 1885 and India's oldest political party, is in the twenty-first century a party of earnest greenhorns (including Party Chief Sonia Gandhi and former Prime Minister Manmohan Singh) who are honest in their purpose but are completely ignorant of the consequences of such earnestness. Rajiv Gandhi, after assuming the office of prime minister in 1984, had spoken about India having missed out on the industrial revolution. 'But we will not miss the IT revolution,' he had said.

The process of opening up the Indian economy began at that time, and computers and the latest in communication technology began to arrive in India in the late 1980s. This technological advancement was resisted by the BJP—former Prime Minister Atal Bihari Vajpayee, who was then opposition leader, came to Parliament House in a bullock cart, signifying his party's opposition to the modernization of technology. It might have seemed rather strange to neutral observers that the BJP should oppose growth in such terms, but Vajpayee, perhaps, had an inkling of the kind of damage that such modernization might cause to the large sections of poor and agrarian masses in the country.

Today Congressmen are among the first to admit that it is the liberalization of the Indian economy undertaken by Congress Prime Minister P.V. Narasimha Rao in 1991 that is the root cause of the decline of the Congress, not just in Maharashtra but across the country. Anant Gadgil, national spokesperson of the party and a member of the Maharashtra Legislative Council says, 'The Congress was always seen as a champion of the poor. I am not saying that we should not have opened up the economy. Today, there is a computer on every desk in every home in India, and every citizen has a mobile phone in his hands. But have we ever stopped to consider what opening up the economy has done to the poorer sections and particularly the farmers? Predators have got into the system. We have had no solutions about how to protect them against the market forces and how to help them make a smooth transition into the twenty-first century. The decline of the Congress has thus been simultaneous with the liberalization process in the country.'

The arrival of information technology and smartphones in the country has also meant that Congress leaders of the new generation have had to change their style of working and communicating with the masses. A veteran Congressman says, 'You want an appointment with Rahul Gandhi? Well, then you have to send him an email. His team will then sort the request along with others and it might take you days or even never to be able to meet him. The poor grassroots worker may have a mobile phone in his hand, but he uses it only for conversations, he has not even worked out how to send an SMS. How do you expect him to email the party leader?'

Thus, the Congress leadership lacks a connection with the masses. If Rahul Gandhi wants to generate ideas and arrive at the next big thing for the country, he should perhaps revive the old system of communication—the shibirs or camps that were held frequently in all the states and at the Centre as well, and were a place where party workers could interact with their leaders.

'These were the best means of communication. The idea for

the Employment Guarantee Scheme was thrown up at the Nashik shibir by Balasaheb Bharde in 1972. The idea for the cooperative movement came a little earlier at a shibir near Nagpur. The cooperative movement became the backbone of the Congress in Maharashtra,' says Gadgil, who is the son of former Congressman and Gandhian V.N. Gadgil. 'The problem with the party is a great disconnect with the masses, who may be just fourth class pass, but still have great grassroots ideas, whereas the computer whizz-kids are just that and go no further. Then, again, the party has been too reliant on moneybags to win elections instead of depending on the grassroots work of hundreds of supporters to connect with the masses.'

Gadgil's critique is reflective of the majority of party workers who have stayed loyal to the Congress but have found their authority and rights usurped by 'newcomers' from other parties who are entrusted with its fortunes, but are clueless about what resonates with its supporters. For example, in the Konkan region of Maharashtra, the Congress decided to completely hand over the reins to former Maharashtra minister Narayan Rane, an import from the Shiv Sena (he has since quit the party and formed one of his own). He brought with him an abrasive, dictatorial style of working that rubbed party workers the wrong way and alienated its voters in the process.

'That is not quite true,' says Hussain Dalwai who believes the majority of the people in the region are still positively inclined towards the Congress. But though he might wish to soft-pedal Rane, the fact is the style that went down well with the Shiv Sena did not work at all with the Congress, and Rane himself lost his base in his home constituency of Kankavli. While his son lost the Lok Sabha election, Rane lost the assembly election not once but twice, once from Konkan and within months, a by-election in his home turf in Bandra in Mumbai. He soon found himself driven out of the Congress.

'Even Mrs Indira Gandhi who was dictatorial used to know party workers by name. She used to listen to them as much as to her advisers and others. But then she used to make up her own mind. We now have rootless wonders advising our party leaders who are fast losing the connect with the masses,' says another Congressman. Radhakrishna Vikhe Patil puts it succinctly, 'If you look at the two leaders of the two main political parties, Modi is here,' he raises his hand above his head, 'and Rahul Gandhi is here,' he brings his hand down to his waist. 'There is just no comparison.'

Chavan is not as direct but says the Congress was not in such a poor situation until 2013. 'Then we had the phenomenon of Narendra Modi streaking across India—his use of the Hindi language and television medium that brought him to every home in the country, his rhetoric, his in-your-face rather abusive style of campaigning which we, as a party of gentlemen, could not combat. All this lost us quite a lot in 2014 in both elections.'

But this was not the only reason for the Congress Party's defeat in the 2014 polls. The Congress's inability to define secularism, its uncertainty in deciding who it actually stood with in the liberalization debate, its half-hearted challenge to Modi's exaggerations and alleged untruths during the election campaign, all contributed to the party's resounding defeat. 'The Dalits and OBCs moved away from us towards Modi, though not necessarily to the BJP. The arrival of the AIMIM in Maharashtra also helped to swing the disenchanted Muslim vote towards them. There were many nuances and factors in that defeat,' says Chavan.

The failure, however, was also Chavan's, and that of the other Congress-led governments that had ruled Maharashtra for fifteen years and had done a considerable amount for the state without even laying claim to it. If the party had publicized its good work, it may have changed the people's impression that the Congress was just a party of the corrupt that did little for the people.

Anant Gadgil says, 'Only a quarter of the Mumbai-Pune

expressway was built by the Shiv Sena-BJP government from 1995–99. It was actually we who built it.' It was a project brought to the drawing board by Sharad Pawar when he was the chief minister of Maharashtra in 1994. Pawar had to attend an important gathering in Mumbai and had chosen to fly by helicopter from Pune to the state capital. The headwinds were so strong that the chopper could not make it over the Western Ghats. Pawar returned to Pune to shed a couple of passengers, some luggage and fuel. But that still did not make any difference.

He then had to travel by road. But traffic on the old Pune-Mumbai highway was such that it took him five hours to reach the gathering. Highly embarrassed, he decided he must have a road that would enable people to motor down to Mumbai from Pune in less than three hours. Then the government ran into land acquisition problems—the expressway was bifurcating villages on the route, which meant the villagers would have to travel all the way to Pune, Lonavla or Mumbai to reach the other side of the road to visit their relatives. Obviously, they refused to give up their land to this development.

The Pawar government then undertook a major exercise in persuasion. But soon it was out of power and Nitin Gadkari of the BJP arrived on the scene as the state's minister for public works. He bulldozed his way through all the objections of the village residents and started the road-building process in record time. 'Today, he and the BJP take massive credit for the expressway. No one in our party even challenges that or talks of other achievements like the toll-free eastern freeway in Mumbai that can take you from the northern suburbs to the city centre in twenty minutes, which was earlier costing you two or three hours of your time. And who developed the metros and other suburban transport for the masses? Even the coastal road now being considered by this government for Mumbai is our idea. We also brought in rural empowerment by giving the zilla parishads the right to decide their own futures by not being dependent on the MLAs or MPs for funds for development work. But we never talk about these things,' says Anant Gadgil.

Kakasaheb Gadgil, a Gandhian of Pandit Nehru's time, and Anant's grandfather, had once said in the 1960s, '*Prasidhi vina kaame mhanje andhaarat mulgi la dolya maarlya barobar*' (good work done without publicity is akin to winking at a girl in a dark room). That is very true of the Congress not just at the Centre but even in Mumbai and Maharashtra today. Much as they may dismiss Modi's tall claims during the 2014 campaign as hype, it is obvious that Modi's winking at everybody through their television screens blinded them to the Congress's achievements of the past ten years. But it is not just about winking at a girl in the dark—the Congress seems to have been winking in a dark empty room, without the girl even being there. They expected people to see through the dark, which did not happen.

Moreover, the party made poor choices while selecting leaders to head its state units during the years it was in power. Chavan was a good, honest man who tried to do his best as chief minister. But as Sharad Pawar had snorted when he first heard about the Congress move, 'He does not even know which road leads from Karad (Chavan's home constituency) to Mumbai! How does he expect to govern the state?'

That might have been a harsh assessment, but Chavan himself gave that credence when a few weeks later he told a group of women reporters on International Women's day, 'I have only come to Mumbai twice in the last several years, and only to meet the governor relating to some issue in my constituency. Otherwise, I would always fly from Pune to Delhi and back to and from Karad. But now I am learning on the job and I think I will soon have the measure.'

But that learning could not have competed with the learning of the other grassroots leaders whom the Congress chose not to empower out of its own misplaced considerations. Around the time

Chavan was chief minister, Manikrao Thakre, another gentleman with no roots among the people, was the state party president. There was not enough fire in either man's belly to take on Modi or even the state opposition leaders, leading to an inevitable depletion of the party's human resources.

Now the Congress has former Chief Minister Ashok Chavan, who is embroiled in an alleged scam, as its state party president. Ashok Chavan lost his job as chief minister owing to his role in the Adarsh housing scam. However, he was the sole reason why the Congress saved itself from a duck in Maharashtra during the 2014 assembly elections. The party won two seats out of 48— Chavan's constituency of Nanded and the neighbouring Parbhani constituency, both in Marathwada, that he helped to win. 'But without authority in our hand it is hardly possible to do anything for the people,' says Ashok Chavan. Unfortunately, while the Congress was in power, it was 'winking in the dark', unable to consolidate its achievements.

The import of leaders into the party is also manifest in the bitter fight underway between the Congress and the Shiv Sena for the control of the Brihanmumbai Municipal Corporation, which was slated for polls in early 2017. Leading the fight for the Congress was Sanjay Nirupam, the Mumbai Congress president, who came to the party from the Shiv Sena and displays the same aggressive style that is typical of Bal Thackeray's party. This rubbed many blue-blooded Congress loyalists the wrong way, and they were scoring self-goals by attempting to derail his efforts to win the 2017 municipal corporation election for the party.

For example, in December 2015, even as the Congress was celebrating Party President Sonia Gandhi's birthday in New Delhi, there was a report that the party mouthpiece *Congress Darshan* had published a critical article on Nehru and his Kashmir policy, and lauded Sardar Vallabhbhai Patel instead. The writer of the piece was later discovered to be an infiltrator, but no one has so far been able to establish whether he was an opposition mole or simply loyal to another faction in the party. Nevertheless, the leak to the media was accomplished by a rival Congressman who had hoped the exposé would help destabilize Nirupam. But a few days later, Rahul Gandhi stood by his city president and said, 'Everybody makes mistakes. I have decided to move on.'

But moving on might not be so easily accomplished in certain areas and there may be some mistakes that cannot be easily overcome. Congressmen at the grassroots are demanding a clear line of demarcation of leadership and authority in the party so that they know who they must work with in the future. A Congress leader, wishing anonymity, says, 'Soniaji seems to be in a state of semi-retirement. Rahul still considers himself a youth leader though he is long past the age. I do not know why he should be so obsessed with the youth. The youth can rally to an older leader and even look up to him like they did with Bernie Sanders (democratic presidential aspirant) in the United States in 2016. The youth did rally round Modi in 2014. Rahul is being a bit more combative than he was before. But it is not enough. We need to be more proactive rather than just react to the blunders of the ruling party.'

When it comes to blunders, there are many, says Gadgil. 'People are deeply disappointed with the BJP. But I am not sure if they are completely disillusioned as yet. I can see that they are beginning to look at the Congress again, but we need that active push to take us over the huge hump we are looking at now.'

What is troubling most party workers at the grassroots is the inability of the party to take on its rivals head on. For example, except for some taunts and barbs over Modi's suit and boot, and calling the government's black money policy 'fair and lovely' or the infamous 'khoon ki dalali' comment over the attempted politicization of the surgical strikes against Pakistan in September 2016 or the fallout of the demonetization, and labelling of the Goods and Services Tax (GST) as 'Gabbar Singh Tax', the Congress leadership at the Centre or even the state, has been unable to call a spade a spade. This was never more apparent than in the Maharashtra Legislative Assembly, when the Congress sided with the Shiv Sena and the BJP in March 2016 to suspend Waris Pathan, a member belonging to the AIMIM, who had refused to chant 'Bharat Mata Ki Jai'. However, he did not have any problem saying 'Jai Hind' or 'Hindustan Zindabad'.

'Jai Hind' is what Mrs Indira Gandhi used to say at the end of each public address, a practice started by Subhas Chandra Bose when he set up the Indian National Army, and which today is followed by both Sonia Gandhi and Rahul Gandhi. Yet Congressmen did not know how to react to this chant. Vikhe Patil, who is the leader of the opposition in the assembly, says rather sheepishly, 'I was having lunch in my office at the time and everything happened in such a blur that we did not have time to think and react.'

But that is a poor excuse and symptomatic of the directionless party that is slowly imploding. The Congress was startled by the AIMIM's success in the assembly elections of 2014, and its state leaders were for a long time toying with the idea of seeking an alliance with the party. While they did not get a green signal from their high command, they went to the other extreme, hating the AIMIM when its younger leader, Akbaruddin Owaisi, said, 'If the BJP and the AIMIM get together, we could finish the Congress completely.'

That was reminiscent of Modi's call for a Congress-mukt India, and so the Congress found itself stuck between the two extremes. It is unsure of challenging the Hindutva-oriented policies of the government full throttle, and at the same time it is clueless about how to combat parties like the AIMIM. However, Anant Gadgil believes they must let all other parties well alone. 'This entire era of coalition politics has had a very debilitating effect on all parties in the state. Each one of us is conceding ground to our alliance partners. That is why even the Shiv Sena and the BJP broke up and each did far better. We should now stay away from seeking alliances.'

Despite such sound advice, however, the Congress in Maharashtra is a party that has been left to fend for itself. No one is listening to the sane voices, and party leaders are in no hurry to change their style of functioning and broaden the party's base once again. If Rahul Gandhi does not come up with that definitive idea soon—for the state as well as for the country—the Congress Party could be left winking at no one at all, in broad daylight!

17

Fish Out of Water

*The Nationalist Congress Party finds it
impossible to survive without power.*

When I asked the late Dr Ramesh Prabhoo, a former mayor of Mumbai and at one time Shiv Sena supremo Bal Thackeray's physician, why he quit the NCP in just a few months to join the Maharashtra Navnirman Sena of Raj Thackeray, he told me rather tartly, 'Have you looked at that party closely? It has only leaders, there are no workers. Everyone wants to be chief minister there. Nobody wants to work for the party.'

Dr Prabhoo was the first ever Indian citizen to be disenfranchised by the Election Commission of India for making use of Hindutva in a 1987 by election to Maharashtra's assembly from Mumbai's Vile Parle constituency. He was then with the Shiv Sena and Thackeray, at the time, was making a paradigm shift from region to religion. Dr Prabhoo's sacrifice for his party leader was not valued enough by the GenNext of the party, and when he fell out with Uddhav Thackeray in 2004, Pawar invited him to join the NCP.

Pawar was then in a tussle with the Congress over Narayan Rane, who had made up his mind to quit the Shiv Sena but was not sure of which way to go. He was then persuaded by the Congress to join its ranks. Former Chief Minister Vilasrao Deshmukh had then advised Rane, 'Ultimately, the NCP will merge with the Congress. You will then have the advantage of being an older Congressman rather than coming along with a bunch of all potential chief ministers in the NCP. They are like bows without arrows.'

That, precisely, is the NCP's Achilles heel even today—it continues to be a party of leaders, all of whom are dreaming about heading the state one day, and no one is willing to work for the party at the grassroots. However, the NCP doesn't only suffer from a plethora of leaders in the party. In the rural hinterland, it has also become synonymous with the rural elite, more with Marathas and even more particularly with sugar barons. They are a much-hated lot in Maharashtra today and are conceding base to other parties, particularly the Shiv Sena, which is emerging as a credible alternative to the NCP's core voters.

When Sharad Pawar first split the Congress to form the NCP in 1999, he had complete faith and confidence, after three terms as the state's chief minister, that he would swing Maharashtra for his party. In the previous election to the Lok Sabha in 1998, at the head of the Congress, he had won 42 of the 48 seats to the Lok Sabha from Maharashtra and, in the mistaken belief that he counted for more than the Congress with the voters, he cold-bloodedly blackmailed the sugar barons into joining the NCP.

We have seen earlier in the book how the Pawars made cynical use of the apex cooperative bank to win stalwarts from the region over to their side. But if Pawar had been cold-blooded in bullying these leaders over to his party, they, too, had taken hard decisions with their heads rather than their hearts. One such leader was Chhagan Bhujbal. The other one was R.R. Patil.

I was sitting with other reporters in Chhagan Bhujbal's office one Sunday afternoon in the summer of 1999 when Bhujbal's phone rang. He was then the leader of the opposition in the Maharashtra Legislative Council. As he spoke into the phone he turned pale and nervous. 'It seems Pawar is planning to split the Congress,' he said, and after a little bit of silent brooding before us, left the room in a hurry. We did not see him for a couple of days after that and, it is said, he had secured himself away from the media's eyes either in Kottakal, Kerala, or in Guwahati, Assam, to take some time to consider if he should stay with the Congress or with the NCP.

His heart was with the Congress; he had been campaigning across Maharashtra, stoking emotions over how the widowed Sonia Gandhi had been raising 'kachcha bachchas' all on her own after the assassination of her husband, Rajiv Gandhi. A huge picture of Sonia Gandhi sat proudly side by side with one of Pawar's in his front office. Under the circumstances, it would be difficult for him to do a U-turn and say he would not support Sonia Gandhi owing to her foreign origins, which was the reason stated by Pawar for splitting the Congress—that he could not submit to the authority of a so-called foreigner.

Bhujbal, however, was not a blue-blooded Congressman. He had joined the party after splitting the Shiv Sena, and Pawar had stood behind him like the Rock of Gibraltar. He knew in his heart that he would not get that kind of support from any other leader in the Congress. So he decided to join Pawar, and the decision paid off when he was made deputy chief minister and home minister of the state.

Bhujbal had a good run for fifteen years, and despite the trouble he got into with regard to the alleged misutilization of funds while in government, Sharad Pawar always stood by him and is still standing by him—Pawar sent his daughter to the Arthur Road jail to meet Bhujbal when he was arrested by the Enforcement Directorate in March 2016. It was a signal to the other party members that Pawar had not abandoned his loyal soldier. It must have been of some comfort to Bhujbal that he had made the right choice in 1999 to support Pawar—for no one in the Congress would have stood by him, then or now, like Pawar had.

The late R.R. Patil, who later became a deputy chief minister and home minster in another Congress-NCP government, was another leader who disappeared underground to think hard about his choices in 1999. When he resurfaced and I questioned him about the long time he had taken to decide to join the NCP, he admitted honestly, 'Until now I have been campaigning round my district asking for votes in the name of Sonia Gandhi. How can I now turn around and abuse her? Will the people not throw stones at me? But then I had other interests to consider.'

Patil was not a sugar baron, but he did have interests in the cooperative sector and he knew these would be hurt if he did not switch sides to the NCP. But it was not just these two loyalists of Pawar who made hard choices—everyone in the NCP is with the party, not out of love for Pawar, but to protect their business interests. To these leaders, their business interests were crucial to their politics and although their hearts were with the Congress, they reluctantly joined Sharad Pawar's party. For they knew Pawar was a leader who did not forget a slight. So, with the presumption that the NCP would do as well under him as the Congress had done the previous year, they hitched their wagons to his star which, a few short months later, however, seemed to be on the wane.

Pawar had split the Congress once before in 1978 and formed a Progressive Democratic Front government of all parties including the Jan Sangh, which was the precursor to the BJP. At that time he had won 57 seats to the assembly. Twenty-one years later, he had added just one seat to his tally and won 58 seats, most of them from western Maharashtra. The Congress, however, won 75 seats, ahead of the Shiv Sena, which won 71. The BJP had 48 seats.

Pawar had wanted to form a coalition government with the Shiv Sena and the BJP, but Bal Thackeray refused to play ball, knowing fully well that Pawar wanted to pull the strings from behind the curtains, much as he attempted to do nearly twenty years later by offering suo moto support to a minority BJP government in October 2014. Legislators in Pawar's party compelled him, in 1999, to tie up with the Congress to form a government in Maharashtra—the five years they were out of power had depleted their resources, and they were desperate to get back into government.

'We should have had the courage to turn down that proposal for an alliance in 1999,' Suresh Shetty of the Congress and a former Maharashtra minister told me during the run-up to the 2014 elections when the NCP was once again playing games with the party. The NCP waited to make sure that the break-up between the Shiv Sena and the BJP was accomplished before announcing, within minutes, that they were breaking their alliance with the Congress too. 'If we had turned them (NCP) down then (in 1999), they would have been finished by now. And we would have consolidated our bases.'

This wisdom dawned very late on Congress leaders. 'We thought that the NCP would merge with the Congress sooner rather than later. But somehow that has not happened,' says Prithviraj Chavan. It has not happened because the ambition to control Maharashtra runs deep in the veins of every single leader in the NCP, including Pawar's nephew Ajit Pawar. When the party tied up formally with the Congress in 2004, it was obvious that the Congress had more well-meaning leaders than the NCP, and they conceded more seats to the NCP than Pawar had hoped for. Former Union Civil Aviation Minister Praful Patel, who was then NCP spokesperson, told me then, 'We would have been content with far less. But we thought, no harm in raising our demands. We were very surprised when they gave it to us.'

But the Congress was not to be fooled twice in a row. For their honesty of purpose had almost lost them a government in 2004 when the NCP won two seats more than the Congress—the Congress had been tricked into conceding seats from its quota to its allies, while the NCP demanded those extra seats for its own allies. But then Pawar faced a classic dilemma—every MLA in his party was a potential chief minister and barring Chhagan Bhujbal, who was an OBC leader, the rest were all Maratha. Pawar knew there would be a bloodbath if authority was placed in any one hand at that juncture, so he 'generously' conceded the chief minister's office to the Congress.

But the induction of Pawar's daughter, Supriya Sule, into the party upset his apple cart. For a long time, Pawar's supporters had been asking for a declaration of an heir and successor and Pawar, conscious of what happened to the Shiv Sena when Thackeray chose his son over his nephew, refused. 'He or she will rise from the grassroots,' he told me. That 'she' was a dead giveaway, and even upset his nephew Ajit who had been groomed for twenty years or more to take over from Pawar. 'Just because Rahul Gandhi is the Congress vice president does not mean he automatically will ever be prime minister,' Ajit Pawar told reporters bitterly. So, his cousin will not automatically pip him to the post of chief minister, it was implied.

This has changed the equations in the NCP. Ajit has formed his own group of core supporters who do not care for Sule, and now they have less loyalty to Pawar. Realizing the conflict that Sule's induction was causing in his party as well as his family, Pawar separated the sphere of work of the two cousins. Sule was sent to the Lok Sabha and Ajit continued with the Maharashtra State Assembly.

However, the fact that there is this internecine war between the Pawars has made its other leaders reconsider their options. Before the 2014 elections, when the party came up short in the Lok Sabha elections, most of them were considering joining the Congress where they hoped they would have a fair chance at leading the state. But by 2014, Pawar realized that despite the ambitious stock of leaders, he had no candidates to contest the Lok Sabha polls. So he pressed all these ministers and sugar barons into fighting the polls. All but Bhujbal refused, angering Pawar no end by this defiance of his authority.

Perhaps Pawar had an inkling of the way his party's fortunes were headed, for the only four candidates who won those polls were Supriya Sule, his daughter; Udayan Raje Bhosale, a descendant of Chhatrapati Shivaji Maharaj from Satara who would have won on any ticket; local sugar baron Vijaysinh Mohite Patil from Madha (which Pawar represented in the Lok Sabha for one term); and Dhananjay Mahadik from Kolhapur. All these candidates were stalwarts in their own constituencies and won more because of their personal reputation than because of the NCP.

The results proved that the sugar barons had been right about not wanting to lose ground by contesting the Lok Sabha polls on an NCP ticket—for even someone like Bhujbal lost the polls and has gone steadily downhill ever since. Pawar's flirtation with the BJP has also not gone down well with these leaders, many of whom have marginal seats and won because of the socialist ethos of their region and constituencies. They cannot but lag behind the Shiv Sena and the BJP if the NCP is seen to be toying with the saffron brotherhood whose focus is on Hindutva, thus alienating not just the Muslim minorities but large sections of OBCs and Dalits as well.

There is another risk that is staring the NCP in the face— the erosion of its core base of Marathas who have found it hard to forgive Pawar for renaming Marathwada University after Dr Babasaheb Ambedkar, and are upset by the failure of the NCP, which was in power both at the Centre and later in the state for a decade and more, to secure reservations for the community. The party is conscious of the fact that it has exhausted its secular credentials and is locked in a battle with the Shiv Sena for the regional vote. The NCP's flip-flops over its alliances, however, have made the people highly suspicious of the party's intentions. After offering suo moto support to the BJP in October 2014, Pawar announced it was no longer propping up the government in Maharashtra.

'But that is because such support became redundant after the Shiv Sena joined the BJP in government in the state,' says NCP spokesperson Nawab Malik, betraying the fact that the NCP had thrust itself upon the BJP and was not welcome to the party. 'Our support at the formation of government was only so that Maharashtra would not have to go to the polls again for the differences between the Sena and the BJP then had seemed irreconcilable.'

That is the best spin the party can put on its unwanted support, for during the election campaign Modi had described the NCP as the Naturally Corrupt Party of India—and indeed the scams under the scanner all seemed to have a bearing on leaders of the NCP, with the exception of the Adarsh scam, which involved both parties. The current dispensation cannot be seen to be cosying up to the NCP. Moreover, the BJP is fast losing ground in Maharashtra, which is returning to its socialist base, and the party is conscious of the fact that at most local self-government elections in the state it is surprisingly the Congress, without much direction from its party leaders, which is leading the NCP in coming up trumps.

'Our core strength in Maharashtra is around 70 seats and the Congress is around 80. We got 40 odd seats each after the break up when we contested the polls separately. A return to the old order is called for,' says Nawab Malik who is, however, wary of claiming outright that the NCP is looking towards the Congress again to form an alliance. For this time the Congress might not oblige. 'We are still contesting separately but we are both doing well at the grassroots. We will form alliances at the local self-government level if we can together emerge in the forefront and keep the Shiv Sena and the BJP from mixing power in the local bodies,' says Malik. He was merely reiterating the NCP's tendency to tie up with whichever political party it can—including the Shiv Sena and the BJP to grab power at the local level, a morally corrupt practice that has contributed to the party losing much ground among its voters.

However, its tie-ups with the Congress will depend on the

generosity of Congress leaders both in the state and at the Centre, for the fact remains that the NCP and its leaders have always needed the Congress for its survival, more than the other way round. Malik says the only thorn in the flesh of the relationship between the two was former Chief Minister Prithviraj Chavan who was clueless and non-cooperative with the NCP. The allegation is only partially correct for the fact remains that when Chavan started out in his tenure as chief minister of Maharashtra, Ajit Pawar, who was the deputy chief minister, appropriated the role that had been assigned to Chavan. He took to calling in ministers from the Congress and seeking report cards of their performance. Ajit also got used to other Congress chief ministers deferring to him and signing any document he placed before them without question.

Chavan was always conscious of the perils of the RTI and refused to affix his signature without a thorough perusal of the documents, which came as a shock to Ajit's authority. He also refused to kowtow to Pawar's crony capitalist friends. The exposé of Ajit's alleged involvement in an irrigation scam worth ₹70,000 crore came about because Chavan had the political will to take on the Pawars. 'He resigned, but then he manoeuvred his way back into government in a few short weeks because he found his authority was much curtailed without having the office of deputy chief minister,' Chavan told me.

But that is true of all leaders in the NCP. Authority is very important to their survival as are their sugar cooperatives. But with many of these cooperatives turning sick, combined with the government's attempts to seize control of them and the entry of private players in the market, NCP leaders are thrashing about like fish out of water. They are conscious that they are losing ground in every direction. However, their image has been tarnished among the masses. And despite the fact that the NCP has a clutch of leaders capable of holding their own, none of them is able to break away from the indebtedness to the Pawars and rise above the petty politics of their respective regions to play a greater role in the state.

This indebtedness keeps them tied to Pawar's apron strings, and they are conscious of the fact that their leader will never allow them to rise above themselves. They realize that the doors to the Congress might be shut to them forever, and if they do not do well in the next elections, the NCP will be headed for the dustbin of history.

18

A Caged Tiger

The Shiv Sena is stuck in a groove, unable to evolve beyond its victimhood.

When Bal Thackeray departed from this world in 2012, the Shiv Sena's critics had concluded that the party had also reached its end. The Sena's ally, the BJP, took Bal Thackeray's son and heir Uddhav Thackeray for granted and believed it could drive the last nail into his coffin by breaking their quarter-century-old alliance mere days before the assembly elections in Maharashtra in October 2014. But then all the Shiv Sena's critics ended up with egg on their faces as Uddhav surprised everybody by single-handedly beating both the Congress and the NCP to second place and netting half the seats of the BJP's tally in the assembly for his party.

In fact, the BJP had to ally with the Shiv Sena again, which was far from becoming irrelevant in Maharashtra politics. Neither was Uddhav the 'pussy cat' the BJP expected him to be. Instead, Thackeray's son and heir is still burning bright and proving to be the proverbial cat of nine lives. The BJP made every effort to decimate the Shiv Sena in the 2017 civic polls, but Uddhav still managed to come out on top, albeit with a slender margin. His party was able to comfortably elect a mayor, nonetheless. The Shiv Sena is now a bigger thorn in the side of the BJP, and is a better opposition party than either the Congress or the NCP.

There is nothing that the BJP does at the state or the Centre that escapes the notice of the Shiv Sena, which raps its ally on the knuckles frequently over various issues, winning the approval of large sections of the Marathi-speaking population. For example, the Shiv Sena's stubborn and unequivocal position on a unified Maharashtra resulted in the resignation of the state's advocate general Shreehari Aney who was rooting for the separation of not just Vidarbha but also Marathwada. The party was also the most vociferous in its opposition to Modi's demonetization move and emerged as a champion of the poor and farmers who suffered the most—a position that brought it rich dividends in zilla parishad and panchayat samiti polls in 2017 where it displaced the Congress and the NCP in large areas as the saviour of these sections. But then so long as the BJP remains an ally of the Shiv Sena in government, it is a given that the interests of the Marathi-speaking people will always be kept in mind. And it is foolish for anyone to think that the BJP could persuade the Sena to compromise on its core strengths so easily. Or even concede its Big Brother status without a fierce fight.

Before the formation of the Shiv Sena on 19 June 1966, Bal Thackeray's father Keshav 'Prabodhankar' Thackeray was among the moving forces of the Samyukta Maharashtra Movement, which was run largely by socialists of various hues. Bal Thackeray, thus, was a socialist at heart but had compelling reasons to turn saffron in later years and became at times too extreme for the Sena's now half-ally, the BJP. Under Uddhav Thackeray, the Shiv Sena has been floundering on some issues and has been unequivocal on others. However, although Uddhav has kept his neck above water, the party is still looking for the ideal twenty-first century issue that will keep the flame burning for many more years. It will have to do this on its own, without any help from either the Congress or the BJP—unlike in the past half century of its existence—which might prove to be tough since the party has never been strong on ideas that have not been borrowed from other parties or organizations. But it has always thrived on opposition to the ruling forces—and the BJP today is providing it with ample opportunity to oppose.

To understand why finding an issue that will keep its flame burning might prove to be a difficult task for the party, one has to go back to its roots. Emerging from the intensity of the Samyukta Maharashtra Movement's agitation for a unified state—which took the lives of 106 martyrs—Bal Thackeray's Shiv Sena was bitterly opposed to both Gujaratis and South Indians. By the 1950s, the South Indians had almost taken over government offices and private enterprises at both the officer and clerical level positions. While Morarji Desai's 'bhandi ghasaa aamchi' taunt provoked great ire against the Gujaratis, Bal Thackeray had a more personal reason to be annoyed with South Indians—Thackeray and the legendary R.K. Laxman were colleagues at the *Free Press Journal* (FPJ), where the editor, news editor, chief reporter and other senior staff members were by and large South Indians.

These senior leaders routinely preferred Laxman's cartoons to Thackeray's and when Thackeray unexpectedly won a contest for cartoonists held by *The New York Times*, the management held back his cheque on the grounds that the payment was to the paper and not to the individual. An outraged Thackeray walked out of the FPJ and started his own cartoon magazine titled *Marmik*. Subsequently, he took to riffling through the pages of the Bombay telephone directory and publishing lists of the South Indians employed by various organizations, which immediately touched a chord with the local Maharashtrians.

Acharya P.K. Atre had been an ideologue of the Samyukta Maharashtra Movement and had used the daily newspaper he edited at the time (the *Maratha*) to good effect to generate public opinion among the masses. He was also an old friend of Bal Thackeray's father, and he advised his friend that publishing lists would not have the effect his son wanted. So, Thackeray was encouraged to set up an organization to achieve his goal—Atre believed that his Shiv Shakti press had given the Samyukta Maharashtra Movement its strength, but now the need of the hour was an army—hence the Sena. The Shiv Sena was not just named after Chhatrapati Shivaji Maharaj but also drew inspiration from Shiv Shakti to bring it luck.

The Shiv Sena had good support from the Congress in its establishment and sustenance. The Congress was a divided house during the Samyukta Maharashtra Movement, with Desai bitterly opposed to the bifurcation and insisting that Bombay should be the capital of Gujarat, and Y.B. Chavan and others equally opposed to Desai's views. After the bifurcation, senior Congressmen in Maharashtra began to hate the continuing domination of non-Maharashtrians. But, more importantly, they hated the control of trade unions, led by the communist parties, over the textile workers in Mumbai. This hatred was shared by the rich businessmen who owned the mills, and they teamed up with the Congress to break the backs of the trade unions.

In those days, the Congress, freshly emerged from the freedom struggle, was mostly peopled by khadi-clad Gandhians, who were, nonetheless, not beyond a trick or two of their own. Thus, they found a very convenient tool in Bal Thackeray—the businessmen and the Congress Party got together to fund him (as they funded Raj Thackeray forty years later to break away from the Shiv Sena and form his own party, the Maharashtra Navnirman Sena) in order to destroy the Communists and take over the movement from the left parties.

After the war with China in 1962, Maharashtra's Congress leaders had a convenient common goal—to defeat V.K. Krishna Menon who was denied a ticket by the Congress to contest from Northeast Mumbai, then mostly populated by South Indians. Though Krishna Menon was offered a ticket by the chief minister of his own state, Kerala, he decided he would contest with the support of all the left and socialist parties who had ganged up together against the Congress. But he had reckoned without Bal Thackeray. The Northeast Mumbai constituency stretched up to Kalyan in those days and went beyond the South Indian areas, and was populated mostly by Maharashtrians. Thus, Thackeray turned the tide against the Communists, Krishna Menon lost and the Congress and the Shiv Sena were closet partners for the next thirty years, with the Congress using Thackeray time and again to do its dirty work.

The fact is that Thackeray was never interested in turning the Shiv Sena into a political party. For many years it was just a cultural organization doing good work for the people. Nonetheless, at the same time, goondas and musclemen also joined it, and spread terror throughout Maharashtra. Although in 1968, two years after its formation, the Shiv Sena won a large number of seats in the Brihanmumbai Municipal Corporation in alliance with Madhu Dandavate's Prajatantra Socialist Party, Thackeray and the Shiv Sena really came into their own in 1969 when they took to violence against the state for failing to integrate the Marathi-speaking areas of Belgaum, Nipani and other towns in Karnataka, with Maharashtra.

The Shiv Sena decided to petition Morarji Desai, who by then was India's deputy prime minister, on his next visit to Mumbai. There might have been a conspiracy against Desai hatched in conjunction with the Maharashtrian Congress leaders for they hated Desai and his abrasive ways as much as Thackeray did. Desai also sensed the conspiracy that was afoot, which is why he refused to stop when Shiv Sainiks tried to prevent his vehicle from entering the city from the airport. That fired the Sena's temper and soon Shiv Sainiks were on a rampage, uprooting government property like milk booths, telephone exchanges, street lights etc. They even took their protest to private enterprises, mostly those belonging to South Indians. Thus, Thackeray's hatred for both Gujaratis and South Indians came together in violent form this time, and this became the party's USP over the years.

It was only much later that the Sena turned from regional violence to religious violence, which also had more to do with personal pique and pride rather than ideological moorings. Thackeray was the only leader in India who had no roots in any ideology—his politics was always dictated by the need of the hour and existential reasons. By the mid-1970s, the Shiv Sena had run out of steam and Thackeray was already being labelled as a paper tiger. His agitation had ensured that at least 80 per cent of all the jobs in Bombay went to locals and there was nothing more to gain. The outsider issue did not bother people living outside Bombay in other parts of Maharashtra, even nearby areas like Pune or Nashik.

There was a crying need for a change of course. Thackeray sensed the mood of the people ahead of the BJP. Although he had teamed up with the Indian Union Muslim League (IUML) in the municipal corporation to be able to appoint his own mayor in 1973, and had addressed a couple of meetings along with G.M. Banatwala of the IUML, he decided to raise the party's pro-Hindu rhetoric to the highest pitch possible. That put off even the BJP, which had just metamorphosed into a party of Gandhian socialism in the early 1980s, from its earlier avatar of the Jan Sangh. When Thackeray started his Hindutva campaign, the BJP was on the side of the non-Congress Socialists.

The 1987 by-election to the legislative assembly from Vile Parle was a turning point for the Shiv Sena, with Thackeray making a paradigm shift in his politics. He made incendiary speeches during that campaign, exhorting the people to vote for his candidate, Dr Ramesh Prabhoo, on the grounds that he was a fellow Hindu. To the surprise of the Congress and other parties, which had dismissed Thackeray as more of a ranter than a serious player, the Sena candidate won the by-election. However, soon afterwards, Dr Prabhoo and Thackeray became the first ever Indians in independent India to be disqualified by the Election Commission for six years from voting or contesting elections, for using religion as the basis of their campaign.

But while that ruling ruined Dr Prabhoo's career, Bal Thackeray, to whom it just did not matter if he could vote or not, only went from strength to strength. The BJP finally realized that Hindutva rather than Gandhian socialism was the way for it to go forward, which prompted Pramod Mahajan to seek an alliance with the Shiv Sena to prevent the division of the saffron votes. While the Congress had only been using Bal Thackeray and the Shiv Sena for its own gains, the BJP was serious about using them to win elections— hence, in less than a decade after this alliance was forged, the Shiv Sena stormed to power in alliance with the BJP in Maharashtra.

A year later, in 1996, the Shiv Sena became part of the NDA government led by Atal Bihari Vajpayee in New Delhi. But the Shiv Sena's victory was also its defeat, since Shiv Sainiks had tasted power and were no longer interested in real bloodshed, preferring instead to safeguard their interests. By then, the Shiv Sainiks had developed major stakes in the system and were no longer willing to risk their all for Bal Thackeray. It also brought forth a fight for the spoils of war between Thackeray's son and nephew, which would end only with a split in the Shiv Sena.

Neither Uddhav nor Raj Thackeray probably ever contemplated that they would one day be abandoned by their long-time ally, the BJP. For many years, the BJP had needed the kind of militancy that the Shiv Sena brought to the polity, but it had fewer qualms than the Congress about setting up its own fighting arms. By 1992, when the Babri Masjid was demolished, the BJP had a very strong force in the Bajrang Dal, which drew its modus operandi from the Shiv Sena—storming the citadels of power, moral policing etc. Thus the BJP had less and less need for the Sena's storm troopers in such matters.

Very soon it would even stop needing the kind of incendiary speeches that Thackeray was wont to make to unite the masses on the basis of religion. Instead, a leader would grow from their own ranks who would leave the Shiv Sena and even his own party men far behind and end up as the prime minister. That leader was, of course, Narendra Modi. Until the BJP felt it needed the Shiv Sena, Narendra Modi took Uddhav Thackeray along. But the BJP's massive 2014 Lok Sabha victory prompted the party to dump the Sena in the next assembly elections.

Raj Thackeray had already floundered in the game he had been playing—running with the hares and hunting with the hounds, as he had done in the Lok Sabha polls when he put up candidates despite requests from the BJP not to do so, while at the same time avowing support to Modi if the latter won the polls. Unsurprisingly, he won not a single seat in the Lok Sabha polls in May 2014, and barely got a representative in the assembly six months later. He did not do much better in the 2017 civic polls either. Now, despite a few intermittent noises here and there, he is mostly silent and seems to have become a spent force. Most of his party workers have abandoned him, preferring to return to the Shiv Sena or join the BJP, and he has been reduced to becoming an occasional blackmailer, threatening to burn autorickshaws driven by non-Maharashtrians, or arm-twisting film producers into parting with their money to make up for their perceived lack of nationalism or even threatening the construction of the infrastructure for a bullet train to Mumbai.

The BJP's hope, however, was that their actions would sound the death knell for both the Senas, but Uddhav Thackeray surprised all with a stunning comeback victory in not one but two elections without any support from the BJP—in fact, despite all state power being used against it in the civic polls of 2017. Even his father had not been able to win more than a single seat at a time in the legislative assembly on his own and had always needed allies in the BMC to win. Uddhav now took half the BJP's tally and left even the Congress and the NCP far behind in the assembly and surged ahead of the BJP in the crucial BMC. A stunned BJP had to take the Shiv Sena on board in the government in Maharashtra and abandon the BMC to the party. Theirs is now a troubled alliance with Sena leaders taking continuous potshots at the BJP, and the BJP warning it off time and again. This is a far cry from the time BJP leaders begged Thackeray not to break their alliance under any circumstance, or swallowed the filthiest of his abuses for their leaders in the interest of keeping their alliance intact.

The BJP has been gradually making its intentions clear—to see an end to the Shiv Sena. Unlike Thackeray, who propped up the BJP when the Sena was at its zenith, the BJP has no desire to return the favour. Thus, the Sena is at a crossroads and there are some hard choices before Uddhav Thackeray. He was always of the view that militancy and violence had little future in an increasingly aware polity, and it has been his effort to clean up the party's act to attract more gentlemen to its ranks, rather than just the musclemen of yore. He has succeeded to an extent—some would say the fire has gone out of the Shiv Sena's belly—but it is my considered opinion that it is necessary to remodel the Sena to suit modern times and ensure its survival.

Yet, transforming the Sena is easier said than done. Violence and militancy is in its DNA and party workers are happiest when they are in the opposition—indeed they continue to act as an opposition party even when they are in government, as was obvious by the party's actions against Pakistani singer Ghulam Ali and former Pakistani Foreign Minister Khurshid Mahmud Kasuri, in October 2015. While the Sena succeeded in preventing Ghulam Ali from singing in Mumbai, essentially because the organizers of the event gave in for security reasons, the organizers of the launch of Kasuri's book—*Neither a Hawk Nor a Dove*—did call the Sena's bluff and held the event amid tight security.

But the writing on the wall for the BJP is clear—it is not going to be easy to contain the Shiv Sena, which is an unleashed tiger even when it is caged within government. And the Shiv Sena cannot help but fall back into its old ways from time to time in order to keep its claws sharpened and its militant workers satisfied.

The challenges to modernize and remain relevant are innumerable and very complicated for the Shiv Sena. Despite its commendable showing in the 2014 assembly elections, the Sena cannot cash in on the sympathy vote for too long as was obvious from the results of the BMC polls—it barely inched ahead of the BJP. In the October 2014 assembly elections, it was not just a vote in the name of Bal Thackeray, but a major Gujarati versus Marathi divide in Mumbai as well, borne out of a sense of wrong done to Bal Thackeray's party by the BJP, now firmly in the grip of two Gujaratis (Modi and Amit Shah). But more than two years later, the battle raged on, somewhat quietened only by the Sena's victory at the municipal polls. The Sena leaders have also shown no signs of evolving a twenty-first century strategy to attract the masses.

Modi's victory in the 2014 Lok Sabha polls and then in Uttar Pradesh was not just on account of Hindutva. It was also due to an aspirational class of youth and backward classes who had hoped that his victory would lead to their mainstreaming. While it is debatable if that has been achieved by the Centre, the Shiv Sena, which continually labels Modi as a dream merchant with no wares to sell, also needs to address the needs of the youth, beyond just street fighting and driving a wedge between various communities and religions. The Sena has so far been lurching from election to election, saved each time by the numbers.

Even a possible coming together of the two estranged Thackeray cousins—that suggestion is becoming fashionable in view of the Bihar experiment when all the parties united against the BJP and renewed talk of a nationwide alliance of all non-BJP parties post the 2017 Uttar Pradesh elections—is unlikely to sort matters out because Raj Thackeray has even fewer innovative ideas than his estranged cousin. It is quite remarkable that while Bal Thackeray was fighting for clerical and officer-level jobs for local

Maharashtrians, Raj Thackeray and to a certain extent the Shiv Sena, were beating up North Indians in the unorganized sectors for jobs that no self-respecting Maharashtrian would aspire to today.

It is not enough to repeat their old arguments about jobs and housing to locals, or to make the BJP a favourite whipping boy because it seized power at the Centre, as both Raj and Uddhav do so often these days. Those arguments ring hollow and the attack on the BJP is rather unconvincing in view of the common ideology they share.

The Shiv Sena must evolve a strategy far removed from the one of its founder. Bal Thackeray had needed nothing more than his magazine *Marmik* to rally the masses to his side. That was because even at independence, a majority of Maharashtrians, including those in the rural areas, were at least literate, if not educated. In the subsequent decades, Thackeray discouraged such education among his supporters because he feared higher education would lead to questioning minds, and many of them would raise objections to his means of growth through violence and political bargaining. If left uneducated, Thackeray's 'boys' would be in need of jobs, which were secured for them by the party—but these jobs never went beyond menial ones such as loaders, turners, fitters, etc., commensurate with the low levels of their education.

Never in the past half-century has a Shiv Sainik reached academic heights though many may have become rich through businesses and extortion. But in a globalized world where competition has become very edgy and Indians are scaling global heights, it is quite telling that there are very few Maharashtrians among the toppers, and if they are toppers, they or their families have never been subscribers to the Sena philosophy or supporters of its leaders, including Bal Thackeray. But even after two generations wasted due to this lack of higher academic pursuits, Shiv Sena leaders do not seem to have a broader understanding of the aspirations of the third generation of their supporters, who do not want to be reduced to the level of the taxi drivers and peanut vendors from North India who have migrated to Mumbai for jobs.

However, in this matter of addressing the aspirational youth, the Shiv Sena could find itself in a catch-22 situation. How does it address the issue without losing its supporters, for when they are educated they will not need the party to take care of their basic needs? Thus, the party needs to address larger issues, but how does it do that without being in government? The BJP is not likely to act on its suggestions and it has already been in the municipal corporation for over twenty years without having anything to show for it—not even in the matter of tarred roads that do not develop potholes as soon as it starts raining every year.

A former Congress minister once told me that he was very surprised that despite offering facilities to the municipal corporation, the government had never received a single proposal from the Shiv Sena, which had control of the BMC, that might be in the interest of the people: 'Not for one school, college, hospital or even a playground for children [...] They could have taken the credit for all this despite provisions by our government (for that). But they did not even have a clue on how to begin and where to begin, or if at all to begin! We had to step in and bring forward the proposals ourselves.'

This is somewhat similar to a public taunt that Ajit Pawar had made towards Bal Thackeray: 'In his entire lifetime he has not built a single institution that might benefit the people—like an educational institution or even a cooperative factory. He has only amassed personal wealth for himself and his family.' There is, therefore, a deficit of ideas among Shiv Sena leaders and I suspect that even the third generation in the party has not yet developed the maturity to recognize this fact. Former Bombay University Vice Chancellor Rajan Welukar had once told me that every time he tried to discuss academics and the need to improve courses and teachers at the university, the University Senate members belonging to the Shiv Sena came down to prioritizing the building of new toilets and canteens and cared little about academics.

Why toilets and canteens? Probably because they were trying to build up Aditya Thackeray, the first generation of Thackerays to go to college, and believed students who would be future voters would remember toilets and canteens better as the physical embodiments of Aditya's skills than they would their teachers and courses! With that kind of blinkered understanding of what matters most to youth, one wonders if the Sena leaders have it in them to take the party from its past moorings to the future, and compete with the best in a globalized world.

And although both the central and state governments have the bulk of the responsibility in making Mumbai a capital and commercial city on a par with the best in the world, I wonder if the Sena will be able to give up the temptation of tendering for roads and other infrastructure every year and instead focus on the quality of construction. This will make people believe that the party wants to help raise them above the miseries of their daily existence—to take them from slums to comfortable homes, from potholed roads to smooth runways and highways, from a state of uneducated and ignorant bliss to one of informed support and participation; and, of course, from violence to democratic dissent. I am not even touching upon the Shiv Sena's past role in riots and other conflagrations because I would like to believe that it has matured under Uddhav Thackeray and is coming of age.

The Sena does not need to be in government to improve the lives of the people of Maharashtra. I believe its own Mahila Aghadi can show it the way—for, in the aftermath of the 1992–93 riots when they had organized themselves to cook meals for the men who had been rioting all day, they extended that impromptu enterprise to their sakhi kutumbs. This was almost cooperative in nature—women who were incapable or unfit for organized employment used their native skills to produce arts and handicraft products, which were sold at these kutumb outlets to help them supplement their incomes.

This, I believe, is the seed of a cooperative movement, and the Sena can move from just women and other such unorganized sectors to major areas like the Congress and the NCP have done in terms of farmers' cooperatives and educational institutions. For this purpose, the Sena will have to shed its regional bias that keeps it confined to Mumbai. It is seen largely as a party of Maharashtrians fighting against Gujaratis and other migrants.

It must extend its base beyond the shores of Mumbai, perhaps even to the suicide fields of Vidarbha and the drying lands of Marathwada, and help farmers or their widows make a living in case of crop failure. It could also set up private or cooperative banks to offer loans to these farmers where governments and the Reserve Bank of India or the NABARD fail to step in on time. With the kind of ferocity (and I am not advocating violence but passion) that it brings to its campaigns, Shiv Sena leaders can put an end to private moneylending operations instead of continuing to support these sahukars who are exploiting the masses.

It can also tackle the education sector, beginning with the setting up of premium English medium schools (it is good to learn your mother tongue, but in these times it is better to be well-versed in a language that is known internationally, and offers a competitive edge to citizens). These institutions could offer education to the deprived classes at low cost, and the beneficiaries could then move on to college, polytechnics or affiliated universities.

The party has to, in fact, change the entire manner in which it looks upon itself and its supporters—not as a victim but as a facilitator, and its supporters must evolve from being musclemen who are helping it to accomplish its narrow goals, to performers in all walks of life. Those who benefit from the Shiv Sena can in turn spread across the world and bring name, fame and glory to the party for the role it has played in shaping these individuals and institutions.

Without this tectonic shift in its moorings, the Shiv Sena is bound to die out sooner rather than later. For even the politics of the country has changed in recent years and there are only two spaces left in India—right of centre and left of centre. The BJP has successfully occupied one, the Congress and the other parties are in the second space and not about to cede ground so easily. The only way out for the Shiv Sena is to address the problems of its supporters at the micro level and project it on to the big screen at the macro level. It needs to represent the people in small wards, municipalities, towns and cities, and then use its leverage with the governments in the states and at the Centre to bring facilities and succour to its supporters.

The party has to be a sum total of all its parts at the state and national levels, and not remain confined to a city or a region. And it must represent more than just Maharashtrians, like Chhatrapati Shivaji Maharaj, who was not just a Maratha king, did. Shivaji's sardars had spread out far to the north, south and even the east and west as far as Multan and Peshawar in modern-day Pakistan, and his descendants had the ambition to unite India under his banner. That they did not succeed due to the exigencies of circumstances prevailing at the time is quite another story.

The Shiv Sena, which Maharashtrians tend to look towards to keep their pride alive, could take lessons from the ambition of Shivaji's descendants and extend its influence across the country. This way they would realize Shivaji's dream of uniting the people under one banner. It is an immense task, and where Shivaji did not succeed, they might not either, but at least an effort and a start would have been made. I am afraid that if the Shiv Sena does not begin to paint on the larger canvas right away, it may be in danger of extinction.

19

The Saffron Brotherhood

The RSS's attempt at Hindu revivalism is damaging the prospects of the BJP.

*M*ohammad Ansari was an autorickshaw driver in Pune. He was about to go for his bath early one morning when pracharaks of the Rashtriya Swayamsevak Sangh (RSS) came knocking on his door. Sometime in the late 1990s, the RSS, which was not growing despite the existence of a government led by the BJP in New Delhi, decided to undertake an exercise in revivalism. They began to visit homes across Maharashtra, hoping to connect with the people in the state of their birth.

I had decided to accompany the RSS workers on their campaign, and the exercise was very enlightening. Ansari appeared a bit queasy about letting us in, but since there were several women in the group, he relaxed and lowered his guard. The RSS workers entered his one-room tenement, gave a cursory look around but did not deign to sit down or accept refreshments. They just asked Ansari if he had heard of the RSS and what he thought about the organization. '*Acche hain,*' said Ansari, rather warily. '*Par mujhe zyada kuch nahin maloom*' (They are nice people but I do not know much about them).

'You should,' said one woman patronizingly and pulled out a garish sticker—which could be described as calendar art—of Lord

Krishna on his chariot with Arjuna. She promptly pasted it on Ansari's door. The sticker reminded me of Nazi markings of the Star of David on Jewish doors, though it was slightly different in orientation. The RSS workers then left, giving Ansari instructions to visit the nearest shakha to learn more about the organization. As he stared at the door in great pain, I was sure Ansari would pull off the sticker even before he went for his bath. He was obviously not a fan of the RSS.

Before visiting Ansari, these pracharaks had visited the home of a Maharashtrian housewife, Rajashri Supe, living across from him. Her home and furniture seemed rather new and I did not think she appreciated such a garish sticker being pasted on her door without her consent. She had a young son of about six or seven and that came as a delight to the RSS pracharaks. 'Does he go for *vyayam* (gym or exercises)?' they asked her.

'He is too young for that. But the school does take care of all these needs of the children. They have special PT (physical training) classes and I have opted for that,' Supe replied.

'Not enough,' one of the RSS sevikas said patronizingly. 'You must send him early morning to our nearby shakha every day. We are much better at training young children.'

Ansari's neighbour had a reluctant look on her face and said rather weakly, 'I do not like to put so much pressure on my kid. He will have to wake up even earlier than he does now. Not quite right...'

She, however, withered under the look the RSS sevika cast her way and ended with, 'I will try...'

I did not think she would really 'try' to send her child to the nearby shakha early every morning, and I was sure she, too, would remove the sticker as soon as our backs were turned.

Around the same time that Ansari was visited by the RSS pracharaks, another group went to the home of my friend's father, Govind Bhatlekar. When he returned home from work, he was very angry to see a similar sticker on his beautiful door. 'I don't want all this nonsense in my house,' he said before asking his wife to bring a bucket of water and a dish cloth, which he used to remove the sticker from the door. 'Next time, do not allow them to spoil my newly painted door in this fashion,' he admonished his wife.

I noticed, though, that typically, people who were unlikely to support the RSS's ideology were the ones who politely let the RSS pracharaks into their homes. The ones who already believed in their ideology were the ones most angered by the RSS's refusal to change their ways—particularly their khakhi shorts—and move into modern times. The pracharaks had expected a warm welcome from precisely one such home in Pune, but the gentleman of the house, Nitin Basrur, was very dismissive. 'That ugly garment that you are wearing is unlike any other in the world,' he scorned. 'It was probably invented by the angrez who could not bear our hot summers. But do you not have your own ideas and can you not move with the times?'

'We are looking at it,' said one pracharak, rather weakly. 'We will be changing it soon.'

The man was not impressed. 'It has already been more than seventy-five years now. How soon is your "soon"?' he questioned.

It was in March 2016 that the RSS finally replaced its unbecoming trademark baggy khakhi shorts with long brown pants, provoking ridicule from its detractors. The hashtag *Chaddi Nahin Soch Badlo* was trending on the social media site, Twitter, the evening the RSS announced the change in its uniform. *Chaddi Nahin Soch Badlo* is precisely what a group of RSS pracharaks was told by the family of a pracharak's sister in Pune nearly two decades earlier when they had knocked at her door. She had added, 'You do not have to tell me anything. My brother is a pracharak in Nagpur and he has even donated his home to the RSS.'

The group then asked to meet the youngsters in the family— sons, daughters-in-law and daughters—hoping to rope them in to their brotherhood. But the women of the family had other plans and set the ears of the pracharaks ringing with their scathing criticism. 'I know precisely what you are up to,' an older daughter-in-law told them, even as her mother-in-law, the sister of a pracharak, looked on silently. 'You go to the jungles and recruit all those poor adivasi boys and girls who know no better, and pretend that you are doing a great favour to Hindu society. And you want us to use swadeshi not caring that the carbolic you sell us peels off our skin and we end up with infections. I am just not interested.'

At that time, I had felt sorry for that team of pracharaks for it was obvious they believed in what they were propagating, and they had a surety of purpose. But to be shunned by homes they should have been welcomed in was a real eye-opener, particularly because it was an experience duplicated across cities in the state. The pracharaks left the homes of these so-called RSS ideologues without pasting the garish sticker, either out of fear of being severely reprimanded again, or because they had decided the material should not be wasted on people who could not be wooed over. Very soon after, the RSS gave up its campaign of proselytizing people to its ideology. But the change to modern times has been undertaken at a snail's pace.

Soon after the announcement about the change from khakhi shorts to long trousers, more than fifteen years after Basrur had demanded the same, there was a cautious statement from top RSS ideologue Bhaiyyaji Joshi that the RSS did not think homosexuality was a crime. That startled many because the BJP had been bitterly opposed to outlawing Article 377 of the Constitution, which denies homosexuals the right to their sexual preferences. But, says Pradip Maitra, a senior journalist from Nagpur who has been observing the RSS closely for years now, 'What the media outside of Nagpur does not realize is that this is a brotherhood of by and large single men. Just like the Ramakrishna Mission. Hence they cannot oppose homosexuality. But they cannot openly endorse it either. That, in their book, is immoral.'

These announcements from the RSS are the closest the party is likely to get to admitting that it is a brotherhood in need of change. Before Mohan Bhagwat took over as the RSS's sarsanghchalak, his predecessor K. Sudershan had publicly stated that he does not believe women are good for anything but procreation and looking after the men in their families. 'Each woman should produce at least five children,' he had said in support of his belief that this would be the best way to overturn the growing Muslim population in the country. He had added, 'They must be more devoted to their families rather than seek to compete with men in their offices.' He had also commented on their attire, saying they must not wear jeans but wear saris, the traditional attire of Indian women.

These views about women generated a lot of criticism and negative reaction from women's groups, and the RSS's political arm, the BJP, suffered as a consequence of this negative publicity during the 2009 parliamentary elections. The RSS has since decided not to rub women the wrong way, even if they are unable to include women in their scheme of things just yet. Maitra says the RSS is not against modernization, and neither is it against the entry of women into its ranks or the entry of women into the sanctum sanctorum of temples. However, this lenient attitude towards women may be a way to appease women, who are one half of the voting population in the country. The RSS cannot be seen to be overtly against this significant half.

That there are definitely conflicting views on the issue of women within the organization as well as within individual members is apparent from a statement by Pramilatai Medhe, former national chief of the Rashtriya Sevika Samiti, the women's arm of the RSS: 'Sangh never justifies unscientific reasons for gender discrimination,' she said. But in the same breath she disagreed with the attempts by the Bhumata Brigade in Maharashtra to allow women entry into the Shani Shingnapur, and the sanctum sanctorum of other temples across Maharashtra that banned women from entering (The courts have now awarded them those rights).

'I don't think that agitation was necessary. The issue could have been resolved amicably,' she said. In other words, women should be docile and not fight for their rights, or rather, they should wait for the patriarchal men to grant them their rights. This view ignores the fact that the male bastion that is the RSS would never cede control and allow women into temples unless there were protests and the government took active steps to break those taboos—or, as eventually happened, the courts facilitated that entry.

But senior RSS leader Sudhir Warhadpande says diplomatically, 'We are always in favour of equality between men and women in every sphere.' This 'equality' is certainly not visible within the RSS or its other arms like the Vishwa Hindu Parishad and Bajrang Dal, whose members are almost entirely male.

While RSS ideologues have been able to take a neutral stand on women's rights and their entry into temples, the same cannot be said when it comes to the issue of Dalits. Bhagwat had, in 2015, spoken out against reservations for Dalits and it had resulted in a huge loss for the BJP in the elections to Bihar's state assembly later that year. They have since taken a step back from that position, but there are many things that the RSS is still unwilling to let go of—more particularly its two-nation theory propagated by one of its earliest ideologues, Vinayak Damodar Savarkar.

Mohammad Ali Jinnah had borrowed from Savarkar in propagating this theory to demand a separate nation for Muslims, but the RSS continues to cling to its belief that Hindus have had a raw deal, particularly at the hands of the Islamic invaders. A unity of Dalits and Muslims is an unbearable proposition for them, and many of their leaders are attempting to drive a wedge between the two communities. RSS ideologues are also unable to forget the domination that was enjoyed by the Brahminical class across Maharashtra and other parts of the country during the Peshwai, and wish to return to the old order. That is also one reason why they are unable to give up their shastra pujas (weapons worship) on Dussehra day despite calls to the contrary.

Shastra puja was a practice introduced by the Peshwas who always launched their wars on Vijaya Dashmi (the RSS later adopted this practice for its annual Dussehra rallies when they launched a new theme for the year). In the medieval era, the best time to go to war was between Dussehra and summer when the rains had ceased and travel on horseback was easier and faster. The Peshwas hated being mired in the mud in the wet season (the Marathas never learnt to ford rivers and always preferred the dry season), while their enemies always retreated from the hot Indian summers.

But now, says Prakash Ambedkar, particularly with the BJP ruling the country, this shastra puja sends a wrong message to the people. 'The dominance of the RSS and the BJP over the nation in the past few years has already emboldened certain people to be unlawful and kill with impunity. This kind of medieval practice sends the wrong message, that anyone can take up arms and get away with it.'

But the issue is not only related to a medieval practice of arms worship. The RSS wishes for a return to the Brahminical domination of the country that existed during the Peshwai. There is a reluctance to admit to the fact, but the top brass in the RSS is troubled by the takeover of the BJP by North Indians and non-Brahmins. This has contributed to the struggles underway between the faction led by Modi at the Centre and the RSS, which would much rather have Nitin Gadkari or at best Manohar Parrikar at the helm of affairs. In the RSS scheme of things, Hindu domination is not enough. The reins of power must be in the hands of the upper castes as they were during the Peshwai, and Maharashtrian Brahmins must have absolute control of Delhi, which must have only a puppet ruler, as during the Peshwa regime.

'The strains of Hindu revivalism are an inevitable part of the birth of the RSS as it seeks to give moral moorings to disoriented persons trying to find a place in a fast-changing society. Combined with this is the belief that disciplined militancy, as against non-violence, holds the key to the regeneration of Hinduism. Hence the drills and other paramilitary activities are meant to give its members an assertiveness to enable them to take their rightful place in the country's life,' says veteran journalist S. Nihal Singh, writing about the RSS in the 1990s.

This is an assessment that holds true even today. There is very little documentation about the RSS, but in the late 1980s, Walter Anderson and Shridhar Damle attempted to probe what the RSS really stood for in their book *Brotherhood in Saffron*. Reviewing their book, Singh said, 'The RSS is not backward looking in the sense of wishing to freeze aspects of the religion which have kept Hindu society divided. But particularly in Maharashtra, the Sangh still suffers from its Brahmin origins although its appeal lies mainly among the smaller entrepreneurs (traders).'

Contrary to Singh's perception, the RSS is an organization frozen in time. A look back into history will tell us that its founder, Keshav Hedgewar, was associated with the militant faction of Bal Gangadhar Tilak in the Congress. Tilakites were against the rise of Mahatma Gandhi's pacifism. Gandhi was then being more inclusive by involving Dalits and Muslims in the national mainstream, and the Brahminical order in the Congress was deeply offended. During the 1920 session of the Congress in Nagpur, Hedgewar was appointed as the deputy chief of what was the precursor of the Congress Seva Dal. A close look at the RSS cadres today shows that they are modelled on the Seva Dal.

But more significant is the fact that the core reason for Hegdewar's break from the Congress and the setting up of the RSS after Tilak's death was the growing influence of Gandhiji and the inclusion of all sections of society into the Indian mainstream. Thus, though the BJP coined the term 'Gandhian socialism' in 1982 to essentially remain relevant to India, the RSS is the antithesis of Gandhism, and it is an organization that cannot be inclusive even ninety years after its establishment.

'The RSS suffers from an ambivalence in its relationship to politics and political authorities. While it classes itself as a cultural organization, it has had a symbiotic and umbilical link with the BJP,' writes Singh. There are no surprises there for anyone today.

The RSS's insistence on developing a Hindu rashtra that was dreamt of by its founders in 1925, however, is proving to be a stumbling block for the BJP, which achieved a startling outcome in the 2014 Lok Sabha elections. Though the mother organization might have been Brahminical, Modi's emphasis on his humble origins and his backward class status during the elections attracted huge sections of non-Brahminical voters, including a fair number of Muslims, to the BJP.

The party had a similar advantage in Maharashtra, in the persona of the late Gopinath Munde. Belonging to the OBCs, Munde painfully built himself up as a credible leader of the masses, despite the Brahminical opposition by the RSS ideologues and the likes of Gadkari, who was always their rank favourite. Munde's untimely death in a motor accident in June 2014 rendered the Maharashtra state unit of the party leaderless. Chief Minister Devendra Fadnavis has been doing his best, but he is seen as Brahminical again and, along with Gadkari, is rooted in the RSS. The BJP state leadership lacks mettle and its recently acquired power is the only glue that keeps the different warring factions together.

The BJP, as a political party, is unable to break out of its upper caste shackles. For example, Fadnavis has attempted to enact a law that would outlaw ostracism and social boycotts in Maharashtra, which are still prevalent in many parts of this otherwise progressive state. While the law was passed by both Houses of the legislature in April 2016, Fadnavis is facing opposition in this endeavour from his own senior party colleagues who believe the law could seriously hurt their electoral interests. The antisocial boycott law could be the next big idea for Maharashtra and India, and would help to reinvent the BJP as a progressive party able to take on the regressive forces in the state and country. But senior party men in the BJP are too afraid to upset the status quo.

According to Professor Prakash Pawar of Shivaji University, 'But now what has happened is this: after Modi, people in Maharashtra had hoped they would finally get a non-elitist chief minister. Because except for Sushil Kumar Shinde for a brief period in 2003–2004, even the Congress has chosen only upper-caste Marathas to lead the party in the state. The Modi experience had persuaded them that change was on the anvil. However, there is a return to the Brahminical order with no consideration as to what the masses are really looking for.' Professor Pawar believes 2014 was the BJP's most glorious moment in Maharashtra, riding piggyback on the Modi phenomenon. But since then the party has come up with little that is new in terms of ideas or policies, and riding piggyback has become a habit—this time on the previous government's ideas and policies.

Kumar Ketkar says, 'I can understand the RSS. They do have a sense of history even if they are unable to let go of the past and want a return to the old Brahminical order in the state. But within the BJP, as with all other political parties, no one has a sense of history—they are unaware of even the RSS's own history. Everyone is busy only in his or her own self-gratification and no one really cares whether their party wins or loses so long as their interests are secured.'

That does not quite make for a return to power in Maharashtra, and Ketkar is afraid the experience of the late 1990s might repeat itself—a lack of innovative policies led to the defeat of the BJP at that time and it took fifteen years of bungling by the Congress-NCP alliance, and the freshness of Modi's appeal to return the party to power. If the BJP does not evolve a unique identity for itself, an identity that is removed from upper caste and Hindutva moorings in a state and society that has been traditionally inclusive in terms of Maharashtra Dharma, then, whatever its fate at the Centre, it might have to return to riding piggyback on its allies.

TWEEDLEDUMS AND TWEEDLEDEES

Tweedledum and Tweedledee
Agreed to have a battle!
For Tweedledum said Tweedledee
Had spoiled his nice new rattle.
Just then flew down a monstrous crow,
As black as a tar-barrel!
Which frightened both the heroes so,
They quite forgot their quarrel.

—Lewis Carroll

Effective leadership is not about making speeches or being liked;
leadership is defined by results not attributes.

—Peter Drucker

20

Chalk and Cheese

Nitin Gadkari and Devendra Fadnavis are united by power.

The BJP in Maharashtra, at any given time, has always had just
two leaders who have defined the party in the state. Soon
after its foundation in the early 1980s, the late Pramod Mahajan
emerged as not just an ordinary leader. He grew from strength
to strength and at one time seemed indispensable to the BJP even
at the Centre. Gopinath Munde was not just a supporter but also
married to Mahajan's sister. Their combination worked well for the
state because Mahajan was an upper caste Brahmin and Munde
belonged to the Vanjara community, which is classified as an Other
Backward Class group.

Mahajan was the strategist and fundraiser for the party. Munde
was the grassroots man with his finger on the pulse of the masses.
He had a sincerity of purpose that once even challenged the
might of then Chief Minister Sharad Pawar, and the courage to
defy his own party line if it was damaging to his interests and that
of his constituency.

In the mid-1990s, when the BJP was campaigning hard to oust
the Congress from power both in New Delhi and Mumbai, Munde,
who was one of the leaders to have been in Ayodhya when the
Babri Masjid was demolished in 1992, had the courage to take on

his party men to limit the consequences of the demolition. A BJP ideologue, Sadhvi Rithambara, had been addressing meetings in Mumbai and her speeches were very provocative. Much like the Raamzade and Haraamzade comment of another sadhvi in the Modi Cabinet several years later, Rithambara had been drawing contrasts between Hindus and Muslims. 'They are the exact opposite of us. We surrender our dead to the elements, they choose to keep them buried in the earth. We face east while praying, they face west. We eat from our mouths. So where do they really eat from?'

Munde, sitting on the dais, was horrified. Some weeks later, when BJP campaign managers assigned Sadhvi Rithambara to address meetings in his constituency, he put his foot firmly down. 'I get a lot of votes from Muslims in my constituency,' he said. 'She will unnecessarily alienate them and I will lose the elections.' The party leaders gave in and Rithambara was never seen on the BJP's political stage again.

Munde won that year and became deputy chief minister. The BJP came to power at the Centre a year later in 1996 but lost the vote of confidence in the Lok Sabha within 13 days. Mahajan, however, went from strength to strength with positions in his party and later in government when Atal Bihari Vajpayee won the Lok Sabha election in 1999. Mahajan was the architect of the alliance with the Shiv Sena almost a decade before the two parties came to power in the state.

The RSS did not quite care for either Mahajan or the Shiv Sena (a mutual dislike shared by Bal Thackeray), and did not much appreciate what Mahajan had done for the BJP in terms of the alliance. So the RSS cut Mahajan down to size by propping up Nitin Gadkari, a student leader from Nagpur, whose family members believed in the RSS ideology. Gadkari had been a card-carrying member of the RSS since his student days and fit the bill in terms of the RSS's concept of the ideal person to head the BJP and, indeed, lead India—he was Maharashtrian, a Brahmin, a committed worker and he was from Nagpur.

After Balasaheb Deoras, the RSS was headed by non-Maharashtrian, non-Brahmin sarsanghchalaks, and this had become galling to the organization's largely Maharashtrian leadership. So, they set their plans for the future very early on by propping up one of their own as a credible alternative to the Mahajan-Munde duo in Maharashtra; and this was something that was instantly recognized by the two brothers-in-law. To cut Gadkari down to size, Mahajan and Munde in turn searched for and spotted a young law student who also came from a traditional family of RSS believers and equalled Nitin Gadkari's profile in every way. He was a Brahmin like Gadkari and also hailed from Nagpur. His name was Devendra Fadnavis.

There was no way the RSS could fault the younger man or disagree with the Mahajan-Munde duo. But when Mahajan and Munde picked Fadnavis as a challenge to Gadkari on his own home turf, no one could have contemplated that he would not remain a pawn in their hands for very long. Or that both Mahajan and Munde would be dead by the time Gadkari and Fadnavis came of age and would become a more lasting phenomenon in the state's politics than either Mahajan or Munde.

There was little love lost between Gadkari and the Mahajan-Munde duo. There was a time when Munde, attempting to assert himself in the Maharashtra BJP after Mahajan's unfortunate killing by his own brother, had even come to blows with Gadkari in their party office. They were not on talking terms and when Gadkari ended up as the RSS's choice for the party's national president, Munde was hard put to continue with the BJP and, at one time, even contemplated joining the Congress. The arrival of Modi on the scene, however, gave him much relief because that wrecked the RSS's plans for Gadkari—to promote him as the leader of the opposition nationally and as a prime ministerial candidate eventually.

However, Gadkari's involvement in an alleged scam with regard to his various entrepreneurial entities under the name of Purti Group put a spoke in the RSS's wheels. They had to concede right of way to Modi who was seen as a cleaner, more credible candidate who would weave together the masses across India in a way that Gadkari never could. Well aware of the challenge he could still face from Gadkari in the future, after the BJP led all other parties in the Maharashtra assembly elections, Modi, like the Mahajan-Munde duo, chose to set the still relatively unknown Fadnavis against Gadkari and installed him as chief minister of Maharashtra. He did this even though Gadkari had better qualifications for the job as a former minister for public works in the late 1990s and knew the state far better than Fadnavis.

There was much jostling between Gadkari and Fadnavis and much bitterness among Gadkari's supporters when Fadnavis was eventually installed as chief minister. Other BJP leaders were also highly resentful of Fadnavis's good fortune. However, in reality, no one had wanted Fadnavis's job of president of the state unit of the BJP, which was the reason why he was at the right place at the right time to become chief minister. No one had believed that the BJP would make such a remarkable showing in both New Delhi and Mumbai in 2014.

Fadnavis was not a grassroots campaigner like Gadkari. There were other stalwarts within the Maharashtra BJP with stints in the previous government, and each had a better claim than Fadnavis to the top job. The inevitable, however, happened, but, says senior journalist Sarita Kaushik, 'It is only after each came to power at the Centre and in the state that Gadkari and Fadnavis learnt to reconcile their differences.'

As Mahajan and Munde had ensured in the late 1980s and early 1990s when it came to making a choice between them, there was nothing really to choose from between Gadkari and Fadnavis for the RSS. Therefore, despite their preference for Gadkari, the

RSS allowed Modi's choice to prevail. Says Kaushik, 'They are, however, like chalk and cheese in terms of how they work, how they nurture party workers and how they are perceived by their supporters.'

Gadkari is politically incorrect, not beyond speaking of 'kicking officials into acting' when they do not perform, while Fadnavis will politely complain about the lack of cooperation from his bureaucrats and allow matters to sort themselves out. Gadkari will fight bitterly with even his own party leaders to bring the fruits of their labour to his supporters. Fadnavis is more diplomatic and will not nettle his leaders beyond a point, even if it means letting down his supporters. Gadkari is a loose talker and often shoots himself in the foot as he did with regard to corruption charges against the Pawars when the Congress-NCP was in power. 'They are my friends and I will not take them on,' he had said at that time.

Fadnavis, on the other hand, is always circumspect and cautious and will not be seen uttering a word out of place. The competitive politics between them has come as a boon to Nagpur, which is delighted that their rivalry is bringing the city the best in terms of state resources and development.

'Today it has become a fashion for all those politicians who profess the BJP ideology to don their brand new khakhi shorts and to have themselves photographed with Mohan Bhagwat. But Gadkari and Fadnavis are the original RSS ideologues who did not have to display themselves in the RSS uniform just to make a point,' says Kaushik. 'Their shorts, you can say, have gone through wear and tear and the new long pants will fare no better, long after it has ceased to be fashionable.'

But despite their growing reputations, there has been some display of silliness and pettiness on the part of both leaders— Gadkari made himself the butt of ridicule when he avowed to the world that he watered the plants in his Lutyens bungalow in New Delhi with his own urine. He claimed it saved him the money on fertilizer and his vegetables also grew bigger and better. That had the nation in splits.

Fadnavis, on the other hand, may not be as facetious, but he did display a fair amount of immaturity when he threatened to throw his detractors and opponents off a high cliff—just as Chattrapati Shivaji Maharaj had done in medieval times—when the NCP opposed his government's award of the Maharashtra Bhushan Puraskar to Babasaheb Purandare. There was a casteist bias to the NCP's opposition to the award, but Fadnavis's subsequent threat was once again seen as upper-caste arrogance. He had to face severe criticism, particularly since he is a lawyer and ought to have known that Indian jurisprudence does not permit medieval punishment.

Fadnavis is also eager to please his masters, evident from his embroilment in the controversy over the insistence of certain groups that all Indians must chant 'Bharat Mata Ki Jai'. He supported those people who insisted on exemplary punishment for the ones who refused to chant the slogan. The Shiv Sena, which is generally less inimical to Fadnavis than to Gadkari, commented, 'You have to be alive to be able to chant Bharat Mata Ki Jai. If you are dead how can you even say Jai Maharashtra?' That remark was aimed at Fadnavis's inability as chief minister to tackle the severe drought situation in Marathwada and other regions in the state, and the increasing number of farmer suicides.

Gadkari wisely steers clear of such controversies knowing full well that he was elected to the Lok Sabha on a substantial Muslim vote in his constituency of Nagpur, and he cannot afford to alienate any of them. There are many ministers in Fadnavis's Cabinet who owe allegiance to Gadkari, and continue to act as stumbling blocks in the government's performance.

Nevertheless, these two tall leaders of the BJP in Maharashtra have made their peace with each other, and each has demarcated for himself an area of performance, letting the other be. Power is keeping them together for now. However, there is no guarantee that Gadkari and Fadnavis will not end up rolling on the floor, the way Munde and Gadkari once did, when power no longer holds them together.

21

Staying with Seven Out of Ten

All the Thackerays believe less in merit and more in muscle.

'*A*rmies all across the world but particularly in India do not want bright young things to people their ranks. I know because I have many family members in the army and they are all rather silly.' This is a rather sweeping generalization, but Prakash Sawant has good reason for his intellectual arrogance. His family is not just an army family, but also a staunch supporter of the Shiv Sena. However, over the generations, Sawant's family members have begun to feel the pinch of their blind worship of 'Shivaji's Army' and its modern-day leaders. 'When you apply for admission to army academies, they fail you if you score less than four out of ten,' says Sawant. 'But they also fail you if you score more than seven out of ten. Why is that?'

He then answers the question himself: 'Because no army top brass wants any soldier to ask him hard questions or challenge his authority. Which anyone scoring eight out of ten might have the confidence to do. So you need people with reasonable intelligence to execute your orders properly, but never so much that they may have their own views and opinions about what you are doing right and what might be wrong. The Shiv Sena is just like that. Its leaders deliberately chose and surrounded themselves with the unquestioning kind of people and cold-bloodedly kept them undereducated and underqualified so that they would never get above themselves or surpass the leaders of their party.'

Sawant hits the nail right on the head. Bal Thackeray was a man without any qualms about how he might have ruined at least two generations of Maharashtrians by denying them a place under the shining sun of a growing, resurgent India. But he was also a leader without peer. He had built up his party, the Shiv Sena, from scratch, though not without help from friends and support from a large section of people who believed in his initial 'Marathi Manoos' and 'Marathi Asmita' philosophies.

The concept of regional chauvinism and a militant force to look after the interests of the people speaking one language in one state was completely new in the 1960s when the Shiv Sena was set up. The only other party of similar nature to exist at that time was the Dravida Munnetra Kazhagam (DMK) of Tamil Nadu, but it had a larger underpinning in terms of raison d'etre and social agendas.

Thackeray had none of the concerns that bothered other regional parties that came up after the Sena—except to secure jobs at the class III and class IV levels for his supporters. He was under moral compulsion to do so for these supporters were incapable of much else besides lending their muscle to Thackeray, and swelling the streets during his public gatherings. In the years before his death, however, many of these supporters were also beginning to feel that they had not been fairly treated and were not given their due by their supreme leader.

Thackeray preferred to keep his supporters at low levels of education and qualification while his own grandchildren went to the best English-medium schools with international affiliations. So, when a few years before his death, he raged about Maharashtrian families choosing to speak to each other in English rather than Marathi, he left his own supporters cold. What they did not realize at that time was that poetic justice would come knocking at Thackeray's door, and the frustrated Shiv Sena tiger was then actually ranting not at them but at his own helplessness within his own household.

When it came to his own children, Thackeray had, indeed, practised what he preached. He had sent his children to Marathi-medium schools and none of them had attended college, except to seek an outlet for their talents at the J.J. School of Arts in Mumbai. They were seriously challenged in terms of history, economics, politics, sociology and other areas crucial to an understanding of Indian polity in general.

They also could not speak English and even their Hindi, punctuated with Marathi idioms, was only decipherable after long exposure to it. Therefore, Thackeray's children decided their own children would have a better education, and it got to a state when Thackeray's grandchildren were speaking in English to their mothers in front of the entire family, which of course irritated Thackeray no end.

The 'poetic' justice lay in the fact that Thackeray's grandson, Aditya Thackeray, the older son of the working president of the party, Uddhav Thackeray, even published a volume of poems in English but was incapable of doing the same in Marathi. Today, several BJP leaders, rattled by the Shiv Sena's constant yapping at their heels, say rather uncharitably, 'What is the future of a party whose leader does not know Marathi and writes poems in English?'

While that is nothing to be scorned at, the Shiv Sena is most certainly facing a dilemma over its leadership. Bal Thackeray, despite his deliberate under-pitching of his supporters, had also managed to attract a number of qualified and educated men, among them doctors, lawyers, social scientists, writers, historians and the like, to the party. That kind of intellectual mooring is now missing among the new leadership. The two cousins, Uddhav and Raj Thackeray, spend more time agonizing over how to cut each other down to size or put the BJP in its place than on formulating policies for their supporters and setting a course for the future.

In 2006, when Raj Thackeray first split from the Shiv Sena to form his own party, the Maharashtra Navnirman Sena, the general view was that he was a chip off the old block and would do with his party what Bal Thackeray had done with the Shiv Sena in the 1960s. But most critics forgot the fact that the Sena and Thackeray grew from strength to strength essentially because of the patronage of the Congress Party through the 1970s and 1980s, and after that because of its association with the BJP, which was more serious about coming to power than remaining just a fringe player on the margins of polity.

In the modern century, however, there were no takers for the kind of violence that had defined the Shiv Sena and Bal Thackeray in the past decades. On the other hand, Uddhav Thackeray was quick to recognize that the party was losing much of its support base primarily because of the violence they were expected to indulge in and Bal Thackeray's continued insistence on keeping an army of musclemen ready to jump through his hoops at a moment's bidding. Gradually, the Shiv Sena has taken on the personality of its new generation leader Uddhav Thackeray, and become less violent while continuing to stress on the Marathi ethos.

Raj Thackeray's early success in the 2009 elections when his candidates were the runners-up in the Lok Sabha polls in almost all seats in Mumbai and won fourteen seats in the state assembly elections later that year, convinced his critics that he was a modern-day phenomenon. However, what Raj failed to realize was that forty years after the formation of the Shiv Sena, most of its supporters had developed stakes in the system and were no longer willing to risk their business interests to help Raj grow in political stature through violence and militancy.

Beating up North Indians appearing for national recruitment exams in Mumbai, taking on Muslim groups for holding meetings or jamaats in the city, burning autorickshaws because their drivers were not Marathi speakers, were all ideas that were past their prime, and there was only half-hearted implementation of these so-called 'policies'. The half-heartedness apparent in their implementation, however, was partly because Raj's own exhortations to his supporters were made in fits and starts. This gave the impression that the MNS chief was using his supporters to blackmail governments and other institutions into conceding his demands—as was evident in his enforcement of a five crore rupees donation to the Indian army, which the army did not want, from film producers who had worked with Pakistani artistes—rather than making a sincere attempt to define his party's ideologies and programmes, however outdated and skewed they may have been.

Unsurprisingly, as there was no attempt to build grassroots support among potential voters of the party, it took no more than four or five years for the MNS to lose relevance in Maharashtra. Moreover, there was too much reliance on the goonish elements within the party who also did not want to stretch their necks for Raj Thackeray beyond a point. Raj also tried to straddle two stools and fell right in between them during the Lok Sabha elections in 2014. As mentioned in an earlier chapter, he decided on fielding candidates against the BJP-Shiv Sena alliance and also avowed support to Modi should he come to power at the Centre.

'What Raj forgot,' says Prithviraj Chavan who had to bear much of the brunt of the MNS chief's shenanigans while the Congress-NCP were in power, 'is that you cannot build a party by playing one against the other. There has to be something to show for the party at the grassroots level. Otherwise how will the people know what you stand for?'

By early 2016, a whole decade after its foundation on 9 March 2006, it had become apparent that even Raj had no idea what his party stood for and was facing an existential crisis. He has been attempting to be violent, then pulling back from the brink, repeating his uncle Bal Thackeray's 1960s and 1970s policies and programmes. Raj has been more reactive than proactive with regard to his own programmes, thoroughly confusing all his supporters in the process. No wonder he has been deserted by most of them, who have chosen to join the Shiv Sena or the BJP.

Raj's cousin Uddhav Thackeray, on the other hand, is somewhat more focused, but that is essentially because he has to battle the BJP's attempts to decimate his party, as was apparent during elections to ten major municipal corporations in Maharashtra and a series of Zilla Parishad and Panchayat Samiti polls in early 2017. The most important of these, from the Shiv Sena's point of view, was the the election to the Brihanmumbai Municipal Corporation, where the core strength of his party lies—he barely survived. Despite their partnership in the government in Maharashtra, both Uddhav and the Shiv Sena are facing an existential crisis because the BJP is determined to cut them down to size.

Much as critics might dismiss Uddhav as a leader far removed from his father's aura and persona—a pussy cat to his father's roaring tiger—the fact remains that Uddhav has done better than his father in terms of electoral fortunes.

For all his self-effacing ways, however, Uddhav proved a tough nut to crack for the BJP in 2014 and again in 2017. The BJP broke their alliance days before polling, hoping that the move would mark the end of both the Shiv Sena and its troublesome leader. With very little time on his hands and campaigning practically on his own, Uddhav posted a very creditable result for his party, winning half as many seats as the BJP did and eventually leaving the party with no option but to ally with the Sena again. In government, Uddhav is proving to be an even more painful thorn in the flesh, acting as a pressure group on the government and not allowing the party to get away with any wrong moves. And, in 2017, he outsmarted the BJP to get his own mayor elected in Mumbai under the threat of toppling the government to ally with the Congress in the BMC. In between he has given the BJP no peace.

For example, in the wake of the controversy at the Jawaharlal Nehru University in New Delhi in 2016 when some students were arrested for allegedly chanting anti-India slogans, Uddhav Thackeray was not on board with Mohan Bhagwat of the RSS who had said all students must be asked to chant *'Bharat Mata Ki Jai'*. From being limited to students, the controversy took a more sweeping turn by including all Indians, and that brought about a conflict with Muslims, with the Deobandi School even issuing a fatwa saying deifying India was against their religion. Chief Minister Devendra Fadnavis jumped into the controversy by stating anybody who refused to chant *'Bharat Mata Ki Jai'* had no right to live in India.

'But they have a right to die in India,' pat came the reply, tongue firmly in cheek, from Uddhav. For, the Sena leader questioned, 'How was one to chant *Bharat Mata Ki Jai* when one was already dead?' It was a repartee that left Fadnavis speechless and his government with a lot of egg on its face. Then, again, it was not the Congress or the NCP but the Shiv Sena that forced the resignation of Maharashtra's Advocate General Shreehari Aney when he called for the separation of Marathwada from the state. The Shiv Sena also put the BJP in a bind by moving a resolution in the State Legislative Council seeking a commitment to a unified Maharashtra—if the BJP goes along, its hypocrisy over the issue is likely to be exposed. If it does not, it will lose support from the rest of the state, including Mumbai, which is crucial to its existence. Then, after the BJP's massive victory in Uttar Pradesh in March 2017, the Shiv Sena, which had been taunting its ally over the Ram temple issue in Ayodhya by oft-saying, *'Mandir wahin banayenge par taarikh nahin bataayenge!'* (We will make the temple there only, but won't reveal the date), was first off the block to demand that the temple be prioritized on the government's agenda. 'Now you have no excuses,' party leader Sanjay Raut said.

So while Uddhav is conducting himself well, though in fits and starts, the worry remains about the GenNext of the Shiv Sena.

Aditya Thackeray's parents were suitably proud of his conduct during the 2014 assembly elections. He emerged as the first generation of the Thackerays to hold his own with the English language media, and his diplomacy over difficult issues was rare in one so young. Yet even Aditya shows the need to fall back into the old Sena ways, defined by his grandfather and uncle. Bal Thackeray had not wished to set up a youth wing of the party because that would expose the fact that the Shiv Sena was now largely represented by old men past their prime. But eventually he had given in to the persuasions of his son Uddhav to define a role for Aditya by setting up the Yuva Sena.

Yet among the first things that the Yuva Sena did was to bully the principal of a college in Mumbai with gheraos, blackening faces, breaking furniture etc., when she refused to overturn a decision on some disciplinary action against wayward students. Building toilets and canteens in colleges is Aditya's idea of catering to the future generations, instead of academic pursuits and larger intellectual moorings or global programmes for the youth—such as how to prepare them for the competitive world and how to expand the Shiv Sena's appeal. Even the party's leaders cannot deny the fact that not every Maharashtrian is enamoured by what the Shiv Sena stands for today.

Both Raj and Uddhav had been pinning their hopes on the series of civic elections in Maharashtra in the years before 2019, when the next Lok Sabha elections are due; but neither has done too well in these civic elections, Raj worse than Uddhav. However, an inability to evolve beyond their blinkered world view and the attitude of kupamandukas—frogs in the well—who know little of the world beyond their domain, is a major threat to the continuing relevance of a leadership whose GenNext has no solutions beyond hustling and muscling down their opponents. Is the English-speaking Aditya, much-applauded for his stylish demeanour, even clued in to the aspirations of the twenty-first century youth?

Bal Thackeray reinvented his party on many occasions, jumping from regionalism to religion to inclusiveness and back again to Marathi asmita over the decades, to stay relevant. However, in all these spheres the Shiv Sena now has competition from the BJP, the NCP and the Congress. Victimhood, which was the basis on which Thackeray built his party, no longer resonates with even the Marathi masses. The new reality is that not all Maharashtrians are supporters of the Shiv Sena, and not all the supporters wish to keep scoring less than seven out of ten in life. In the absence of a deep understanding of new age issues, the Thackerays may need more than just seven out of ten or a militant opposition to remain relevant.

22

Last Man Standing

Sharad Pawar and Ashok Chavan
are the only hope for their parties.

One day in the year 2001, I was waiting in Sharad Pawar's parlour to speak to him about how he had managed the Latur earthquake in 1993 when he was the chief minister of Maharashtra. There had been a major earthquake in Kutch a few days earlier and the Gujarat government didn't seem to be handling the crisis as effectively as Maharashtra had done under Pawar's regime. As I whiled away the time until Pawar dealt with other appointments, I learnt an enduring lesson about the man's reach and ability to move things around to suit himself and other people.

The first to pop out of Pawar's antechamber was Ajit Wadekar, well-known cricketer of yesteryears. He was as startled to see me as I was to see him. Only a couple of days earlier I had met the man in his office at the posh high-rise of a premier bank at Nariman Point in Mumbai, and he had made several unkind and uncharitable comments about Pawar. As it happened, the Maratha warlord was contesting elections to the Mumbai Cricket Association (MCA), and Wadekar had been propped up by the Shiv Sena to give him a run for his money. However, Pawar preferred to be elected to the post unopposed and his meeting with Wadekar was a step in that direction.

Eventually, Pawar proved to be too much of a handful for both Wadekar and Manohar Joshi of the Shiv Sena who was managing that election, and Pawar had a smooth transition into the office of MCA president that year. When I later asked Pawar what had transpired at his meeting with Wadekar, all he would say was, 'Everything can be resolved by sitting across the table with each other. I was not sure he would accept my invitation to lunch. But I am happy he did.'

I was in for another surprise when, a few minutes into my interview with Pawar that day, a former Shiv Sena minister was ushered in. I was rather bemused by now. 'People from the opposition come to you to seek your intervention in their matters…?' I asked. Pawar was flattered. 'Not just now. Even when they were in government the Shiv Sena leaders were seeking help from me.'

Implicit in the statement was the fact that bureaucrats in Maharashtra preferred to act on Pawar's requests even when he was not the chief minister, rather than follow orders from their own current political bosses. While I was still mulling over this fact, noted film director Jabbar Patel walked in seeking a tax write-off on a recent film he had made. Pawar picked up the phone and obliged. 'Go and meet Chhagan Bhujbal,' he told Patel. Bhujbal was then the deputy chief minister and Pawar's point person for works in the government. 'The job will be done.'

Sharad Pawar was the uncrowned king of Maharashtra at that time, and even today he continues to be a leader of the masses. He knows the state like the back of his hand and is the only leader today with a keen sense of its history, and knows what Maharashtra has meant to the rest of the country. Unfortunately, says Kumar Ketkar, now he does little for the people because he is a very embittered man who is nursing a big grouse at the blows fate has dealt him. The biggest of these grouses is that despite being the tallest leader in India with enviable networking skills, he has not been able to become prime minister.

Pawar came closest to the job when, soon after the assassination of Rajiv Gandhi in 1991, he contested against P.V. Narasimha Rao. However, he could not make it to the office because not all the Members of Parliament from Maharashtra supported him. That was one of the factors that contributed to his decision to split the Congress eight years later, in 1999. The first time he split the Congress was in 1978 to gain, successfully, the chief minister's office.

He had hoped that this time (1999) he would become prime minister, and with the example of former Prime Minister H.D. Deve Gowda before him, Pawar had worked out his numbers. Unfortunately, he couldn't achieve his goal. Gowda had gained the prime minister's office with just 17 MPs in 1996 when the BJP had found it difficult to weave together support for the Atal Bihari Vajpayee government, which had replaced the Rao government after elections that year. Pawar got only six in 1999.

Pawar's bitterness was owing to the fact that while most of the regional leaders like Mulayam Singh Yadav, Jayalalithaa and even Praful Kumar Mahanta of Assam had led their parties to government in their states under their own steam, Pawar, with a larger political persona than these newer leaders, had never managed the feat except at the head of the Congress Party in the state. The previous year, in 1998, he had succeeded in sweeping Maharashtra, but when he attempted to repeat the feat without the Congress in 1999, he managed just about half a dozen seats out of 48 (he had won all but six with the Congress) and he was also displaced from his job as leader of the opposition in the Lok Sabha.

In 2001, then, he was facing the excruciating prospect of seeing his supporters in office while he was merely an ordinary MP eligible for little else than a government bungalow in New Delhi. So when then Prime Minister Vajpayee offered him the job of heading his government's disaster management cell, Pawar accepted with alacrity because it had always been important to him to be seen in a position of authority.

Fate was kinder to him in 2004 when his supporters badgered him into an alliance with the Congress. Considering the comments he had made against Congress President Sonia Gandhi's foreign origins, it was almost a miracle that she chose to ignore that slight and gave her sanction for an official tie-up with the NCP. Sonia Gandhi then led the Congress to victory at the Centre and Pawar was sworn in as the union agriculture minister. It was a job he held for a decade, dreaming throughout his tenure about winning enough seats to make his bid for prime minster. That was a dream completely shattered in 2014 when Modi emerged victorious at the polls with such a massive majority that he had no use for support from parties that had not been the BJP's allies in the elections, let alone one that had been supporting the Congress.

Pawar's bitterness grew but abated somewhat six months later when the BJP ended up with a minority government in Maharashtra. He compelled his legislators to offer suo moto support, but with the Shiv Sena coming on board a few weeks later, the BJP-led government was determined not to spare former NCP ministers for their cases of corruption. An embittered Pawar now finds himself on the fringes of politics with no influence on Maharashtra's ruling dispensation for the first time since he made his debut in politics in the 1960s as a Youth Congress leader.

'The death of R.R. Patil has also broken him,' says Charu Satam, a PR professional who has handled the accounts of several political parties and observed them closely. R.R. Patil, who Pawar installed in the office of home minister and deputy chief minister, was his most loyal soldier. The arrest of Bhujbal has also been a setback as Pawar was expecting Patil and Bhujbal to look out for the interests of his daughter, Supriya Sule, in the future.

There is no one else he can trust in his own party, including his nephew Ajit Pawar who, Pawar knows very well, might be the first one to lead a revolt in case he makes any attempt to impose his daughter as the leader of the NCP. The support bases of the other NCP leaders come from the people rather than a dynasty, and they have had bigger stints in government compared to Sule who has been an MP for only one term. She was re-elected in 2014 with a highly narrow margin and faces election again in 2019.

Knowing the office of prime minister might never be his, Pawar began eyeing the presidency, but it was clear to all his supporters that with Modi firmly installed in the saddle and the RSS pulling the strings from backstage, he would not be able to manoeuvre himself into Rashtrapati Bhavan in the 2017 presidential election. Pawar now finds that all the doors are shut on him, yet, says Ketkar, he is the only leader in Maharashtra who can rescue the state from the mire it is sinking into. 'But he will not do it; he would rather allow the state to slide in order to get back at the people for not voting him to power.' Pawar's pettiness thus defies his greatness and it is essentially this flaw that keeps him from rising above his circumstances.

While the NCP still has a stalwart in Sharad Pawar, the Congress is completely deprived of human resources, more than any other political party in Maharashtra. It had a leader who could match Pawar measure for measure in Vilasrao Deshmukh who, unfortunately, passed away in 2012 due to a terminal illness. It has former chief ministers like Sushilkumar Shinde and Prithviraj Chavan in its ranks, but though they are loyal Congressmen, neither is capable of holding the state together and taking the party to a revival and victory in the next elections. The last man standing for the Congress, then, is Ashok Chavan, also a former chief minister, who unfortunately had to quit his office in the wake of the Adarsh scam in Mumbai.

As revenue minister in the Vilasrao Deshmukh government, Chavan had allegedly sought a 60-40 division in allotments in a housing society being built for widows and veterans of the Kargil war. Unfortunately for Chavan, when the scam broke in November 2010, he was in the wrong place at the wrong time. He was chief minister and it was discovered that among the private allottees in the society were two of his relatives who were army veterans but who had perhaps received the allotments because of their proximity to him. Chavan's decision regarding the Adarsh allotments could have been overturned by two chief ministers—Deshmukh and Shinde—but they either chose to overlook the transgression or found nothing wrong in the allotments.

Chavan had to quit his post as chief minister when the scam broke. But then in the 2014 Lok Sabha elections he was the only person who made sure the Congress, which was mostly wiped out even in its strongholds, did not come up with a complete blank at the polls—he won his seat in Nanded with a substantial margin and also helped his party with the neighbouring seat of Parbhani. He was therefore the Congress's obvious choice for party president in the state, but, says Satam, a close associate, 'He seems rather listless and unwilling to take on the ruling dispensation.'

For example, when the former advocate general of the state, Shreehari Aney, demanded a separate state of Marathwada, Satam asks, 'What was Chavan doing by maintaining a studious silence and allowing the Sena to get away with the credit of forcing Aney's resignation? He is the Congress's tallest leader from Marathwada, so why did he not take Aney up on his lack of jurisdiction on the issue?'

At that time, Uddhav Thackeray had commented that the attempt by the BJP to break up the state into four regions—Vidarbha, Marathwada, Mumbai and Deccan (or western Maharashtra)—was actually an attempt to reduce the influence of the Marathi-speaking people in the country. He said, 'Chavan should immediately have exposed the Shiv Sena's hypocrisy in continuing with the government even while recognizing the attempt by its ally to hurt the Marathi ethos of the state. That, too, did not happen.'

But, says Ketkar, that does not quite mean that Chavan and the Congress are not working on the ground. 'He is working silently. The media is not interested in anything that does not give them headlines and TRPs, and the Shiv Sena's intemperate language is always what makes the news.' Chavan, says Ketkar, is keeping his head down while paving the ground for his party, quietly implementing measures that may see the Congress make a startling recovery in the next elections. This assessment proved right when in the municipal elections in Nanded, Chavan's home constituency, in September 2017, Congress won 73 out of 81 seats and surprised even itself. This has infused new energy into the party.

And even though Chavan is hamstrung by the investigation into the case against him, the fact remains that he is his party's only hope for the future in Maharashtra. Indeed, like Pawar vis-à-vis the NCP, he is the last man left in his party from the old guard who has an understanding of the state and its history, and the only one who can save the Congress from complete decimation in Maharashtra.

QUE SERA SERA

(Whatever will be, will be)

It is not in the stars to hold our destiny, but in ourselves.

—William Shakespeare

*You cannot evade the responsibility of tomorrow
by evading it today.*

—Abraham Lincoln

23

A Bleak Future?

The leaders of Maharashtra today are men of straw.

'Chief Minister Devendra Fadnavis is often seen these days with the beautiful people of Mumbai at events like fashion shows and beauty contests sponsored by leading brands of creams and cosmetics. You wouldn't see Ajit Pawar dead or alive at such an event. He prefers to attend a rally of farmers in Marathwada or western Maharashtra, which were facing a severe drought for at least three years. So, if you ask Fadnavis to tell you the difference between a drought and a famine, he will have no clue. The BJP believes it is one and the same thing, and does not know what is a natural calamity and what might be man-made,' says Kumar Ketkar without mincing his words.

Although his remark cuts very close to the bone, there is truth in Kumar Ketkar's assessment that the ruling BJP has no knowledge of the history, economics, agriculture and industry of Maharashtra. 'They are versed in only the tertiary sector of the economy like the building industry and real estate. These are not the sectors that sustain the economy. But what does? Ask any BJP minister and see for yourself if he knows,' says Ketkar.

The Congress and the NCP were voted out of power in a major ouster in both the Lok Sabha and the assembly elections in 2014 but, says Ketkar, that victory was essentially a 'freak' one for Narendra Modi and had nothing to do with his party per se. As things stand in Maharashtra today, the BJP is entirely a party of the urban middle-class, people who believe only in malls and markets 'but that is trading, not industry'.

The Shiv Sena, on the other hand, which is the BJP's ally in government, is a party with a presence in just four highly urbanized centres of Maharashtra—Mumbai, Thane, Pune and Nashik—and somewhat in Aurangabad because of the sharp Hindu-Muslim divide in that city. 'It is full of lumpen elements connected more to builders than even to real estate. They have absolutely no understanding of the rural economy,' says Ketkar.

Sharad Pawar had recently said that Uddhav Thackeray does not even know whether groundnuts grow on trees or beneath the ground. He was also rather annoyed that the Sena chief had no idea that 'parati' and 'kapaashi' or 'kaapoos' all meant cotton, like 'ruiee' and 'kapaas' in Hindi. These may be harsh judgements of the leaders, but they are based on the truth of what is happening on the ground in Maharashtra today.

The state was reeling under successive droughts, but not much was done by the people in government. Bureaucrats in Mantralaya admit that they are constrained by the lack of knowledge on the part of most ministers in the Fadnavis government who have no idea how to tackle issues beyond Mumbai, Nagpur or Pune. Most of the programmes now being implemented, whether in the urban or rural areas, were designed by the previous Congress-NCP government and once the current dispensation runs through them, 'they may also run out of newer ideas for the state,' one serving bureaucrat said candidly, though on condition of anonymity.

'The choice for the people,' says Ketkar, 'is thus between corruption and connectivity or corruption and disconnection. They are choosing the former.' By that he means that even if the Congress and the NCP came up as among the most corrupt of governments in Maharashtra in the past fifteen years, the smallest of their leaders had a fair idea of the connection between production and productivity in the areas of industry and agriculture. These are the two areas that move the economy and therefore the people's fortunes to greater heights.

But since the current dispensation is clueless on this issue, Ketkar believes the Congress might become the biggest beneficiary of the people's disenchantment with the BJP and Shiv Sena in the next elections. Much evidence of this is available at local self-government elections where, unexpectedly, the Congress has been posting the better results than the Shiv Sena and NCP, notwithstandng the fact that the BJP has had to use much muscle and money power to win the polls. The Congress, today, has neither.

Activist and sociologist Tushar Jagtap says, 'It might not be quite visible to all just now but the state is already a mess. There is no logical and concerted thinking on the part of administrators, there is no uniform implementation of policies or ministration of the resources, there are no fresh new ideas, there is large-scale unrest in society and there is no faith in the people towards their leaders.'

It is startling, he says, how disconnected the two ruling parties are with the masses. While Uddhav Thackeray does make some noise against the government, it is essentially to distance the Sena from a party he knows is swiftly losing ground at the grassroots. There is an understanding among Shiv Sainiks that they must 'sacrifice' something quickly and break loose from the BJP before the advent of the next phase of elections in the state. For, if they cling to the BJP until the end, the people will not be impressed and will turn to other political parties, notably the Congress and the NCP, even in the urban areas of the state.

Perhaps that is why Uddhav asked his party men to be prepared to face the series of elections in the four urban centres they are strong in, all on their own. It was a move that startled the BJP for realization is now dawning on the party that it may need the Sena after all—its experiments in going alone in the local self-government polls have not proved to be as fruitful as they had expected.

Thus the alarm bells are ringing for all, but there are a few people who know the measures required for a course correction and how to implement them. There are some rural MLAs who understand the distress the people are facing in the villages, but they are entrants from either the Congress or the NCP, and do not count for much within the party hierarchy.

'Unfortunately, the BJP thinks the Congress does well in the rural areas because of the cooperative movement or the banks they control. So, they set up several banks of their own. But since they have no understanding of productivity and economics, all that these banks ended up doing was to give a few housing and car loans. That is again trading, not industry. Not surprisingly, many of these banks have been shut down. Others are barely surviving but even those have not been able to connect with the people in the manner that such institutions run by Congressmen or those in the NCP have.'

Several years ago, Ajit Pawar, in a searing critique of Bal Thackeray had said that all the Sena supremo had done was to build a house for himself with twenty-seven air conditioners. 'Show me one institution he set up for the people. When he will do nothing for them why should they care for his party?' he asked. That is true of the party even today.

In fact, despite its toning down, the Shiv Sena is returning to extortionism and lumpenization of the polity, which might prove to be damaging to the state's interests. There is a growing realization in the BJP that its disconnection with the masses is increasing, as seen in the strike by farmers in June 2017 for loan waivers, but the party does not have the intellectual resources to come up with ideas that will make a lasting difference to the everyday lives of the people. 'If you ask me today what the future of Maharashtra will be in the next couple of years, I can only say it might be very dark and bleak,' adds Ketkar.

Maharashtra, however, has never been a state plunged into darkness even during the period of Islamic rule in past centuries. Chhatrapati Shivaji rose from within the heart of these Islamic dynasties to shape the destiny of Maharashtra and the rest of India through succeeding generations. Maharashtra Dharma was the philosophy that was the underpinning of the state for centuries. Later, it was a philosophy that drove leaders like Yashwantrao Chavan to ensure that their state remained in the forefront of nation-building in independent India. Even if most of Maharashtra's political leaders don't have any idea what that might mean today, enough of Maharashtra Dharma's tenets have been absorbed by the common man in the state to ensure the tradition does not die out altogether.

The state is passing through a dark phase but, as before, it is not confined to Maharashtra alone. There is a general disconnect between the masses and the leaders across India. As Professor Pawar of Shivaji University puts it succinctly, 'There is a turmoil happening beneath the surface. When it erupts the lava could burst in any direction, one does not know who will be burnt the most.'

The only certainty is that there aren't any low-hanging fruits that can be plucked easily, like there were in 2014. All the political parties will have to work hard and even then the fruits might still be out of their reach. The people then will have to be their own saviours. For Maharashtra must not be allowed to crumble. A Shivaji or a Yashwantrao Chavan must rise again to give a new direction to a state that has always been a crucial entity, a gateway to the rest of India.

Acknowledgements

I was an infant when my father was posted to a defence installation in Maharashtra in the 1960s. Working for the Government of India he should have been transferred out every three years but somehow once he stepped into the state, there was never any question of leaving. That is because Y B Chavan, without whom Maharashtra, as we know it today, would never have come into being, as India's then defence minister was setting up arms and ammunition factories left, right and centre all across Maharashtra and my father and his colleagues had their hands full getting those factories on track. Governments and regimes changed but we stayed put. My love affair with Maharashtra began right then in my childhood—I grew up knowing little else, apart from occasional visits to my parents' home states. Every such visit reinforced the impression that Maharashtra was a uniformly safe, progressive and highly conducive state for growing up in and, of course, for education and livelihood.

So when I chose to become a journalist and was reluctantly pushed into political reporting by one of my first editors, I began with an advantage that most non-natives of Maharashtra might not have had—an understanding of the state and its society, of course, but also something that came to me almost by default—a sense of complete belonging to Maharashtra, while not being quite a Maharashtrian, that enabled me to take a critical view of its society and polity as a well-wisher would of a good friend and yet be immensely proud of its progressive and socialist ethos at the same time.

So when the editors at Rupa Publications offered me this opportunity, I welcomed it as it would help me return to Maharashtra a little bit of what it had given me in ample measure over the years. This is my labour of love for a state that has given me my roots and the only place I can feel completely at home today.

I must, then, begin by thanking all my editors, past and present, at Rupa for their patience and painstaking work on this book that had to keep pace with the changing political situations through the writing and the editing.

Despite my vast experience of reporting on Maharashtra, this book could not have taken the shape it has without the tremendous help I received from peers and colleagues and all those people we refer to as our 'sources'.

To my eternal regret, noted Marathi editor and littérateur, Dr Aroon Tikekar, who began guiding me for this book, passed away too soon (in February 2016). I would have treasured and valued his opinion on the final outcome.

Many elements in the book were not part of any historical records and happened before I began my career as a journalist. In gathering information on these events I was greatly helped by my senior colleagues D K Raikar, group editor of *Lokmat*, and veteran journalist and commentator Kumar Ketkar, who has also been kind enough to allow me to reproduce his opinions in the book. I am indeed grateful to both of them.

My contemporary Praveen Bardapurkar and Sarita Kaushik and Pradip Maitra, who were both my colleagues at *Hindustan Times*, were also very helpful and kind in not only sharing their perspectives with me but also providing me with rich sources and information that I have used generously in the book.

Every named and unnamed source in the book has added to its richness and perspective. For this I am grateful to all of them—including the state's political leaders and professors at many of the state's universities—for taking precious time off their busy schedules to speak to me. I thank all the persons quoted in the book for enhancing its quality and content.

All statements are original and appear in the book as a result of painstaking interviews conducted through the course of its writing. Some comments have been taken from press conferences and public meetings—particularly the one by the late Bal Thackeray—where I was present and can vouch for their verity and authenticity.

To Vir Sanghvi and Anil Dharker, I am forever grateful for taking the time to read the manuscript through their extremely busy schedules and enriching the book with their perspectives in the introduction and foreword respectively.

I cannot end without thanking both my sisters, Sushama and Aparna, to whom I have dedicated this book, who saw me through trying personal times even as I was researching and writing the manuscript. Their silent support and dedication to my interests and well-being kept me going through the writing and their gentle prodding was always a source of encouragement. I am indeed fortunate and may God keep both my sisters blessed forever.

Index

242 • MAHARASHTRA MAXIMUS